FAMILY MINISTRY

FAMILY MINISTRY

The Enrichment
of Family Life
Through the Church

Charles M. Sell

ZONDERVAN
PUBLISHING HOUSE
OF THE ZONDERVAN CORPORATION
GRAND RAPIDS, MICHIGAN 49506

Copyright © 1981 by the Zondervan Corporation
Grand Rapids, Michigan

Library of Congress Cataloging in Publication Data
Sell, Charles M 1933–
    Family ministry.
    1. Church work with families. 2. Family. 3. Marriage. I. Title.
BV4438.S44   248.4   80-29335
ISBN 0-310-42580-8

)

Unless otherwise indicated, the Scripture version used in this book is the New International Version, copyright © 1978 by the New York International Bible Society. Used
by permission.

Edited by Arnold Jantzen and John Iwema
Designed by Gerard Terpstra

This printing: July, 1981

Printed in the United States of America

For their enriching love to me,
I dedicate this book
to my wife, Ginger,
and to our children:
Chuck, Larry,
Becky, and Howie

CONTENTS

Preface

The small Claviger beetle moves inside the ant hill, unalarmed by the fact that ants are one of its most ferocious enemies. The ant hill offers it easy access to life's necessities: it's warm inside and the ants stock a variety of tasty foods.

The beetle soon stops in its tracks—it spots a fast-approaching ant, one of the hungry predators that call this hill home. The ant, in turn, stops when it reaches the motionless beetle. But, instead of striking out, it strokes the beetle. A secretion then appears on the beetle's body; and the ant eagerly consumes it and goes on its way, leaving the visitor unmolested.

These two species, the Claviger beetle and the meadow ant, have a pleasant arrangement; biologists call it "symbiosis." Though they should be enemies, they live together in a mutually beneficial way. The beetle gets a warm home with a lot to eat, and the ant has its portable refreshment stand.

We might expect the church and the family to display some of this, to work together in a sort of social symbiosis. Yet, these two institutions haven't always gotten along so well, nor contributed to one another's welfare as they should. In fact, I know of many church members who have sacrificed their family life to build the life of the church. And it is quite obvious that many churches fail to offer much to enrich their families.

I have always believed there should be full cooperation between the church and the home. Both are created by God. Like the Claviger beetle and the ant, they should live in harmony.

Family Ministry grows out of my strong conviction that the church should support the family. I am indebted to the many people who share this belief and who have forged the programs that are described in this book. I also acknowledge my indebtedness to one of the early leaders in family ministry, my friend Howard Hendricks. He was a major source of encouragement for me to start in this field twenty-five years ago.

My thanks also to the people at Trinity Evangelical Divinity School. I receive much personal support and encouragement in the faith from the faculty, students, and administration there, and the two quarterly sabbaticals granted to me made it possible to write this book. Thanks also to the staff of St. Mary of the Lake, a nearby seminary. They provided me with a quiet and comfortable place in their library where I could write without interruption.

I also express my appreciation to my secretary, Beverly Faugerstrom, for her promptness and precision in typing parts of the manuscript in its final stages.

I owe most to my wife, Ginger, who has provided massive doses of encouragement through the six years I have been occupied with this project. She also typed the manuscript, persevering cheerfully through the seemingly endless writings and rewritings.

We share with many others the conviction that life in a family is one of God's greatest gifts. We offer this work to our Lord with the prayer that He will use *Family Ministry* to help churches to, in turn, help families realize what God intends family life to be.

Introduction

Recently, a friend of mine, an educator, said to me: "Sometimes my daughter will ask, 'Dad, may I go out tonight?' It is then that I appeal to what I remember from adolescent and educational psychology courses from my college days. Next, I draw on my advanced training in secondary education. Then I dip into the wide resources of my Ph.D.-level administration classes. After all this, I confidently reply, 'Go ask your mother!'"

What this man says in jest is all too real and serious for many of us. It underscores one of the basic problems in the enterprise called family ministry: the difficulty of transferring knowledge to life.

While true of other areas of life, this transfer is especially difficult in the area of the family. This is due in part to the fact that family living is such an emotionally laden sphere—a sphere that involves the ongoing interplay of dynamics that are woven into the total fabric of our personalities. Training to be a competent mechanic or chemist is different from training to be a successful husband or wife. Training to be a family member requires in-depth personal changes and adjustments. Thus, the wisdom of courses and sermons has a tough time penetrating the front doors of our homes.

Introduction

Because family living involves the whole person, family-living skills are best learned in the family rather than in a classroom. Our own childhood family experiences should prepare us for relating to our own spouses and children later on. But so many of us, despite all our formal education, have not learned the art of family living because the homes in which we grew up were so problematic. If we did not develop skills for effective communication early in life, we carry this handicap into marriage. Sometimes we also bring into our marriages extremely negative attitudes, habits, and emotions that need to be modified or "unlearned" if we are going to relate well. Such "unlearning" and changing is painfully slow, sometimes even requiring extensive counseling.

The crux of the family-life education problem lies here. Since dysfunctional families tend to produce dysfunctional families, it is difficult to provide training that will overcome this influence of the past on the present. That families do pass on their problems to the next generation is evident from the divorce statistics, for children of divorced parents divorce at a higher than average rate.[1] This also raises questions about children who grow up in other types of difficult family circumstances.

For example, how will abused children (estimated at one million per year in the U.S.) fare as parents themselves some day?[2] How will the family conditions of today's generation of ten million adult alcoholics affect the families of the next generation?[3] With the number of children who are being raised by only one of their parents continually increasing, what effect will the absence of a father or mother in the home have on their ability to be effective parents later on in life?[4] Such questions make us realize that family life in the West is caught in a deteriorating downward spiral, generating guilt among those involved and pessimism among the professionals who are trying to help families.

But we should not permit this awareness of the problems to breed hopelessness. Stopping such a vicious cycle is difficult but not impossible. We Christians know that God supernaturally intervenes in tough situations. He is able to bring redemption to all of life's spheres, including that of the home. And the growing numbers of creative family-enrichment programs are, for a fact, bringing renewal to many families.

John R. Quinn, former president of the U.S. Catholic Conference of Bishops, is one church leader who refuses to be pessimistic. He states: "At a time when many in our society are predicting the demise of family life . . . a new-found hope is appearing in the pastoral life of the church."[5]

This hope for the renewal of family life is based in part on the recent development of family-education programs in both Catholic and Protestant circles. Evangelicals are very much a part of this, developing innovative, biblical forms of family ministry.

Family Ministry is in part a compilation of some of these more creative efforts to help the home. However, it is not a mere encyclopedia of church programs, for it deals with the church's task of Christian education *of* the home, or "family-life education" as it is often spoken of, and it looks into the matter of "family nurture," or Christian education *in* the home as well. In discussing these two aspects of Christian education, I have drawn on a range of educational, psychological, and theological sources.

This material is presented under seven major headings. Part One establishes the need for the church to conduct family ministry, and Part Two examines the theological basis for this endeavor. In Part Three we look at the need for interaction between the home and the church in family ministry. Christian education of the home, or family-life education, is examined in Parts Four and Five; and in Part Six, Christian education in the home, or family nurture, is discussed. Various family-unit ministries are then presented in Part Seven.

The Suggested Readings at the conclusion of key sections in Parts Four and Five are intended to point the reader to resources for dealing with specific problems and issues in family-life education.

The Selected Bibliography at the close of the book includes the sources listed in these Readings, and it also lists additional works that can help the church in family ministry. It is my hope that this bibliography will also serve to encourage wider reading in the areas of the family and family ministry.

Family Ministry, then, is not a mere catalog of programs. It grows out of several basic personal convictions. These convictions have prompted me to write; they have been my guide in the organization of the material; and they give the book its major distinctives. They are as follows:

Family ministry needs to have a theological base. I am persuaded that theology should regulate all that the church is and does. Therefore, it is an important part of this book. The doctrinal viewpoint of the text is evangelical. From that position, the theology of the family is fully developed in Part Two, "The Theological Foundations." Theology also pervades the entire book. Programs and movements, both secular and religious, are viewed in the light of biblical truth from an evangelical perspective.

Family ministry must be contemporary. Our greatest challenge is to relate biblical dictates of the past to family life in the present. The family in an industrial, technological world experiences unique problems and challenges, and both of these cry out for attention.

To help the family contend with the situation it finds itself in today, I have leaned heavily on data and programs from a broad range of sources, both secular and religious. It is my conviction that credible analyses of and solutions to the challenges and problems that confront the modern family can be found among those who work closely with families, whether or not they are professing Christians. Whether the material taken under consideration in this book arises out of a secular or a biblical perspective, I have sought at all times to scrutinize and evaluate these theories and programs from the evangelical viewpoint. We can then select and use principles and practices for family living that are both relevant and biblical.

Family ministry must be realistic. Being contemporary requires that we be realistic. In this book I have sought to grapple with the family as it *is* as well as with how it *should be.* I know that the family can be a place of great happiness; it can also be the scene of terrible hurt. So I have incorporated struggle and conflict in my view of the home.

I have also sought to avoid stereotypes and clichés, such as speaking of the Christian home as "heaven on earth." Such thinking and expression only serve to confuse and disturb those for whom the home is a place of struggle.

Realistic family-life education, I believe, must deal with the pain of disappointment, crisis, and failure. It should teach family members how to cope with failure as well as how to handle success. *Family Ministry* attempts to deal with the complicated struggles that are part of life, while avoiding simplistic or idealistic solutions that stir up guilt rather than stimulate growth.

It ministers to every kind of household. In the past the church has tended to gear its teaching and design its programs with the "typical family" in mind. This family has traditionally been thought to consist of a husband who is the provider, a wife who is the homemaker, and several children. In his most recent book, *The Third Wave,* Alvin Toffler reminds us that such a family now comprises only 7 percent of the households in the U.S.[6] Even if we consider the typical family to include one or more children, with both the husband and the wife working outside the home, this still accounts for only 34 percent of the households in the U.S.[7] It is clear, then, that our stereotype of the family is inaccurate.

Moreover, with 38 percent of the nation's households now being headed by single persons, this means that these households actually outnumber what we have thought of as the typical family.[8] When the

14

church plans its ministry to families, it will have to take into account the many forms of the family in today's society. The church needs to give careful thought, in particular, to its ministry to singles.

While this work does not deal with special programs for singles, I have emphasized that they be included in all of the activities and programs that the church offers to its families. For example, intergenerational experiences (chapter 18) and family clusters (chapter 19) are designed to include singles and single parents and their children, as well as the members of the church's nuclear families. In other words, whenever the church, itself, becomes to some degree an extended family, everyone can find a meaningful place. This is the dominant thesis of *Family Ministry;* and it deserves further development in the next section.

Family ministry works best when it is part of the church's attempt to be a community of believers. The most favorable context for family ministry is the church. But not just any church. The best context is a church that is attempting to build family kinds of relationships in the spirit of community.

Family ministry is, therefore, not merely a matter of adding additional committees, classes, programs, and personnel. Certainly, these things play a part. But family enrichment that relies too much on additional activities and programs often adds to the time and energy demands that the church places on the family and on individuals. Frequently, these demands short-circuit the wholesome relationships they intended to foster.

Family ministry, then, needs to be integrated into the life of the church rather than being merely one more program among many others. This integration can happen in at least two ways.

First, an emphasis on family life can be inserted into existing programs. For example, the church can offer elective courses on Christian marriage in Sunday school classes. Or, a church might periodically substitute intergenerational events for Sunday school or the evening worship.

A second form of integration is even more substantial than the first. This approach requires educational programs, patterns of organization, and a style of leadership that conform more to the family-like character of the New Testament church than to the more institutional form of the church of today. Then the larger, redemptive community of life, warmth, and unity will provide the nurturing context for training in family living. Those whose childhood homes denied them experiences in wholesome family relationships will find them in the church.

We will thus improve the quality of family life by improving the quality of our church life. The church's role is crucial. With its message and its life of love perhaps it alone has the power to stop the deteriorating spiral in which the American family is now caught. At least it can reverse the cycle for many families.

Developing the family church, "the family-church-family," as I refer to it in Part Three, will not be easy. It may require significant modification in churches that fiercely resist change. It will probably occur over a long period of time. But creating the family church may be our most crucial task—both for the sake of our families and our churches.

PART ONE

THE
PRESSING
PERSPECTIVE

1

In Defense
of Family Ministry

The pastor's voice was sad. His tone and inflection signaled deep concern.

"You simply wouldn't believe how many families in my church are in deep trouble," he said.

But I did believe him. I had heard enough from pastors and lay leaders in similar situations, and had myself seen so much evidence of family problems in the church, that I knew what he was experiencing.

This sense of urgency prompted him to ask me to lead a three-day conference on family living in his church. He and I both knew that a weekend of lectures and workshops could not possibly be a cure-all, but it might help toward solving some problems, and, hopefully, prevent others from occurring.

This pastor's concern and his almost frantic attempt to help the families in his church is typical of evangelical leaders across North America. This situation has made *family ministry* one of the most relevant terms in church life today.

Among evangelicals, this intense interest in the family is a rather recent phenomenon. As a seminary student twenty years ago, I was introduced to family-life ministry by Howard Hendricks, who had left the starting line far ahead of most. At that time only one substantial book on Christian marriage from the evangelical viewpoint was available. It was written by another early starter, Dwight Small.[1]

There is still some resistance to family-life ministry, but pressing reasons for such a ministry are fast overcoming the indifference and resistance. The need for family-life ministry is so urgent that the church's ministry to the family often resembles a rescue effort more than it does an educational venture. As an institution the family is truly facing a crisis.

THE ILLS OF THE FAMILY

Church leaders were among the first to be alerted to the problems endangering the home. In 1937 Regina Wieman sounded this warning in *The Modern Family and the Church:* "The family is going through a long and perilous crisis. Nobody noticed just when it started; nobody can say just how long it will last; nobody knows what the outcome will be."[2]

More recently, Nathan Ackerman writes, "I am a psychiatrist who has devoted a lifetime to studying emotional problems of family living. I have pioneered in the field of family therapy. From where I sit the picture of marriage and family in present day society is a gloomy one."[3]

Scores of writers agree with this assessment. "The home is falling apart and wall to wall carpeting will not hold it together," quipped Methodist bishop Hazen Werner.[4] Kenneth Gangel paints a dark picture of family disintegration and disorganization as a backdrop for his biblical answers to family problems in *The Family First,*[5] and Howard Hendricks implies that the family is in a critical state with his imploring title, *Heaven Help the Home.*[6]

One hour's thumbing through the dozens of texts devoted to the family in any library will convince one that the prophets of family doom are not all within the church. "The United States," says Betty Yorburg, "is regarded by many analysts as a bellwether in the trend toward the disappearance of the family as a social form in urban, computerized societies."[7] And in the words of Edward Shorter: "The nuclear family is crumbling."[8]

It's not just that families have troubles; the family itself is in trouble. Sociologists are suggesting that the crisis is of such proportions that the family as we now know it may not survive.[9] Some futurologists are even forecasting what may take its place rather than arguing for the survival of the family.[10]

Almost daily, American press and television remind us of the family's plight. Our own friends, relatives, and neighbors, with their baffling and sometimes tragic family situations, bring the crisis even closer

19

for most of us. A recent survey by *Better Homes and Gardens* confirmed that the public is aware of the problem. Seventy-one percent of the respondents thought that American family life is in trouble.[11]

Family Instability

Even if we avoid the extremists' swear words—fragmentation, disintegration, and disorganization—we are left with what they represent, instability.

Instability in the family is evident, first of all, in the fact that there are more people terminating their marriages through divorce than ever before. We need not argue about the precise nature of the divorce statistics or whether they are the latest. The fact remains that there is an increase in the dissolving of marriage bonds that is unprecedented. Edward Shorter describes the situation this way:

> Since the mid-1960's divorce rates have accelerated dramatically in every country in Western society. . . . The long, gradual climb (interrupted in the 1950's by a plateau in most places) gave way in the 1960's to an unprecedented explosion. Save for France and Portugal, divorce rates accelerated sharply everywhere around the mid-1960's.[12]

While many different statistics could be summoned to support the claim that there are an increasing number of divorces, the data on divorced women are sufficient proof. Paul C. Glick and Arthur J. Norton, demographers in the U.S. census bureau, calculate that about 12 percent of the marriages contracted by women born between 1900 and 1904 ended in divorce. In contrast, they estimate that between 30 and 40 percent of the marriages of women born between 1940 and 1944 will end in divorce.[13] Glick and Norton also estimate that between 5 and 10 percent of these modern-day divorcees will be divorced a second time.[14]

Still, establishing the reality of this increase in divorce does not reveal exactly what it means. For example, some argue that the divorce rate shows a high, not a low, esteem for marriage because more than two-thirds of divorced women remarry, as do three-fourths of divorced men. It is probably true to say that people are not turning from marriage, but rather from bad marriages. Also, there are some signs that marriage is prospering, since more people are remaining married for a longer period of time than ever before. Of course, given the higher life expectancy of modern times, this would naturally follow. Compared to the past, it's like having two lives to live—and with the same partner. Some, like Lyle Schaller, have concluded that the family in America has never been stronger than it is today.[15]

The rising divorce rate creates a situation of great concern to the church—that is, marriage today is more fragile than it was previously. In the words of Arlene and Jerome Skolnick, "Marriage as a normative institution . . . has lost its taken-for-granted, lifelong quality."[16] Perhaps what is most important here is that the possibility of divorce is an unspoken but significant part of the marriage vows. Today, both partners remain permanently available on the marriage market until death do them part.

This loss of commitment between marriage partners is a matter of concern for both the church and Western society as a whole. It is a sign that there are many unhappy marriages and that couples are not using necessary skills in human relations. And the misery within such homes and the resulting breakup of families are immeasurably destructive to the emotional life of children.

One factor in this problem of divorce and its effects on the family is the disregard for the biblical view of marriage as a permanent bond. It is only within a continuing, secure commitment that true, mature love can develop. People who expect *not* to spend their entire lives together, who will dissolve their marriage when they think friction might warrant it, do not have the necessary basis for constructing a quality Christian marital relationship. Such persons cannot relate to each other in a mature, lasting way.

Marital instability, then, is one of the church's greatest challenges. For this reason, examining the theological structure of marriage is a crucial task. Evangelical leaders at the Continental Congress on the Family recognized this and spoke to this need in their combined statement to the church.[17]

The church also needs to be alert to its ministry to single parents and their children. During the 1960s the number of families headed by single women was twice as great as it was during the 1950s. This problem is concentrated in the black population, where 35 percent of the households are headed by women and only 52 percent of the children under eighteen are living with both parents. For the white population, 10 percent of the homes are headed by women, and 13 percent of the children under eighteen do not live with both parents.[18]

Urie Bronfenbrenner, a professor at Cornell University, maintains that if the present divorce rate continues, one child in six will lose a parent through divorce by the time he or she is eighteen.[19] Though studies show that children of divorced parents seem to fare better than children in unhappy homes, it is still true that the home ruptured by divorce is damaging to children. That there is a higher divorce rate among the offspring of divorced parents underscores this fact.[20]

Most important for those of us in the church, we can teach how a truly satisfying, meaningful Christian marriage can be built on a di-

21

vinely sanctioned commitment. The Bible doesn't demand that marriage be continued as a marathon of misery. It stresses the fulfillment of marriage, not merely the duty of remaining married. Church leaders are not discharging the whole of their responsibility if they warn against divorce but do not teach about marriage. Marital fidelity includes more than avoiding an affair; it demands that there be a growing, satisfying relationship between marriage partners.

There are also social factors that suggest divorce will not soon diminish. The individualism of our capitalistic society contributes to the independent attitude of both marriage partners, and our industrial society provides women with the economic freedom to extract themselves from bad marriages. We can add to these factors the secularism that has reduced a divinely sanctioned commitment to a mere human contract. This divine sanction for marriage, formerly a part of Western culture, is for the most part gone.

The end result of this loss of commitment may result in a postmodern society lacking the family structure as we now know it. One scholar ventures to guess that, with the entire structure of the family shifting, formalized marriage will be replaced by the *free-floating couple*—"a marital dyad subject to dramatic fission and fusions, and without the orbiting satellites of pubertal children, close friends, or neighbors . . . just relatives, hovering in the background, friendly smiles on their faces."[21]

No one knows for certain what the extent of this shift away from societal and religious pressures regulating marriage will be, but a statistic to watch is the number of marriages that occur in a year's time. A sharp reduction would show there is a trend away from traditional marriage. Census figures do show a slight drop, but it is not enough to call this a trend.[22]

While divorce is eroding marriage on one end—the termination of marriage—the sexual revolution is eating away at the other end—the beginning of marriage. Though some sociologists argue that a sexual revolution is not taking place, a sober appraisal of the data makes it obvious that this is the case. From the vantage point of the 1980s, it appears that the revolution had its beginnings in the 1950s and 1960s. "In these decades," Shorter explains, "adolescents in particular began to strip away the sentimental layers from the romantic experience to get at its hard sexual core, thinking eroticism most precious in what human relationships have to offer us and impatient with the delays that feeling once imposed."[23] Surveys dealing with the attitude of youth toward premarital intercourse support the conclusion that there has been a dramatic change in thinking.[24]

Shorter uses a barrage of statistics to support his view that this revolution took place in two steps. First, there was an incursion of premarital intercourse into the lives of the unmarried late in the eighteenth century. Intercourse once again became prevalent among the unmarried after the mid-1950s. In the 1960s the chances were very great that young people who were strongly attracted to each other would extend their relationship to include sexual experiences. And if things did not go well in the realm of sexuality, Shorter contends, "the couple would dissolve and the dance of courtship would recommence with someone else. And that would have been unthinkable in times past."[25]

Causes of this sexual revolution are not too difficult to uncover in our society. Once again, secularism is certainly a major factor. But discovering where this attitude will lead is not so easy. Yorburg maintains that living together prior to marriage will become universal in our society.[26] Whether this prediction will come true will depend on how much value future generations place on marriage as a sanction for promoting security in the relationship of a man and a woman.[27]

The sexual revolution places tremendous demands on the church, because it holds that, according to Scripture, socially sanctioned marriage is the only proper context for explicit sexual expression. The church's position will require a defense of marriage. We will need to explain why God has given the marriage institution—in part to regulate sex for man—and that it is urgently important to maintain it in view of the Fall and the consequent human tendency toward perversion and selfishness. We will need to be more open about the quality of sex within marriage in order to counteract the attention given to sex outside of marriage by the modern media. Youth will need to be convinced that true sexual fulfillment occurs only within the marriage bond, in which there is both love and responsibility. By discovering together what the Bible has to say about sexuality, we can teach parents how to convey right attitudes and information to their children. And we can at the same time teach husbands and wives how to enrich their sexual experiences, as Tim LaHaye has done in his forthright book, *The Act of Marriage.*[28]

Those who are preparing youth for marriage will need to include counsel on how to select a mate without entering into the same premarital intimacy being practiced by most of their peers.

Breakdown of Traditional Roles

Another variance between the church's ideals and the circumstances of the contemporary family is in the matter of roles. The traditional family pattern provided defined roles for males and for females, rendering the marriage institution more secure, though more rigid. Departure from some of the more restrictive aspects of these traditional roles has provided greater creativity for many, but that departure has brought to many couples a disturbing perplexity—a perplexity they have brought with them into the counselor's office. Family counselor Richard Mechem of Santa Fe, New Mexico, speaks of a "hopeless confusion of roles" as one of the most divisive elements in American life.[29]

Part of the upheaval of traditional roles is a result of the democratic and industrial context in which the Western family lives. The industrial revolution began in England about 1760 and later took hold in the United States also. The major consequence for the family was that the home was no longer the production center and the father was absent from the family for most of the day. In the more agricultural society of pre-industrial times the father's role as parent was reinforced by his role as foreman of the work, but with the decline of cottage industry and the rise of factories, work became a much more individual matter for each family member.

The changes brought on by the industrial revolution have resulted in a democratic structure that stresses the individual rather than the family unit. The role of the father has changed from that of economic patriarch to a role built on affection. Individual freedom for other family members has increased because government and industry cater to the individual, not to the family as a unit.

The evangelical church has adapted fairly well to the changing roles of family members. Evangelicals have had no problem asserting the essential equality of married partners. The Continental Congress on the Family in St. Louis stated: "In Christian marriage, the husband and wife strive to become one spiritually, intellectually, emotionally, physically, and function interdependently as equals."[30]

The pronounced dissatisfaction with the traditional role of women expressed by the women's liberation movement has been more difficult to understand and to alleviate. The proportions of this challenge are hard to measure, but at this point they do appear to be far-reaching. There are at least three major problems here for the church to deal with.

First, data confirm that modern women in the home tend to hold themselves and their work in lower esteem than they do the person and the work of men.[31] Thus, a life devoted to the care of children is deemed less rewarding than it was in the past. Of course, the possibility that there are social causes for this attitude toward child care and that it is not merely a product of women's desire for freedom needs to be carefully considered.

Second, this unrest with the traditional role of women puts a severe strain on the nuclear family. "The major unsettlers of the [marital] nest have been the women themselves," notes Edward Shorter.[32]

Third, the role of wife and mother in the nuclear family is often blamed as the source of the modern woman's lack of self-esteem and her inferior vocational status.[33] Thus, the more radical theoreticians maintain that change is not possible within the context of the nuclear family. They insist that some type of communal environment is necessary to liberate women from domestic responsibilities.

Certainly the evangelical church can do no less than proclaim biblical principles describing the divine ideal for the roles of individuals within marriage; but it must also seek to understand the dissatisfaction of modern women and support legitimate remedies to help them. Biblical principles need to be creatively fitted to marriage in modern times.

Powerless Parents

Deprived of clear-cut roles, modern parents seem hard-pressed to achieve one of their major functions—the successful rearing of children. Current books on child rearing call attention to parental helplessness by using the word *power* in their titles. Helen DeRosis informs parents of their power.[34] Others remind fathers to take heart, there is still such a thing as father power.[35]

The avalanche of books on parenting, some of them best sellers, is testimony to the troubles parents have in socializing their children. A major and basic function of the home in almost all known societies, socialization is the process of teaching one how to behave in a group or society.[36] If the home fails its children, it fails society. Radical social engineers maintain that the home has already failed in this task and that alternatives to the nuclear family must be found.

How bad the situation is in the average family is difficult to determine. Juvenile delinquency rates reveal serious deficiencies in many homes. Tension between parent and child is also evident from the numerous cases of child abuse. Physical abuse that involves bodily injury is at epidemic proportions, according to some experts. From a recent survey of over thirteen hundred American families, it was estimated there are two to four million cases of such abuse per year.[37]

Much of the failure in child rearing is due to the problems arising out of an industrialized society. Before a congressional hearing Urie Bronfenbrenner stated:

> Parents find themselves at the mercy of a society which imposes pressures and priorities that allow neither time nor place for meaningful activities and relations between children and adults, which downgrade the role of parents

and the functions of parenthood, and which prevent the parent from doing
things he wants to do as a guide, friend, and companion to his children.[38]

These conditions are especially difficult for the blacks and other
minority groups experiencing poverty. Five percent of American children are living with a mother who is working outside the home and
who is also the only parent. In fact, 43 percent of the nation's mothers
are employed in jobs outside the household. The greatest increase in
such jobs has occurred for mothers of preschool children. One in
every three mothers with children under six is working today.

Fathers also seem to be hard-pressed to find time for their children. The typical father sees home and job as two separate domains.
Fairchild reports that difficulty in combining occupational and family
roles successfully is among the most common sources of guilt and
anxiety for the middle-class male.[39]

A survey of changes in child-rearing practices over a twenty-five-
year period revealed a decrease in all spheres of interaction between
parent and child.[40] Probably the most visible aspect in the wane of
parental influence is to be found in the parent-adolescent sphere.
Shorter maintains that the current reshaping of the family includes the
loss of control by parents over adolescent children.[41] While the young
children continue to learn the basic social skills in the family circle,
"the new development is that adolescent children have begun to
manifest a massive uninterest in their parents' values."[42] Shorter is
careful not to call this a generation gap, to prevent us from thinking
that there is open hostility between adolescents and their parents. He
explains that adolescents are indifferent to parental values, rather than
being opposed to them.[43]

Bronfenbrenner contends that "at every age and grade level, children today show a greater dependency on their peers than they did a
decade ago."[44] Such peer orientation and alienation from parents has
resulted in the rising rates of running away, dropping out of school,
drug abuse, suicide, delinquency, vandalism, and violence.[45]

The conclusions of Shorter and Bronfenbrenner are true beyond
question for some American families. The slackening of parental
power and the corresponding rise of peer-group influence is especially true for families in which one parent is frequently absent.[46] How
true this situation is for the average family is a much-contested question. When Daniel Offer reported the results of his extensive study of
what he termed "the normal adolescent," he assured his readers that
their values were essentially the same as those of their parents.[47]

No matter what we conclude concerning the power of parents, we
can say that they are having great difficulty fulfilling their child-rearing

task. For many years their cries for help have brought forth a response from the church as well as from secular agencies.

As early as 1890, child-study groups and child-welfare organizations organized parent classes. When the term *parent education* came into vogue in 1924, it became clear that many parents were at sea when it came to controlling their children. Earlier, parenting practices were handed down through family lines like family heirlooms.

The church was not far behind the sociologists, psychologists, and educators in turning its attention to the family. "We have been aware of the troubles of the family for more than seventy years," reported John Charles Wynn.[48]

Because the nuclear family has always been the major socializing agent, many sociologists are desperate in their pleas to government and society to help the home. Sociologist Betty Yorburg warns, "The nuclear family . . . needs massive help."[49]

Larry Richards is also urgent in his plea:

> Today the church is on the edge of many great decisions. But certainly one of the most significant is this: Are we willing to do what must be done for the church to help the family face the future? Or will we abandon the nuclear family to face essentially alone these forces it was not designed to overcome without the support of the body?[50]

INSTITUTIONAL FAILURE AND THE POTENTIAL OF THE HOME

More than crisis in the home bids the church turn its attention to the family. The family itself has great potential for providing family-life education, especially when one reviews the record of the church's programs of Christian education. The Peninsula Bible Church, of Palo Alto, California, was a front runner in the second half of the twentieth century in dealing with the church's failure to minister adequately to the family. It declared its dependence on family nurture because of the ineffectiveness of traditional educational programs in the church: "The church's system of educating children . . . has been a relative failure for twenty-five years."[51]

For this same reason early-twentieth-century churches had also turned to the home for Christian education. Changing times rendered the Sunday school insufficient for mainline churches, particularly because of the changing theological views. Before that time Protestants had relied on both the public school and the Sunday school for religious nurture.[52] But a rising secularism crept into public schools, making them less of an ally and more of a liability to the church. Alone, the Sunday school did not have enough of the character-building force the church needed.

This condition spurred an effort on the part of church leaders to supplement the Sunday school with other educational programs. What followed was the "agency period" of religious education, which gave birth to the following familiar institutions: vacation Bible school, weekday boys' and girls' clubs, day schools, youth fellowships, summer conferences and camps, denominational boards of religious education, and religious education departments in seminaries. Since all of this institutional machinery needed specialists to organize and supervise it, each church was installing a desk for its brand-new staff member, the director of religious education.[53]

The Great Depression slowed this trend toward church programs of Christian education. During the economic crunch, religious education directors learned that they were the last hired, the first fired. Programs disintegrated because most pastors were then saddled with a work for which they had little interest and little training. This left the churches with inadequate Sunday schools and ailing supplementary agencies.[54]

The church then turned back to the home. During this difficult time, one leader lamented, "The active concern of the home with religious education is our only hope."[55] Although the home was already busy contending with its own crises, in 1940 it was obvious that the family must also be the chief religious teacher.[56]

We evangelicals are reliving in our own way this shift in the home base of religious education from the church to the home and back again. Until the sixties evangelicals had not become disheartened with the Sunday school, though the liberals had. On the contrary, evangelical Sunday schools enjoyed revivallike growth in America after World War II. Between 1945 and 1960 Sunday school enrollment had almost doubled.[57]

In the sixties, however, many institutions were challenged to prove their worth against charges of ineffectiveness, obsolescence, hollow traditionalism, and uselessness.[58] Church renewal was in part spawned by the insistence that the church's educational agencies, among them the Sunday school, were no longer productive. It was not that the enrollment statistics in evangelical churches proved the Sunday school obsolete. As Dean Kelley's revealing analysis showed, enrollment figures continued to climb.[59] Rather, it was the suspicion that church programs were not capable of producing mature Christians in modern circumstances. The agency approach being inadequate, the home must be enlisted.

The modification of the traditional approach to Christian education that is required in a home-centered approach is one of the most controversial features of current family-life education. The lingering popularity of the agencies is just one aspect of the issue. The larger question is whether the home can really be an effective center for discipling, an issue we will consider later.

HELPING CHURCHES THROUGH THE FAMILY

The church today wants to help the home in training future generations in the faith but it is also interested in the way home life affects church life. Some evangelicals maintain that programs to rescue the home are in turn necessary for the survival of the church. Robert Lynn sees this argument put forth already in the literature of the thirties, and he quotes one such writer: "The family needs the church, the church needs the family."[60] Many evangelical writers today take the same position. One writes: "As goes the family—so goes the church."[61]

The Christian church and the Christian home, as institutions, are as closely bound together as Siamese twins. If they are cut apart, a major artery may be severed and cause one or both to die. The church cannot function as it should in a disordered world if it cannot rely on the home to play the major part in Christian nurture.[62]

The challenge to the church, then, is crucial in our day, when many are speaking of the death of the American family. Educator Ted Ward takes this position in his address to the Continental Congress on the Family, and he makes it the basis of his forthright plea to help the home. He maintains, "The family serves a particular and apparently indispensable role with the church."[63]

FAMILY ENRICHMENT

Of course, family enrichment is a major topic of interest for many non-Christians as well. Ever since World War II, the North American continent has been experiencing an era of familism. "Sometimes dubbed togetherness, this vogue has permeated the social value of a generation," says Wynn, "and has come in particular to characterize suburban living."[64]

Moreover, the market for publications and seminars on family matters, such as marriage, is by no means all a crisis-based phenomenon. Couples with good communication are urged to improve. Husbands and wives enjoying some degree of intimacy are taught how to have more. In summary, the Christian's search for a better home life is part of the search for the abundant life that Christ tells us can be ours in all spheres of life.

THE OTHER SIDE: CONSIDERING THE CRITICS

Despite the strong case for family ministry, it has met often with indifference and resistance. On the basis of his own survey, Norman

The Pressing Perspective

Wright indicated that the churches that had a concentrated ministry to the family were the exception rather than the rule.[65] Out of five hundred directors of Christian education and youth directors who received Wright's questionnaire, ninety-six responded. Among these, only one-third indicated that their church members had heard any sermons on the family during the previous two years. And one-third reported that there had been no program related to the family during that same period of time.

Marriage counselors and family-life educators also note this shortcoming of the church. Sixty-six percent of twenty-five hundred of these professionals agreed with the following statement in another survey: "The churches are not doing an adequate job of promoting and maintaining family life as a contemporary concept."[66]

This weakness of the church may be due in part to the sense of inadequacy among church staff members for carrying out this ministry. It is significant that no seminary requires a course on the Christian home. That there is no lack of interest in family ministry on the part of pastors was confirmed by a recent survey by Larry Richards. Richards states that nearly all the respondents were sensitive to the need for developing the home as the center of Christian nurture.[67]

Nevertheless, through the years family-life ministry has drawn much criticism. Though perhaps not openly expressed, it can be seen in the tensions arising over programing in the local church. Resistance to family-life ministry has produced some insights that are instructive.

The Home–Church Conflict

Underlying much of this reluctance has been the sense of competition between church and home. Julie Gorman, writing from years of experience in family ministry, describes a lingering either-or complex. "Historically, there has often been a tendency . . . to focus on one or the other. Churches outstanding for their large membership and growing Sunday schools are not, by and large, correspondingly known for a strong focus also on the home."[68]

Much of this tension has probably been due to the fear that the church's programs would die. Positions of leadership in these programs took up the time of faithful church leaders, and this often involved sacrificing family life for church service. Jesus' own statements concerning the priority of the kingdom prompted pastors and laymen to justify this neglect of the family. Because the church relied so heavily on so few to staff its growing number of organizations, its progress resulted in fragmented homes and lonely children. When laymen began to give priority to their families, key programs threatened to collapse; so a competitive spirit was fostered.

One church leader told how far misguided zeal for the church's ministry can go. He had motivated a man in his church to devote more than thirty hours a week to the bus ministry. This situation alienated him from his wife and eventually brought about their divorce. Hopefully, such examples are becoming fewer in number. There is a growing sensitivity in the church to the needs of church leaders' families and a realization that church programs should be constructed so they cooperate, rather than compete, with the home.

The Conflict With Mission

The neglect or rejection of family-life ministry may also be due to the enormity of the local church's task. Concerned with evangelism, Christian education, worship, missions, Bible study, sharing and serving, and administrative matters, church leaders may tend to see family-life education as one more burdensome chore. Family-life ministry could make such demands on church leaders and modify established programs to such an extent that it would dwarf the outreach of the church.

In times past, critics of the family-centeredness of mainline churches have contended that this was a "new idolatry."[69] These critics said that the emphasis on the family would cause the church to ignore its mission to influence social structures. Schooled in liberal theology, they balked at the idea of applying Christian ethics to personal relationships if this meant ignoring the church's mission to society.

Such criticism should not be dismissed lightly. *Hyperfamilism*—a virtual idolatry of the home—is always a danger.[70] No doubt one source of such idolatry is the spirit that has captured the American suburb. There the home has become a fortress that shields the individual from the larger community.

Caution should keep us from permitting family ministry to jeopardize the church's larger task of evangelism. There are at least three basic principles that should guide the church's family-life ministry.

First, we need to recognize the importance of the family—that it does have a theological priority. Scripture emphasizes the importance of the family. We cannot consider it perilous or impractical to act on the promptings of Scripture.

Second, there has to be a realization that the church and the home should not be in conflict. If the traditional church's approach to evangelism does harm to family life, it has to be changed because both family and church have biblical mandates. In turn, should the family emphasis hurt evangelistic outreach, something is again wrong.

31

The Pressing Perspective

Third, accomplishing its evangelistic task while also preserving the family may require a modification of the church's program. Larry Richards says it forcefully: "The local body must be designed (and in some cases drastically redesigned) to affirm the significance of the family."[71] In certain instances it is obvious that the church's programs do not support family life. Continuing in that direction in the name of evangelism is an obvious justification of the means by the end. Yet, before us are creative examples of churches that have overhauled programs in order to accommodate the family, while continuing to have an effective outreach. If we are too busy to minister to the family, we are too busy.

Ignoring Atypical Households

Perhaps the most serious charge against making family ministry one of the major concerns of the church is that this neglects the many church members who are not living in a nuclear-family household. Atypical households, such as single people and childless couples, may be neglected because the ministries of evangelism and education are deficient in a church that is wrapped up in its families. Single persons often report that they feel most alone during the church's worship service, a time when they are surrounded by families. Unless there is a concerted effort to make single persons as well as those who are divorced and widowed feel comfortable in church, they may stay away. An informal survey conducted by a member of an organization called Parents Without Partners showed that in a significant number of cases the relationship of the divorced person to the church changes: some stop attending church, at least for a while; some change churches; and some stop going to church altogether.[72]

That we should be very careful in our approach to family ministry becomes even more obvious when we look at the profile of the North American home. Fewer than 50 percent of the people in this country live in what we consider to be the "typical" family—a nuclear family that includes husband, wife, and at least one child. (If we modify this stereotype to include only wives who are not employed outside the home, the percentage is reduced to 23 percent.[73]) The rest of the people are single, divorced, widowed, married with no children at home, or children not living with both parents. Census data on living arrangements show that the number of people living as single persons is increasing, with the greatest increase occurring among young males and relatively older females.[74]

2

Today's
Family

A desperate situation often occasions short-term solutions that fail and lead to sullen resignation. For example, in the area of Christian education, Larry Richards warns against "a plastic packaging of highly promoted curriculum revisions which never touch the real needs."[1] And in contemporary family life, complex issues require long-range solutions, not simple answers and faddish programs.

Remedies will have to be based on an in-depth analysis of the family, just as effective treatment follows careful diagnosis. Church literature on family-life education too often reveals a superficial and alarmist approach that lacks objective insight into what is happening to the Western family. Such literature tends to produce myths, half-truths, or generalizations. These inaccurate ideas are like blurred x-rays that prevent accurate prognosis.

It is not correct, for instance, to think that people in modern society consider the family unimportant. That idea is a myth. Popular terms like *disintegration* and *fragmentation* are no doubt responsible for perpetuating this hollow concept. According to this view, working mothers don't care about the home and fathers no longer enjoy family life. Or else the word *unimportant* is used to convey the idea that the family no longer has a strategic function in society. Some Christian leaders cite secular sociologists who maintain that the responsibilities and roles of the family of earlier times are now being handled by larger social groups. Thus, such leaders maintain, the home is less important today than it was then.

Despite the claims of such theorists, the family is still important to the majority of people and to society's well-being. When questioned, Americans affirm that the family has a strategic place in their lives. Among youth eighteen to twenty-five, for example, 81 percent of the noncollege segment rated the family as a high personal value, as did 68 percent of college youth.[2]

As for the family being stripped of its functions because it is no longer necessary to modern society, that too is false. "In many ways," says J. Richard Udry, "the nuclear family has become more important as a social unit."[3] The family is in jeopardy in our culture not because it is of little consequence but for the opposite reason—because it is so significant. It would be more helpful and accurate, then, to speak of the contemporary family as being different than the family of earlier times.

Another myth is that we need to return to the recent past in order to improve the family. "Too much church literature," wrote R. W. Fairchild, "betrays a wish for today's families to remain just as they were in the 1890s."[4] This wishful thinking is unrealistic for two reasons. First, today's society is so different from that of the nineteenth century that such a retreat is impossible. Second, what people want to get back to may never have existed in the first place.

Family sociologist William Goode has aptly described the difference between the actual family of a century ago and what he calls "the classical family of Western nostalgia."

It is a pretty picture of life down on grandma's farm. There are lots of happy children, and many kinfolk live together in a large rambling house. Everyone works hard. Most of the food to be eaten during the winter is grown, preserved and stored on the farm. The family members repair their own equipment, and in general the household is economically self-sufficient. The family has many functions; it is the source of economic stability and religious, educational and vocational training. Father is stern and reserved, and has the final decision in all important matters. Life is difficult, but harmonious, because everyone knows his task and carries it out. All boys and girls marry, and marry young. Young people, especially the girls, are likely to be virginal at marriage and faithful afterward. Though the parents do not arrange their children's marriages, the elders do have the right to reject a suitor and have a strong hand in the final decision. After marriage, the couple lives harmoniously, either near the boy's parents or with them, for the couple is slated to inherit the farm. No one divorces.

Those who believe we are seeing progress rather than retrogression often accept these same stereotypes but describe the past in words of different emotional effect. We have progressed, they say, from the arbitrary power of elders toward personal freedom for the young, from cold marriages based on economic arrangements to unions based on the youngsters' right of choice, from rigidly maintained class barriers between children to an open class system, from the subjugation of the wife to equalitarianism and companion-ship in marriage, and from the repression of the children's emotions to per-missiveness.

Like most stereotypes, that of the classical family of Western nostalgia leads us astray. When we penetrate the confusing mists of recent history, we find few examples of this "classical" family. Grandma's farm was not eco-nomically self-sufficient. Few families stayed together as large aggregations of kinfolk. Most houses were small, not large. We now *see* more large old houses than small ones since they survived longer because they were likely to have been better constructed. The one-room cabins rotted away. True enough, divorce was rare, but we have no evidence that families were gener-ally happy. Indeed, we find, as in so many other pictures of the glowing past, that each past generation of people writes of a period *still* more remote, *their* grandparents' generation, when things really were much better.[5]

If Goode's observations are true, and more recent studies show that they are, our task is not to retreat to the nineteenth century but to forge modern families based on biblical principles.

Another fanciful concept is that the nuclear family will soon be obsolete. It is true that there are signs of the inadequacy and deterio-ration of the family, as we have already shown in chapter 1. The threat to the family is not mere idle propaganda invented to sell family-survival kits. But it is also correct to say that more people *think* the family is obsolete than previously did. In 1968 only one in four stu-dents (24 percent) believed that marriage was an obsolete institution. In the past few years the figure has increased to approximately 32 percent.[6]

It is true, moreover, that alternatives to the family are being suggested and tried. Letha and John Scanzoni mention a number of alternatives practiced in some degree today, including communes and group marriages.[7] There is also a trend toward the casual "living together" arrangement, sometimes called "unstructured trial mar-riages" or "ad hoc arrangements." Single life is another alternative, although research does not confirm any certain trend toward lifelong singleness.[8] None of these alternatives has taken hold in a fashion that suggests a revolutionary change is around the corner.

In fact, reversals are occurring in some experimental situations designed to modify or replace the family. Nuclear and extended family customs are beginning to appear once more in the widely publicized Israeli kibbutzim, where the traditional family was modified to fit the purposes of a collectivist society.[9]

Even in the Soviet Union, where there has been strong government encouragement of communal living, the nuclear family still seems destined to survive. "Long live the Soviet family," exclaimed Urie Bronfenbrenner.[10]

Writing about the future of the nuclear family, Betty Yorburg, well aware of its history and the present crisis, is quite optimistic: "The nuclear family will not only persist into the twenty-first century, but it will be stronger than ever."[11] So it seems best to speak of the nuclear family as changing, not vanishing.

Predictions that the family will survive must not rob us of our zeal to help, however. That people are suggesting and even practicing alternatives indicates more than a rebellion against God's design. Perhaps the search for alternatives shows that the nuclear family is hard-pressed to meet the needs of both individuals and society. If so, we need to learn to live within the nuclear-family pattern and to adopt changes that will make that pattern more functional and satisfying. Helping others make that adjustment requires an understanding of the contemporary nuclear family that is not distorted by myth.

The factors that formed the nuclear family are complex and varied. Two that are frequently cited are industrialization and urbanization. When families moved from the farm to the city, vast changes resulted. But by no means are all the changes attributable to these two social factors alone.

Some sociologists maintain that the family as we know it today was being formed prior to the industrial revolution.[12] Probably the greatest factors influencing the family are the individualism and secularism that are fostered by modern democracy.

But whatever the factors in its formation, the family today is rather novel and, as we shall see, under unusual pressures. The following description of the contemporary nuclear family is like a yard of cloth. The characteristics in this description are like various patterns interwoven into one piece of material. This interweaving will result in some necessary repetition and overlapping.

The Nuclear Family

The focus of family life in America is on the nuclear family—a family that consists of both parents and their child or children. This statement does not overlook the existence of other family types, primarily the single-parent home, which has become more prominent in recent years. It has already been noted that there are many persons who live alone, particularly elderly men and women and young adults. The local congregation is being stirred to action by the needs of individuals in all types of family and nonfamily situations.

Despite the fact that a significant number of people are not part of a nuclear family, we can say that the concept and existence of the modern nuclear family is central to the well-being of modern society. Its unique characteristics dictate that any changes made must be grounded in creative and informed thinking. Searching for its major features, we find first of all that the modern family is primarily a *conjugal unit.*

The Conjugal Unit

A mistaken notion that has recently dissolved under closer sociological scrutiny is the idea that industrialization has forced the nuclear family to replace the extended family. For some time now, Americans have tuned in the Waltons, supposing that the passing of that era is the basis of most of our social ills. Like most generalizations, this notion contains an element of truth but is not fully accurate.

First, *it is clear that, technically speaking, the extended family was never a part of life in America.* Some definitions are required here. The term *extended family* refers to a husband, wife, dependent offspring, and married sons with their spouses and their offspring, all of whom reside together. This type of family is seldom encountered in any society, and it has certainly had little place in American life.[13]

If, however, a nuclear family along with one or more other adult relatives is considered an extended family, we can speak of the extended family in America. Such was the case in rural America, where the farm was turned over to one of the sons, who then went with his family to live in the farmhouse with his parents. Yet in most cases this occurred during the time between the retirement of the parents and their deaths. Thus, even this situation did not constitute an extended family in the strict sense of the term. What is relevant for us here is that in our affluent and mobile society there has been a reduction of the number of other adults living with the nuclear family. The existence of even this modified form of extended family in America has been a declining phenomenon, and this is one reason that the nuclear family is left very much alone.

The extended family plays a less important role now than it did in preindustrial society. Controversy swirls around this proposition. John Demons offers evidence to show that one's relationships to cousins, uncles, and aunts are no more intense today than they were in seventeenth-century New England. He explains that these relation-

37

ships were as functionally irrelevant in the seventeenth century as they are today.[14]

The question arises, How do sociologists such as Demons deal with the fact that it is the nuclear family that occupies most residences today? These sociologists explain that though there may not be other adult relatives present in such homes, the nuclear family is not isolated from its kin. "The completely isolated nuclear family with no relatives within easy visiting distance is relatively rare," says Yorburg.[15] Studies show that extended family members are called on in emergencies and for financial help, as well as for companionship; and this happens even in the urban centers.[16]

The issue of the isolation of the nuclear family is crucial for those of us in the church who want to minister to families. A large share of the crisis of the nuclear family has been blamed on its being isolated from its kin. If this is true, this is a pressing problem that needs a solution.

The experts line up on both sides of this question. The evidence, however, seems to be inconclusive. What does emerge is that, in general, there is a qualitative difference in the relationship of nuclear family members to kin nowadays, compared with preindustrial times. Yorburg concurs with others in concluding that today's patterns are different "from the daily contact and interdependence based on economic necessity that characterized extended families in traditional societies."[17]

Thus, there is some foundation for speaking of the decline of the extended family. Functions that were formerly taken care of within the extended family are now performed by specialized agencies not based on kinship (functions such as caring for the elderly, one's occupation, etc.). For many Americans the extended family has gradually ceased to perform any function besides that of being a vehicle for friendship.[18] This phenomenon may be true in a special way for evangelicals, a topic we will consider next.

Weakened extended-family contacts may be a major factor in the loneliness within many evangelical homes. Several factors make this a highly plausible assertion. First, studies have shown that the extended family is more intact in Jewish and Catholic homes than among Protestants.[19] Second, the evangelical constituency includes a major proportion of the upward-mobile middle class living in suburban America.[20] A compelling description of such families is made by Seeley, Sim, and Loosley:

> What is most characteristic of the upper middle class families is their geographic and social isolation from the extended family, despite the fact that contact may be made from time to time. The ideal for these families is that of

separateness—both in terms of their physical habitation and the kinds of influence they encourage or sanction for their children. For such families, a man's home is indeed his castle.[21]

French historian Philippe Aries says this isolation results in the suburb becoming a form of ghetto.[22] A third factor is the isolation many evangelicals experience when non-Christian kin misunderstand or oppose their Christian commitment.

The families to which the church ministers, then, are largely families cut off from their kin. This disjoining is perhaps even more significant because it has a chronological dimension as well.

The nuclear family has lost touch with its history and tradition. While this generalization is not true of all nuclear families, it appears to be the case for the majority. Edward Shorter develops this thesis in his portrayal of the modern family.[23] The modern nuclear family, often without contact with older generations to keep family memories alive, lacks a history, a family tradition. In the past, the family was held fast to the larger social order by ties to generations past and future, as well as to kin living presently. Shorter writes: "Awareness of ancestral traditions and ways of doing business would be present in people's minds as they went about their day."[24] "Now, in its journey into the modern world," he continues, "the modern world of the family . . . has parted from the lineage, that chain of generations stretching across time."[25] Thus, the nuclear family has drifted onto the high seas, alone on its voyage; and it is in need of help.

The independent nuclear family is less equipped to face its tasks and hardships. The first and most obvious problem for the nuclear family is the loss of counsel and practical help. The psychologist represents the loss of the first of these, and the baby-sitter is a vivid symbol of the loss of the latter. One man, who with his wife is harrassed by the hectic pace of life, partly caused by the need to chauffeur two teen-agers too young to drive, sighed, "If my father lived nearby, he would be happy to drive the kids around." This man was envisioning but one of the many ways in which the extended family could be significantly helpful to the nuclear family.

Second, in today's nuclear family children lack exposure to adult models other than their parents. The superficiality or lack of intergenerational contacts outside the home leaves the children with no other adults, and in particular no adults other than their parents, to emulate.

Third, what happens to the emotional tone of the home may constitute the most serious aspect of this loss of contact with kin. The members of the modern family have more intimate relationships with one another than earlier families did, and these relationships must now bear a heavier emotional load. If relatives were present, they could dilute family tensions. But friction in a nuclear home dedicated to togetherness produces an atmosphere in which every quarrel can become a crisis, and each misunderstanding threatens to result in the isolation of one person from another. "Under contemporary circumstances," says Udry, "it is easy for families to become boiling cauldrons of emotionality."[26] Left with the task of being the major source of emotional security of adults and children during most of life, the nuclear family becomes almost explosively emotional. That climate is such a major component of the modern family and of our own lives that it demands further description.

The Intimate Unit

In this context of loneliness and the loss of history and tradition, we see the modern family moving in the direction of intimacy, not dissolution. Having heard so much about the family's disintegration, it is jolting to realize that the modern family desires intimacy. It is also a surprise to recognize that this quest for intimacy is something relatively recent in Western society. Philippe Aries notes this trend in his influential book, *Centuries of Childhood.*[27] Dominating this book is the thesis that since the thirteenth century the family has moved from a large, corporate form strongly enmeshed in society at all levels to the more or less nuclear form we see today.

Today's companionship form of the family has replaced the institutional model, which was more of an economic and social arrangement. This is not to say that love was entirely absent in the traditional family; it simply did not have the primary place in maintaining family solidarity. This fact shows up in the courtship practices of those times and in the decision to marry, a decision that was in most cases made by the parents. And parents gave more consideration to material welfare and social standing than to anything else. Sexual intimacy, so highly valued today, may well have been of less concern then, especially to lower-class couples who had little opportunity for privacy in a home where everyone slept in the same room.[28] Thus, the major concern was whether each person fulfilled the explicitly defined tasks expected of him or her.

This priority of economic factors in earlier times is shocking to those of us in modern times who prize intimate family relationships. Yet, there is ample proof that the medieval peasant would call a veterinarian for a sick cow before he would call the doctor for his ailing wife. In the peasant's value system, because of his poverty, the cow was more dear to him than his wife was.[29]

A comparison of the modern family with the traditional family shows several major differences between the two.

40

TRADITIONAL	MODERN
(Prior to the nineteenth century)	(Today)
There was a lack of privacy. (Except for upper and middle classes, houses were small; whole families slept in one room.) Often other adults lived in the home.	Privacy is highly valued. The nuclear family lives alone. Sometimes pregnancy is delayed or even precluded for the sake of companionship.
Tasks were explicitly defined. The expectation was that each person would do his or her work faithfully.	The expectation is that of companionship. Other roles are secondary to this.
A measure of economic security was the major consideration in the choice of a marriage partner.	The major consideration in the choice of a marriage partner is romantic love.
Sexual relationships in marriage (all evidence seems to suggest) were not as developed or as important as today. Religious views and a lack of privacy inhibited the development of the couple's sexual intimacy.	Sexual intimacy in the relationship is highly valued.

What accounts for the change? Edward Shorter uses an impressive array of statistics to demonstrate that the Western world underwent a sexual revolution that brought about the present-day emphasis on intimacy. Romantic love unseated economic and other practical concerns during the time he dubbs "the revolution of sentiment."[30]

This revolution affected not only the relationship between husband and wife but also the ties between mother and child. Shorter makes a convincing case for his contention that there was a lesser degree of motherly love and devotion prior to the nineteenth century. Maternal indifference to infants characterized Western society prior to this time.[31] (He follows Aries's thesis here.) Babies were frequently shuttled off to faraway places for the first two years of life to be cared for under filthy conditions by wet nurses. Going off to work in the factory or fields, the mothers had little choice. In some places in Europe the mortality rate for such children was as high as 90 percent.[32]

This high mortality rate no doubt contributed to the parents' lack of attachment to their children. Knowing the great possibility of losing a child made a close emotional attachment to babies too costly. In some countries, parents did not give names to their babies. Frequently parents forgot how old their children were, gave the name of a baby who had recently died to one newly born, or couldn't even remember how many children they had brought into the world. Mothers indifferent to their babies? It sounds unbelievable to the modern man and woman. Yet a band of scholars has for some time been arguing that it was so in earlier times.

Those of us accustomed to insulated living in the nuclear family can hardly identify with the following record of a seventeenth-century Englishman's family:[33]

NAME	DATE OF LEAVING	AGE IN YEARS AND MONTHS	PLACE AND OCCUPATION TO WHICH BOUND
Jane	21 April 1656	10.6	Cholchester, education
Thomas	15 May 1659	15.5	London, bound apprentice
John	9 Jan. 1667	15.4	London, bound apprentice
Anne	24 June 1668	14.0	London, bound a servant
Mary	2 Feb. 1668	10.0	White Colne, education
Elizabeth	23 April 1674	13.9	Bury St., Edmunds, education
Rebecca	17 April 1677	13.5	London, bound a servant

While Shorter's view of the "traditional" family is not without its opponents, it does provide a helpful backdrop for understanding the phenomenal onrush to intimacy during the last one hundred years. Most of us so wrapped up in this longing for intimacy in the family find it difficult to imagine that it could have been otherwise. But Shorter's research shows that this is a new emphasis.

What is the significance of this modern emphasis on intimacy? First, if today's family has been preceded by a less-personal institutional form, the modern family is put in a different light. We would judge that since the beginning of the nineteenth century, the family has more, not less, intimacy than families living prior to this time. Shorter says,

> Is there, for example, a growing lack of communion between the spouses? Not at all. As much openness in communication between husband and wife as we're ever going to see was laid down during the nineteenth century in the form of romantic love; spontaneous exchanges between husband and wife were achieved when what I call *domesticity* was hammered into place a hundred years ago.[34]

This statement helps us see the extent of our preoccupation with romantic intimacy. Societies tend to hold certain relationships as primary. The twentieth-century United States has chosen to emphasize the significance of the heterosexual peer relationship above all others. Not only does popular literature and music focus on it, but child rearing is pointed toward it. The protracted period of adolescence in the United States now provides an entire decade for exclusive preoccupation with each other for the *sex-pair.*

Udry states: "The family system is built upon it [affection between sexes]. Americans expect the [male-female] relationship to be the most important source of emotional satisfaction and support."[35]

This does not suggest that intimacy is achieved in every case; the important point is that it is so highly valued as an ideal. Modern individuals look to the family for their primary relational satisfaction. This phenomenon above all others boldly and forcefully marks the modern family and accounts for its strategic place in our emotional lives. This makes the family more important than ever, since it provides the longest and most significant relationships in life.[36]

Second, this emphasis on intimacy reminds us, by contrast, that traditional marriage expectations are still present in modern society, and that the nature of the marriage relationship is being questioned. Vestiges of traditional marriage patterns persist in the contemporary scene.

Sociologist John Hostetler, himself raised in a church community, calls attention to this fact in his description of the Amish family. "Personal relationships between husband and wife," he reports, "are quiet and sober with no apparent demonstration of affection. The relationship is strikingly different from the way sentiments are indicated and affection is expressed in American society."[37]

That this traditional style can also be found among modern blue-collar workers should indicate to us that it is important to provide biblical justification for the intimate and romantic relationship between husband and wife advocated by books and conferences on marriage.

Third, the preoccupation with romantic intimacy in modern marriage helps explain the high regard for sexual expression in current marriages and in society in general, since physical intimacy is the most unique and intense expression of affection. Sometimes it seems that little else holds the marriage together. Pressure on couples to perform well sexually may account for the fact that when there are marital problems, the sexual relationship is also affected. Thus, the quest for intimacy is a significant factor in the high divorce rate of modern times.

It is to be expected that as friendship becomes more important in marriage, more marriages will end in divorce. It is more difficult to be a friend than to be a master; it is more difficult to be a friend than to be just property. By the same token, it is much easier to lose a friend than to lose one's property; and is much easier to lose a friend than to get away from one's owner.[38] It is ironic that the desire for togetherness in marriage plays a major part in its fragmentation. It is a tragedy that divorce is becoming more prevalent as affection becomes the cement holding the nuclear family together.

Fourth, there is value in seeing that this strong intimacy basis of the nuclear home is a contributing factor in one of the major problems of the nuclear family—its loss of contact with the community. The search for intimacy works two ways. It is a centripetal force, moving family members toward emotional fusion; but it is also a centrifugal force, pulling them away from the larger community.

Richard Sennet argues that Americans, upon reaching middle-class status, "turned in upon themselves and fashioned a family of great intensity at the expense of extrafamilial diversity."[39] Is it possible that this thirst for intimacy in the home is related to the drying up of other meaningful relationships? Some persons identify this longing as one of the major faults of modern society, and of the nuclear family in particular.

The Isolated Unit

The desire for intimacy in the home is not without its cost, according to Aries and Shorter. After citing a host of statistics to show that married couples of all ages are achieving greater sexual intimacy, Shorter writes:

> One can conjure up visions of these legions of couples fiddling and fooling with each other in this tremendous forward leap of marital eroticism—and yet, if I am right, one price paid for this new capacity to explore one's sensory responses has been the abandonment of meaningful emotional life outside the home. . . . Nothing is free in this world.[40]

This hypothesis is supported by many other experts. When Sennett compared modern suburban families in America and working-class immigrant families living at the turn of the nineteenth century, he reached the same conclusion that Shorter did—we have lost community. And in that loss the family has not merely become important, it has become all-important. "The character of city life," writes Sennett, "was such as to break down the insularity of the ethnic enclaves that formed in the immigrant sections."[41] Prior to the revolution of sentiment there was a round of daily activity that brought adults and children into contact with a variety of people and experiences.

When these contacts were lost, the demands on relationships within the family were intensified.

Shorter disagrees with Sennett in regard to the cause of this loss of community. It was the demand for affection in the family that cut into community ties, he claims. In traditional European communities life was centered in community. Capitalism and urbanization unleashed the individualism and freedom that allowed husbands and wives to strengthen the ties of affection between themselves. This, according to Shorter caused them to become isolated from the community.

The story of community loss has been told and retold in popular presentations, beginning with David Riesman's *The Lonely Crowd*. In *We, the Lonely People* Ralph Keyes summarized his findings in these words: "We feel daily our sense of community loss."[42]

But the answer to the question, What should the relationship between the nuclear family, and the community be? is not so obvious. The need for a connection between the nuclear family and the community is a reality of major proportions in understanding the family. It means that the church ministers to many families who are adrift from both kin and community.

Think for a moment about this family portrait: it is not a home with walls broken down, its occupants forced apart by community demands and relationships, but a castle, its wide moat neatly dug, within which members press and implore one another for more love, openness, closeness, identity, and togetherness—the emotional stuff of human existence. Shorter adds substance to our imagination: "A New York existence in the twenty-first floor apartments that overlook the East River differs from domestic life about the tanner shop in eighteenth-century Memmingen, partly because the one seals out the outside world, while the other is punctured by it at many points."[43]

And what has this loss of community, this break with kin, and this turning toward itself done to the nuclear family? First, it has placed unprecedented demands on the parents to provide for the basic emotional needs of their offspring with little help from the outside. Prior to the emergence of the modern family, emotional attachments were diffused over a wider group than just the immediate family. Today the child's emotional attachments are in most cases confined to the few people in her or his immediate family.

Second, the nuclear family's isolation forces the couple to concentrate on their relationship to such a degree that a tremendous pressure to succeed sometimes makes that success elusive. Studies show that this expectation is clearly a factor in the degree of marital satisfaction attained. "Blue-collar" housewives who do not have nor greatly expect to have a close relationship with their husbands but who do have close friendships with other housewives are, on the whole, more satisfied with their marriages than the wives of white-collar workers.[44]

These blue-collar wives have female confidants who serve as the functional equivalents of their husband's work mates. As blue-collar workers are less geographically mobile than many white-collar workers, the wives of the former have more time to develop and maintain close friendships. Blue-collar wives are also likely to have kin living nearby.[45]

The more isolated white-collar couple has to rely heavily on their own resources. Seminary students are in some cases an example of this. Sometimes their isolated experience contributes to an eventual rupture of the relationship. It starts when these newlyweds leave extended family and friends and arrive in a new area. They move into their first apartment, often with high expectations of living together in intense closeness. In building their relationship, however, they may neglect to settle down in a church. They seem like butterflies, flitting from church to church, establishing no meaningful relationships.

In the meantime, the husband is busy with studies; but not so busy that he cannot develop some close friends among the student body. But his wife may lack outside contact and long for extended family and friends who are now out of reach. Her relationship with her husband may become her only in-depth bond. The demands on the marriage to supply so much for her leads to dissatisfaction, particularly when the husband's studies interfere. Eventually, the relationship that is supposed to be everything becomes nothing, and she announces, "I'm leaving."

While few seminary marriages deteriorate to this point, many of these couples do experience similar pressure. Perhaps character faults and ignorance are factors in this pressure. However, the social context is also significant. Within the surroundings where there are relatives and friends, the desire to become linked so intimately so soon would be reduced. When there are meaningful relationships outside the marriage, the marital union is not the sole supplier of emotional support. A wife in this situation might be more patient and content with what companionship was developing in her home.

The loss of community may also explain the dissatisfaction of some housewives with their role in the home. These women say they feel isolated there. This is true particularly when the marriage is faltering, for then empathy and companionship are lacking.[46] And in addition, she is separated from the outside world because the nuclear family is isolated. And although it may be true that the doors of her home are not open to the community as they once were, it can also be said that the community does not enter into her life and it is not easy for her to enter into its life in a meaningful way.

The one sure entrance she does have into the community is through vocation. Gainful employment provides a sense of identity and a sense of usefulness, as well as being a means for social contacts. Surely this is one of the reasons that more women are entering the work force.

The isolation of the modern nuclear family causes distress to those without as well as to those within. The elderly, in particular, often take the brunt of the results of the exclusiveness of the American family structure. Having to transport their wife's mother on numerous errands is too much for some husbands; they won't allow the widowed mother-in-law to move in permanently. Therefore, she is forced to live alone. Relatives interrupt rather than complete the picture of the American home.

It is true that the majority of elderly people prefer to live alone,[47] but there is still a significant number who do not. Society at large and the government in particular has responded to their needs, constructing special housing units that provide much-needed social life with those of their own age and offering the "meals on wheels" program that assures them of basic nutrition. But whether their emotional needs are met is another matter.

In summary, stresses in the modern family were brought about in part when, in the words of Edward Shorter, "the couple terminated its association with . . . outside groups and strolled off into the dusk holding hands."[48]

THE CHURCH'S MINISTRY TO NUCLEAR FAMILIES

In what way should this picture of the family shape the ministry of the church? The evangelical church has already responded to the needs of the isolated nuclear family. It has been pouring its energy into making this family a more effective unit. Most of the many books on the teaching and training of children are intended for the family in its nuclear form. Literature on marriage reflects this approach too. And couples who are cut off from other satisfying relationships, are taught the skills of intimacy in special encounter sessions. Pastors and conference speakers have searched concordances for words relating to intimacy, romance, and communication, while the Song of Solomon has come to rival the Twenty-third Psalm for first place in many households.

Seeing the family structure as the lonely strand of rope holding society a few feet from destruction, the church has sought to fortify the family in its insulated form. That this ministry has made a great contribution is quite evident. And the continuing enrichment of the nuclear family will be essential even if community life in America were to return to earlier patterns, which is as unlikely as the resurgence of the extended family.

But this approach of directing all energy toward family enrichment may ignore the impoverishment the family experiences when it is cut off from other people. Writers of evangelical literature on the home may be overlooking the individual's desperate need for community life as well as for a rich family life. Surely, meaningful outside relationships play a tremendous role in a person's life. When Oscar Feucht, for example, pointed to the successful example of Amish parents in raising their children, he neglected to mention the solid community support the family had. That part of the Amish lifestyle is surely a major key to the successful socialization of children.

Larry Richards stresses that the family needs the community life of the Christian congregation.[49] We have begun to realize that the nuclear family is overloaded, in that it is expected to contribute more than it can to family health and well-being. The church's strategy should include finding means for the family to discover companionship and help outside itself. This companionship is being increasingly developed in the larger family life of the congregation; but it is also appearing in other forms, particularly family-cluster and intergenerational groups. Perhaps practical steps in this direction will be the most far-reaching and effective contribution evangelicals can make to the family.

PART TWO

THE
THEOLOGICAL
FOUNDATIONS

3

The Nature
and Basis
of Marriage

Our technological society introduces considerable stress into marriage. Roles, for example, are not as clearly defined as they once were, and they are often more difficult to perform.

For example, in many cases the husband of today is not the sole breadwinner. With both husband and wife working outside the home, it often becomes necessary for them to discuss household duties, a task that was formerly the exclusive province of the wife.

The challenge to modern marriage hits at the theoretical principles and their practical applications. The jackhammers of modern theorists have been shattering the foundations of marriage, and this has resulted in confusion of thought and practice. So the twentieth-century person looks down on the bits and pieces of what once were unquestioned concepts and ideals. If the church is to minister to those who are married, it must do so with the certainty and conviction that is the result of an approach that is based on Scripture.

At this juncture the task of the theologian is basic and strategic. It is basic because it must deal with the most elementary questions; in our revolutionary society nothing is above questioning. It is strategic because we need definite guidelines in our rapidly changing times.

The theologian must lay a foundation for the nature and basis of marriage without succumbing to the temptation to merely use proof texts. The gap between pulpit and life is nowhere wider than in the area of marital relations. Dedicated and conscientious men and women are caught between society's pressures and proclamations of the church; this dilemma causes sizable amounts of stress and guilt for them. We must be careful not to place a yoke on Christian couples that they are unable to bear.

THE ISSUES

A student in one of my classes once asked, "What is marriage supposed to be like when you are living in a Christian commune?" Since he and his wife were part of such a commune, this was not an academic question for them. Though sexual intimacy was confined to married couples there, he wondered what other things should be reserved for married partners. For example, should one be closer to his wife than to his sister in Christ?

The question before us is, What kind of marriage should the church foster and support? Marriage today should include at least three features.

First, it should consist of one wife and one husband living in a permanent bond. The challenge to this monogamous arrangement is not new; missionaries to polygamous groups have wrestled with the theology of monogamy for centuries. However, polygamy and group marriages are not a serious problem in American society today. As we have seen in chapter 1, the challenge comes in the matter of permanency. Easy divorce laws and live-in arrangements make possible a "serial polygamy," in which a person has many spouses in a lifetime —one at a time!

Marriage should also include intimate relationships with the children in the family. In modern society this intimacy is more difficult to achieve because family members are so often separated. The child's relationships with peers and the parents' relationships with friends and business associates are often more intimate than the parent-child relationship. This concept is questioned by those who advocate communal forms of the family, in which a close relationship to many others is the ideal for each member of the family.

Third, definite roles should be part of the marriage relationship. Both of the marriage partners have special responsibilities to one another and to the children as well.

There are many forces that threaten the institution of marriage. This requires a defense of the biblical concept of marriage. The theological base must be laid with care.

The Theological Foundations

While the family as we now know it has been the most universal and the most prominent form of the family, it has not been the only one in Western tradition. Despite the monogamous ideals in Old Testament theology, polygamy was the norm during preexilic times. And while Genesis states that a man will leave his father and mother, the patriarchal family gave particular place to the extended family rather than to the nuclear form. Marriages were arranged and given approbation by parents, not by the individuals who were marrying. And the tribe seemed to be a more prominent unit than the nuclear family was.

By the time Jesus came to earth to minister, however, the nuclear family was the prevailing form amongst the Jews. Rome, too, supported the nuclear family. The medieval church perpetuated this more individualistic view of marriage and family and handed it down to the Western world of today. In this medieval society the primary justification for marriage and the family was that they were necessary for the continued existence of the state. This, then, was a purely functional rather than a spiritual view of these two cornerstones of human society.

Of Divine Intent

It appears that in the area of marriage, some of the early Hebrews accommodated themselves to the social practices of neighboring cultures. For example, Abraham married his half-sister (Gen. 20:12); Sarah gave her maid to Abraham as a wife (16:1–3); and Jacob obtained two wives (29:26–28). These examples might suggest that marriage and its customs were the mere invention of men, subject to the definition and control of society. But both Testaments view marriage as being of divine origin and under God's regulation.

The second chapter of Genesis provides the basic ideal: "For this reason a man will leave his father and mother and be united to his wife, and they will become one flesh" (v. 24). Both the fact that Moses offers this principle as foundational and the fact that Jesus appeals to it make it compellingly normative for us. Marriage is founded, not in Mosaic law or in the patriarchal social system, but in the creative order that precedes these. Thus, Christ appealed to God's order in "the beginning" (Matt. 19:4–6). For this reason Luther warned against speaking of the "Christian family." He contended that the family is not part of the gospel; it is part of creation. Marriage has been established by God.[1]

There is continued biblical justification for seeing the first couple as a human prototype created in the beginning by God, and this prototype remains a perpetual model and example for the whole human race.[2] Three of the Ten Commandments relate directly or indirectly to the family—honoring one's father and mother, and the prohibitions against adultery and covetousness—as do numerous Mosaic regulations, thus confirming that it is a norm for humankind. In his appeal to Timothy to combat those "liars" who would forbid marriage (1 Tim. 4:1–5), Paul seems to be including marriage in his statement that "everything God created is good" (v. 4).[3] Perhaps he had in mind the pronouncement made by God after He had created man and woman and given them the cultural mandate (Gen. 1:27–28): "And it was very good" (v. 31).

Monogamous

Not all scholars of the Bible hold to the view that Scripture promotes monogamy. Gerhard von Rad, a German theologian, maintains that no recognition of monogamy should be extracted from Genesis 2.[4] Karl Barth said: "We can hardly point with certainty to a single text in which polygamy is expressly forbidden and monogamy universally decreed."[5]

In fact, polygamy was the norm in the nation of Israel until the time of the Exile. Marriage customs, moreover, were much different than they are today. For example, in most cases the parents of the groom chose the marriage partner and also made the marriage arrangements.

On the other hand, some scholars maintain that monogamy *is* taught in Scripture. In an excellent article on the nature of the family in the Old Testament, Walter Wegner, a professor of Old Testament and an evangelical, provides convincing evidence for his contention that throughout her history Israel's ideal for marriage was monogamy.[6] He points first to the prototype of Adam and Eve, which was clearly monogamous. And, he explains, the Old Testament proposes a one-husband and one-wife pattern, even though Israel's actions did not always match God's plan.

In particular, the prophets, who cover half a millennium of Israel's life, affirm monogamy in their messages. Using the marriage relationship as a metaphor of God's relationship to Israel, Hosea is a shining example of love and faithfulness to one's partner in marriage. David Schuller asserts, "The portrait of Hosea's marriage suggests that a monogamous union is under discussion and that such a marriage would be regarded as normative by the prophet's audience."[7] The exclusiveness of the marriage relationship, for both partners, comes through most clearly in the Book of Hosea. And God, too, will have no other wife but Israel, just as Israel is to have no other husband but

Jehovah. This emphasis on faithfulness can be found in both Isaiah and Ezekiel as well (Isa. 54; 62:1–5; Ezek. 16).

Koehler explains the exceptions to monogamy in Israel as being primarily the practice of the kings, but, he says, this does not cancel the standard of Genesis 2:24. Departure from the ethical and religious will of God was frequent among the kings. It is erroneous, however, to conclude from their marriages that polygamy was the norm for the ordinary people.[8]

For the Christian, Jesus' interpretation of Genesis 2:24 is definitive (Matt. 19:1–12). In maintaining that remarrying after one is divorced, except for marital unfaithfulness, constitutes adultery for both the man and the woman (v. 9), He by implication upholds the ideal of monogamy, in that He is assuming that God is speaking of a one-woman–one-man relationship in Genesis 2. Also, Jesus quotes the Septuagint, the most important Greek translation of the Old Testament. In Genesis 2 the Septuagint uses the word *two,* who become one in marriage. This indicates that only a pair is to be involved in a marriage, not more. Paul, too, supports monogamy when listing both qualifications for church leaders and criteria for church support of widows (1 Tim. 3:2, 12; 5:9; Titus 1:6).

An Intimate Relationship

We now turn to the nature of the marriage relationship. That it is set apart by sexual intercourse is, of course, clear. The sex drive is part of the natural order. The fact that Eve was created out of Adam's body is the basis for the impulse to be once again united as one flesh, now in sexual embrace. The sensuality of that embrace can be seen in the terms *unite* and *one flesh.* But the question of what the relationship between husband and wife is to be brings into our discussion the matter of intimacy. Do the Scriptures provide warrant for the trend toward cultivating what is suggested in the titles of books like *The Intimate Marriage* and *Magnificent Marriage*?[9] Can we justify the shift from marriage as a practical arrangement to marriage as intimate companionship?

The context of Genesis 2 provides part of the basis for that shift. Intimacy is decidedly there. Eve was created for more than propagation. Her creation was occasioned by Adam's aloneness. "It is not good for the man to be alone" (Gen. 2:18). That this statement does not refer merely to the need to procreate seems to be settled by the requirements for Adam's partner. It had to be someone who was a helper, a counterpart to him. While this does suggest a procreative sexual relationship, it also conveys Adam's need for companionship. This companion had to be someone who was unlike him, yet complementary to him—someone who could be one with him, being made from his own flesh and bone.

Second, the parallel words *leave* and *unite* suggest a companionship beyond mere sexual union. The man leaves his parents to enter a new relationship—a relationship with his wife. In addition, the definition of the Hebrew word for "flesh" can be called in as evidence that God intended marriage to include companionship. This word does not always refer merely to the body. It sometimes denotes the whole being. Thus, the two become one in marriage. The lack of shame in their nakedness may also indicate that there should be emotional intimacy as well as physical intimacy.

Old Testament scholars cite examples of marriage after Genesis 2 as conclusive evidence that marriage is a special relationship. Jacob's love for Rachel and Isaac's for Rebekah include both romance and intimacy. But the view of the prophets is most decisive. The fact that they chose marriage as the most appropriate analogy of God's love for Israel reveals more than anything else the Hebrews' lofty concept of the marriage relationship. As the husband of Israel, God says, "Though the mountains be shaken and the hills be removed, yet my unfailing love for you will not be shaken" (Isa. 54:10).

Marriage in the Song of Solomon is portrayed as a romantic, sensual, and intimate companionship. She is his "darling" and his "beautiful one" (Song of Solomon 2:13). Her voice is "sweet" and her face "lovely" (2:14). He is handsome and pleasant, her beloved and her friend (5:16).

Thus, in the Old Testament marriage is more than a contract for economic and sexual purposes. It includes this but it is also much more. The most explicit statement of this truth is made by the prophet Malachi. Speaking of the wife, he says, "She is your *companion* and your wife by covenant" (Mal. 2:14; italics mine).

The richness of the marriage relationship reaches its fullest expression in the New Testament. Paul, following the example of the Hebrew prophets, compares the union of Christ and the church with the union of husband and wife (Eph. 5:22–33).

Marriage, then, is a relationship that pervades the totality of life and calls for marriage partners to cherish and support one another. In this way they pursue perfect union of mind and full communion of life. Husbands are told to love, not merely to lead and provide (Eph. 5:25). Wives are enjoined to be lovers of their husbands, not merely obedient partners (Titus 2:4). Typical of contemporary theologians, Cornelius J. van der Poel makes the following summary statement about the biblical view of marriage: "In the text of Scriptures the union and mutual exchange of husband and wife is so deep and all-embracing that it is in the fullest sense of the word a mutual expression of total self-giving."[10]

There are many sides to this communion. Two will be mentioned here. First it is a *complementing* relationship. It is possible for two to become one because the woman is the same kind of being as the man. Having been taken from Adam, Eve qualifies for union with him. But her distinctness also makes oneness possible. She qualifies for union with him because she is "opposite," that is, complementary, to him. Their personal union, like their sexual union, is made possible by their differences.

Although marriage is the joining of two halves so that they become one whole, it has also been said that "one plus one equals three." This maxim accents the fact that the whole is more than the sum of its parts. True oneness is an amalgamation of two into a special new entity. Partners must bring all that they are to the relationship. Marriages in which one of the personalities is stifled falls short of true oneness. Partners must respect their differences. The man must allow the woman to assert herself just as she must allow him to assert himself. Each partner will need to adjust to the other. Requiring one to make all the concessions amounts to annihilation rather than amalgamation. In fact, couples should learn to see strengths in their differences and to capitalize on them, instead of allowing them to become the basis for competition.

Marriage is also a *multifaceted communion*. The Clinebells have described intimacy as an instrument of many strings. Sexual intimacy supplies the axis around which other forms of intimacy cluster. Sharing feelings and ideas is also part of the whole. Aesthetic intimacy is the in-depth sharing of beauty. Creative intimacy is closeness through the creating together of, for example, a painting, a garden, or a song. The intimacy gained when tasks are done together is part of the marriage union, as is recreational intimacy. Going through crises together and sharing convictions and commitments also serve to strengthen the marriage bond. Finally, the Clinebells describe spiritual intimacy as the nearness that develops through sharing in the area of ultimate concerns, including a vital relationship to God and His universe.[11]

Although a particular couple may not experience all of these phases of oneness, Scripture fully supports the contemporary trend toward intimacy in marriage.

THE BASIS OF MARRIAGE

The nature of marriage is also its basis. Thus, it is not an exclusively legal matter. Von Rad maintains that the Genesis narrative is not concerned with legal custom.

Whence comes this love strong as death? (Song of Solomon 8:6). Whence this inner clinging to each other, this drive toward each other which does not rest until it again becomes one flesh in the child? It comes from the fact that God took woman from man, that they actually were originally one flesh. Therefore, they must come together again and thus by destiny they belong to each other.[12]

Although a legal basis for marriage is perhaps only implied in Genesis 2, there is a clear legal basis for marriage elsewhere in Scripture. Malachi refers to marriage as a covenant (2:14). And the idea of contract might be found in the term *unite* in Genesis, since the Hebrew word means "to adhere to" or "hold fast to," as in a commitment (Deut. 4:4; Josh. 22:5). The erosion of the permanent nature of marriage today makes it necessary to emphasize that marriage involves commitment.

Personal Commitment

Marriage is a personal commitment, a responsible covenant of love. Even in the sacramental view of marriage held by the Roman Catholic church, the personal aspect of the contract, along with physical consummation, renders it complete. In the Catholic view: "The parties, not the priests, are the ministers of the sacrament."[13]

An emphasis on legality should not obliterate the personal nature of this pledge to one another.

Social Commitment

Marriage is also a social commitment. There is no biblical sanction of marriage as a private, live-in arrangement. The public nature of marriage is clearly seen in that the man leaves his father and mother and is united to his wife; this involves the families of both the bride and the groom (Gen. 2:24). Later marriage customs such as the public procession from the bride's home to the groom's home reinforced this concept of social commitment. And the legal sanctions in the Old Testament make it clear that marriage is a legitimate concern for all of society. These commandments regulate marriage for the welfare of both the couple and society. Furthermore, social pressure may be necessary to help some couples fulfill their obligations through the rough spots of their relationship. And since the welfare of women and children who are deserted becomes the responsibility of the extended family and of society, others besides the marriage partners do have a stake in the success of a marriage.

A Divinely Sanctioned Commitment

Another aspect of this commitment is that it has divine sanction.

Jesus said that God joins couples together. This joining takes place in the "uniting" that makes a couple become one flesh. Secular society lacks this Godward aspect of human pledges, especially those made in marriage. We have lost what Peter Berger calls "the sacred canopy," his term for an awareness that human affairs should be conducted with a heavenly sanction.[14] Perhaps this loss, more than anything else, makes people today what one psychologist calls "commitment cripples."

The marriage contract is also a permanent, unconditional commitment. Or so it would seem from the Scriptures. Yet this is a hotly debated issue, one that we will grapple with in the next chapter.

4

The Permanence of Marriage
and the Nature of the Family

Ideally, marriage is to be dissolved only by death. Those who hold to an inerrant view of Scripture agree on this point. Confronted by the Pharisees with a question concerning divorce, Jesus appealed to God's standard "at the beginning." This clearly indicates that marriage is an exclusive and lasting relationship.

At the same time, however, most evangelicals agree that Christian standards cannot be forced on non-Christians. John Warwick Montgomery states: "In a society where most people are now getting married on a non-Christian basis, we make a great mistake if we insist on them being divorced only on a scriptural basis."[1] For this reason, Montgomery argues for the acceptance of no-fault divorce laws.

In addition, some agreement seems to be emerging in regards to how divorced and remarried persons in evangelical churches are to be treated. Editors of the conservative periodical *Christianity Today* separate the issue of the way the church should treat divorced and remarried people from the moral question involved.

The Theological Foundations

> The church must clearly and unhesitatingly teach the biblical condemnation of easy divorce as the moral equivalent of adultery. But it must also learn to forgive and to minister to the fallen. . . . It must be prepared to bind up the wounds of the broken-hearted, to comfort the lonely and grieving, and to restore to spiritual wholeness those whose lives have fallen apart in the breakup of their marriages.[2]

There is little consensus, however, among evangelicals in regard to the many practical, much less the theological, issues related to divorce.

Practical Issues

Here are but two of the many practical questions that confront the Christian student of family life today.

One issue relates to the results of a lax view of divorce in our day. The traditional view of marriage as being indissoluble made it more stable and even more successful than it is today. Couples who entered marriage knowing that divorce was an impossibility tried hard to make the marriage work.

The results of entering marriage with this view about its permanence have been difficult to assess. Such a no-exit view could motivate a couple to strive harder to succeed in marriage. On the other hand, it could also cause a lackadaisical attitude. Without any fear of being left by one's partner, little effort might be expended by a partner who takes the relationship for granted.

On the other hand, knowing that divorce is an option might weaken a couple's efforts. Attorney Bernard Kaufman blames the increase in divorce cases on today's lax view toward divorce: "There is the social factor of people not feeling the same way toward marriage and family as they used to. They try marriage out, and if it doesn't work they get a divorce."[3]

The question of whether tough divorce laws reduce the number of divorces and result in more successful marriages is a complicated issue. Montgomery, cited earlier, does not attribute the rising divorce rate to the weakening of divorce legislation. He maintains that this rise is caused instead by a weakening of marriage relationships.[4] Max Rheinstein, a professor at the University of Chicago Law School, after extensive study of divorce in many countries, has concluded that there is no connection between the strictness of divorce laws and the divorce rate.[5] John Scanzoni comes to this same conclusion in regard to church laws: "There is no way that religious edicts themselves can deal with the root problem, which is not divorce but the difficulties involved in maintaining satisfactory marriages in today's fast-changing world."[6]

Another practical issue relates to the pastor's responsibility. The pastor is to be directive, say some, refusing to marry those who have not followed his interpretation of what Scripture says about the permanence of marriage. A pastor, in order to spare himself from attack by others or from personal affront, may merely stand behind his denomination's stance; or if his church is not in a denomination, he may choose to abide by the decisions made by his church board. But many consider this a display of cowardice, maintaining that the pastor should decide for himself whom he should and should not marry, in fairness to those he counsels. Some recommend that the pastor take refuge in nondirective counseling; they maintain that the decision to marry is the couple's. Thus, the pastor washes his hands of the matter and is relieved of responsibility in regard to their decision.

The Strict Protestant View

The major debate among evangelicals is, of course, not practical but theological.

Foremost in this debate is the matter of theological change itself. Some maintain that theology concerning marriage must change due to contemporary marital problems, but only after a careful scrutiny of the Bible. The historical Protestant position has been to permit divorce in cases of adultery or desertion, but remarriage was denied. Bernard Ramm accuses those who hold to this view of divorce and remarriage of "being naïve or unrealistic in facing the thousands of facts we now know about marriage and divorce from medicine, psychology, and sociology."[7] And Dwight Small's departure from the traditional view is based in part on his belief that new insights have been forged by the pressure of changing times.[8]

On the issue of a biblical ethic of divorce and remarriage, there are scores of opinions, yet basically they may be subsumed under two major viewpoints. Ramm calls one of these approaches "the strict Protestant view." In general, those who hold this view believe that Matthew 19:9 and 1 Corinthians 7:15 allow divorce in cases of unfaithfulness or desertion,[9] but they deny divorced persons the right to remarry. Many evangelicals today, as well as earlier Protestant ethicists, however, allow the innocent party the privilege of remarrying, because the marriage was broken by the unfaithful or deserting partner. There is, therefore, they say, no sin in the innocent partner's remarrying.

The hallmark of this viewpoint is the strict interpretation of Jesus' words on the subject of divorce: "What God has joined together, let man not separate" (Matt. 19:6). Proponents of this view hold that there is additional biblical evidence that Jesus taught a strict view of divorce: "I tell you that anyone who divorces his wife, except for marital unfaithfulness, causes her to commit adultery, and anyone who marries a woman so divorced commits adultery" (Matt. 5:32).

Those holding this view are divided primarily over what exceptions there are to the general rule. Some dispute the textual validity of the exception clause in Matthew 19:9, denying that there is any exemption whatsoever that allows divorce. Others would permit divorce and remarriage in the case of unchastity, explaining that the exception clause applies to unchastity but not to desertion. They would disagree with the interpretation of 1 Corinthians 7:15 that puts forth what has come to be known as the "Pauline privilege." This verse is instead taken to mean that the Christian should remain unmarried.[10]

The Broad Protestant Principle

Ramm calls the opposite viewpoint on this matter of divorce and remarriage the "Broad Protestant Principle."[11] Those who hold this view maintain that the New Testament gives the church the fundamentals of Christian marriage but not an exhaustive treatment on the subject of divorce.[12] On the contrary, they say, only a minimum treatment is given. Thus, the traditional camp is accused of using a simple proof-text approach to a complicated ethical problem.

Ramm argues that the pastor who thinks the New Testament contains an exhaustive body of ethics concerning marriage and divorce is at a loss to handle the kind of problems he faces in modern society. As an example, he points to the person with neurotic or psychotic symptoms that were masked during courtship. Also, there are the alcoholics or persons dependent on alcohol who marry. Again, what should be done with homosexual spouses, especially those who marry to conceal their sexual orientation? And, certain states allow automatic divorce if either partner is sentenced to prison for ten years or more. None of these matters are specifically discussed in Scripture, yet the Christian church must deal with these problems, argues Ramm.[13]

Modern society contributes in another way to the wide range of problems confronting marriage partners, according to those who hold this view. They explain that it has become more difficult to succeed in marriage in the last five decades. In our complex society, divorce is seen as a necessary safety valve for the preservation of the institution of marriage. Historian William O'Neill argues that divorce prevents explosions in the family that might undermine the very foundation of marriage. If there were no divorce, dissatisfaction would build up suddenly, and could result in violence. People might repudiate the institution of marriage, much as governments are overthrown.[14]

As more and more people turn away from a view of marriage as an orderly, practical structure to the idea that marriage is an arrangement for facilitating companionship, Scanzoni believes we can expect more marriages to fail now than in the past. His comparison of past and present marriage concepts is given as an argument for a newer understanding of the phenomenon of divorce:

> In order to eke out a mere subsistence, husbands and wives worked from dawn to dusk. And for those who did manage to survive, what we call marital satisfaction was not an issue. There was no time to worry about whether your spouse really "understood" you or whether you could achieve mutual orgasm. Such matters never entered the picture. Women were the property of their husbands—not their friends. . . . It is to be expected that as friendship became more important, more marriages would dissolve by divorce.[15]

Those who hold the broad view of divorce and remarriage accuse adherents to the strict view of having impractical solutions to marriage problems. They point to Roman Catholics, for instance, who have their own version of a safety valve for marriage—annulment. In spite of the strict stand of the Catholic church on the indissolubility of marriage, there are more than 250,000 divorces in the Catholic church every year. And eighty percent of these people eventually remarry.

Many Catholics apply for annulments; and such requests, according to one writer, are granted on a routine basis.[16] All that is required is the submission of a written application. And cases have been piling up following the extension of grounds for annulment to include "psychological incapacity."[17] Couples whose marriages deteriorate after fifteen years of seemingly happy marriage are now granted written statements to the effect that they were never "emotionally married."[18]

Some evangelicals suggest that such solutions are unrealistic and even embarrassing. Ramm says there is now a "divorce underground," caused by "American evangelicals who have kept to a very simplified view of marriage and divorce."[19] Great numbers of evangelical lay people and ministers, who have quietly been divorced, have remarried and carried on as though nothing happened. This, Ramm calls "stark unrealism."[20] Furthermore, who knows how many Christian husbands and wives, convinced that the strict view of divorce is correct, secretly wish for their spouse's "timely" death? Or else, consciously or unconsciously, a husband or wife may pressure his or her partner into an adulterous relationship that provides a legal and "moral" basis for dissolution of the marriage.

Advocates of the broad view of divorce and remarriage do not seek to break from a conservative view of Scripture. They attempt, rather, to get a different perspective on the statements of Jesus on this subject. Dwight Small takes a dispensational approach to Christ's statements on this matter, explaining that they pertain to the kingdom age of the future. Small does not deny that Christians of today should take their standard for marriage from Christ's words, but he maintains that there is a different application of these words during the present age of grace than there will be during the kingdom age. Thus, the indissolubility of marriage is the ideal, as stated in the beginning of Genesis and as it will be again in the kingdom age; but because of our continued sinfulness and hardness of heart, there is forgiveness for those who fail today.

Small maintains, moreover, that divorce is possible only because of grace.[21] Marriage is supposed to be permanent. Divorce is always wrong. It is allowable only under special circumstances and then only under the permissive will of God, not His ideal will. Small builds his case on the concept of "realized forgiveness," a term put forth by Presbyterian James G. Emerson, Jr., in 1961.[22] Realized forgiveness is the Christian's awareness that one always lives in the presence of God's forgiveness. Christians are to realize this truth to such a degree that they are free from excessive guilt. Therefore, according to Small, pastoral ministry in cases of divorce and remarriage should be based on God's forgiving grace, not only on His ideal law.

According to those who hold the broad view, even if Jesus' words were meant to be directly applied to present-day Christians in situations of divorce and remarriage, they were not meant to be used in a legalistic way. They develop this argument as follows. Christ refused to deal with divorce within the confines of Mosaic law. He held up God's ideal standard for marriage, which prevailed before the fall into sin—in the beginning. Jesus' statement about divorce is not unlike other declarations of His, such as, "Be perfect, therefore, as your heavenly Father is perfect" (Matt. 5:48). The indissolubility of the marriage bond is a standard of perfection, just as holiness is. Permanence of marriage was God's intention.

Proponents of the broad view explain that the question of whether this perfect standard can be applied to every couple considering divorce is the major issue. Their explanation is as follows. Even in Old Testament times divorce laws were not always enforced so as to uphold God's perfect standard. To interpret Jesus' words as law does not allow for contingencies such as partners who deny or forfeit their commitment through adultery, perversion, desertion, impotence, frigidity, or severe neurosis or psychosis. Under the Mosaic law there was no difficulty in dealing with, for example, adultery—the guilty person would have been stoned. But situations that were not problems under the law have become problems for Christians under grace.

Those who hold the above view of the words of Jesus concerning divorce call attention to the context of His words. They say that He was affirming God's ideal for marriage against Jewish leaders who made the termination of marriage an arbitrary decision of the husband. As at other times, the Lord intended to show these leaders their own sinfulness. He appealed to the creative order, which constitutes the spirit of the law.[23] These leaders were denying their own selfishness and sinfulness by stretching the letter of the law.

According to those who hold the broad view, it is possible to take Jesus' words and codify them into law, thereby doing exactly what He was trying to avoid. So it is, according to this view, that evangelical pastors and theologians juggle verses and argue about exceptions and motives, much like canon lawyers. And lay people go from one clergyman to another to find sanction for their actions, attempting to resolve their guilt and restore order in their lives by a legalistic appeal to a verse in the Bible. Rather, Small and others are saying, we should appeal to God's forgiveness. The answer is not to be found in analyzing an exception clause; it is to be realized in God's indisputable words about grace. Marriage is part of the created order; divorce is part of the redemptive order.

To hold that forgiveness extends to the divorced person who has remarried has been most difficult because of Jesus' explicit statements that one commits adultery by remarrying (Matt. 19:9). However, the editors of *Christianity Today* recognize this problem and come to the following conclusion:

> Murder and theft the evangelical freely forgives, but not divorce. In part, this different attitude is based on the conviction that other sins are completed and have been repented of, but divorce and remarriage involve a continuous living in adultery. The conclusion is not warranted on biblical grounds. The guilty partner in a divorce on the grounds of adultery has already broken the original marriage. . . . The fact that the original marriage is dissolved means also that the guilty party who remarries is not living in adultery, for his original marriage was dissolved. His sin was in the adultery that brought on the divorce. Since he is no longer married, his new alliance is not adulterous. Similarly in the case of divorces secured on trivial grounds, a move to marriage by either partner serves (as does adultery) to break the original marriage; and on biblical grounds the church is not justified in treating the remarried as though they were continuing to live in adultery.[24]

The distinctive mark of this new stance on divorce, then, is that divorce now becomes primarily an ethical issue. While they do not deny that God's standard for marriage is permanence, those of this persuasion place the question of breaking God's standard in the broader context of the whole New Testament ethic. According to this view, divorce and remarriage are moral choices that are sometimes acceptable, though never the Creator's ideal. Dwight Small sees them as being acceptable when it is a matter of choosing between the lesser of two evils. At times, remaining together may be intolerable for a couple and possibly also for their children. James Montgomery Boice concurs with Small's conclusion. He states: "We live in an imperfect world. And this means that there will always be circumstances in which the Christian will have to choose the lesser of two evils."[25] Boice cites an imaginary case in which a woman is married to a brute of a husband, a man who spends her money on drink and deserts her with the result that she must raise the children alone. Should the husband return, he might seize the money she has saved for her children's college expenses. A woman in such circumstances is justified, says Boice, in initiating a divorce.[26]

Small explains that since divorce and remarriage are always wrong, the persons involved must claim the forgiveness of God.[27] But Norman Geisler does not always insist on confession. He explains that whenever a Christian is facing a moral dilemma, he or she must choose the best course of action even if that action breaks a moral standard.[28] Since God would not allow a Christian to be put in a position where he or she would have to sin, a Christian who tells a lie to save a life has not sinned, since he or she has done what was considered best. The lesser moral law was in that instance in abeyance.

Applying this view to divorce and remarriage, some proponents of the broad Protestant principle explain that a couple would not in all cases be sinning if they chose to follow these alternatives, rather than to stay together. Certainly, a Christian husband or wife may have contributed to the failure of a marriage, and they should confess that sin. But divorce in a marriage in which the relationship is becoming more and more destructive is not sin. Following Geisler's approach, remarriage may be best for divorced persons who burn with passion and are continually subject to sensual temptation and fantasy.

Whether it be the "strict Protestant view" or the "broad Protestant principle" that is being set forth, it is clear that no evangelical writer today endorses easy divorce or a low view of the marriage commitment. One sure guideline for individuals and pastors dealing with this complex issue is that only under the most difficult circumstances is a Christian to think of separating what God has joined together.

THE NATURE OF THE FAMILY

Of God's Creative Order

That the church has biblical justification for holding a high view of marriage is quite clear. But this high view of marriage does not at the same time constitute a biblical base for the family. So it is that some scholars do not agree with those who hold that the opening chapters of Genesis include the institution of the family by God. For example, Helmut Begemann, a German theologian, states: "The institution of the family is not a result of the creative command."[29]

Others argue, however, that the terminology in Genesis 2:23 leads us to the conclusion that God is here establishing the family. Those who hold to this interpretation point to Adam's exclamation in this verse—"This is now bone of my bones and flesh of my flesh"—as evidence. In this view, when God created Eve for Adam He was not only instituting marriage but was also establishing what we speak of today as the nuclear and extended families. And the phrase "one flesh" in the next verse encompasses not only the sexual union of a woman and a man in marriage but also the children that result from this union. In fact, children are a concrete manifestation of the two "become one."

It is significant that the phrases Adam used to describe his relationship to Eve are later used to refer to what we call the extended family and the nuclear family. In his excellent article entitled "God's Pattern for the Family in the Old Testament," Walter Wegner states:

> The Hebrew words for bone (*etsem*) and flesh (*basar*) are frequently used idiomatically to express family and blood relationships, either in combination (Gen. 29:14; Judg. 9:2; 2 Sam. 5:1) or as parallels (1 Chron. 11:1; 2 Sam. 19:12–13).[30]

An example of the use of flesh and blood as a reference to the extended family in the Old Testament is when Jacob meets Rachel, and then his uncle, Laban:

> When Jacob saw Rachel daughter of Laban, his mother's brother, and Laban's sheep, he went over and rolled the stone away from the mouth of the well and watered his uncle's sheep. Then Jacob kissed Rachel and began to weep aloud. He had told Rachel that he was a relative of her father and a son of Rebekah. So she ran and told her father.
>
> As soon as Laban heard the news about Jacob, his sister's son, he hurried to meet him. He embraced him and kissed him and brought him to his home, and there Jacob told him all these things. Then Laban said to him, "You are my own flesh and blood." (Gen. 29:10–14)

Later Old Testament regulations offer further proof that the family has been instituted by God. God's commandment to honor one's parents (Exod. 20:12) and His prohibition of adultery (Exod. 20:14) as well as His later commands to parents—for example, the instruction to "impress [God's commandments] on your children" (Deut. 6:4–7a)—show us that the family is an institution of divine origin.

The Theological Foundations

A Family Model

But what is the nature of the nuclear family? It is rather surprising to discover that there is no definition of the word "family" in the Bible, either in the Old Testament or in the New. Sometimes the Greek word for "family" in the New Testament refers to the nuclear family, but it also refers to an entire household, including servants. For many Christians, the family of Jesus is the first to come to mind when we speak of families in the Bible. But the details of His family life are given only incidentally, without any apparent intention of providing an example for us to follow.

There is, nevertheless, plenty of data available in Scripture for constructing a model of what the family should be. The first and most obvious characteristic of the family is that each member has certain *responsibilities* and *roles.* For children, the one explicit command in the New Testament says nothing about love or intimacy; it commands them to obey their parents (Eph. 6:1; Col. 3:20). This command follows the fifth commandment in the law of Moses and the book of Proverbs (e.g., 30:17); in both places the accent is on obedience. And in the New Testament, the relationship of children to their parents is once again phrased in terms of responsibility (1 Tim. 5:8, 16). Responsibility is also central in the roles of both husbands and wives (Eph. 5:22–33; 1 Tim. 5:14; 1 Cor. 7:2–7). Nothing is said in Scripture of any special obligation between brothers and sisters, except the kinsman-redeemer responsibility in the Old Testament, in which a man was to marry his dead brother's wife in order to continue his brother's name and inheritance.

There is some warrant for seeing the family structure in institutional terms, whereby each member has a clearly defined "job description." But other passages in Scripture make it impossible to see the family primarily in these terms.

A second characteristic of the family relates to the matter of *unconditional love.* In current literature, the home is often held up as a place where there is a particular kind of unconditional love. Many sociologists today see this function of providing love as the primary task in the family. Each family member hopes that the family will be a place where persons display unlimited empathy, understanding, and support for one another. Loving interaction within the family thus becomes a means of therapy for personal hurts.

Is the idea of unconditional love included in the biblical concept of the family? Beginning early in the Old Testament, we can see that parental love is characterized by mercy and patience. In the Psalms, for example, God is compared to a father who pities his children (103:13), showing us that the Hebrew concept of a father included this kind of compassion. And a special love parents have for their children seems to be implied in the Psalmist's cry: "Though my father and mother forsake me" (27:10). He seems to be suggesting that his parents would be the last people on earth to forsake him, and this would reveal a high view of parental love.

But, the most definitive description of parental love comes from the New Testament, from the lips of Jesus Himself. His parable of the prodigal son is an amazing display of love. It portrays a father's patience and his acceptance and forgiveness of a wayward son. In addition, Jesus discloses how important He considers parental love to be when He points to God as an example for us. "Love your enemies . . . ," He says, "that you may be sons of your Father in heaven. He causes the sun to rise on the evil and the good, and sends rain on the righteous and the unrighteous" (Matt. 5:44–45). Jesus appeals to the same analogy in Luke 6:36, this time speaking of mercy: "Be merciful, just as your Father is merciful."

These statements not only tell us what Jesus thought about God, they also show to us what He thought about parental love. A parent's love, like God's, is to be characterized by mercy, acceptance, and forgiveness. And it should be steadfast, as is God's love. God is the kind of parent who can love even His evil children. All of this biblical evidence seems to justify the assertion that the home is to be a place with the feel of unconditional love.

A third characteristic of the family that can be established from Scripture is that the family displays the quality of intimacy. A special closeness among family members seems to be referred to in various Scripture passages, some of which relate to the church family and others to the family in the home. Open expression of emotion and of concern seem to be basic elements in what Scripture says about the family. An excellent example of two of the most dramatic aspects of family life, those of repenting and forgiving, is found once again, in the parable of the prodigal son: "His father saw him and was filled with compassion for him; he ran to his son, threw his arms around him and kissed him" (Luke 15:20). And in a description of true friendship in Proverbs 18:24, our relationship with a friend is compared to our closeness to a "brother," that is, to one of our siblings.

If intimacy is defined as kind, sensitive concern for the welfare of another person or other persons, there is no doubt that intimacy in the family is scriptural. In Scripture, Christian love and kindness are presented as going hand in hand with close interpersonal relationships. The author of the second letter of Peter urges that we treat one another with "brotherly kindness" (2 Peter 1:7).

Contemporary research underscores what Scripture says about

the need for meaningful relationships. For example, psychologist James J. Lynch has discovered a relationship between weakened family ties and physical illness. He found that the amount of serious illness was significantly less among people who had deep relationships with other family members than among those whose relationships in the family were superficial. "Simply put," he concludes, "there is a biological basis for our need to form human relationships.[31]

Nuclear Family Compared to Extended Family

There are varying opinions as to whether Scripture establishes the primacy of the nuclear family over the extended family. Today, those who seek to expand the influence of the extended family point to the fact that the words "bone" and "flesh" in Genesis 2:23 refer to the extended family as well as to the nuclear family. The background for this assertion is that in the nation of Israel in the Old Testament, the extended family was seen as something distinctive in God's ordering of His creation. Proponents of this view maintain that this Old Testament emphasis should not be discarded.

Those who hold this view also point out that another distinctive feature in Israel's life in the Old Testament was its grouping into tribes; these tribes were, in effect, extended families. Thus, there is some basis for suggesting that the society that values the nuclear family too highly may be over-looking relationships within the extended family that God intended for the enrichment of our lives.

Despite what Scripture says about the place of the extended family, it is difficult to find an explanation in Scripture of the nature and the responsibilities of the extended family. We can point to the fact that although marriage as outlined by God calls for leaving one's father and mother, the law of God still affirms a responsibility to one's parents. The fifth commandment, which states that children must honor their father and mother (Exod. 20:12), includes the responsibility of caring for them in their old age. And the apostle Paul upholds this responsibility in 1 Timothy 5:16: "If any woman who is a believer has widows in her family, she should help them and not let the church be burdened with them, so that the church can help those widows who are really in need." We can also cite the kinsman-redeemer obligation both in the times of the patriarchs and in the laws God gave to the people of Israel. We do not, however, have extensive information in the Bible concerning the relationships and the responsibilities of siblings when they reach adulthood. Nor is there much information about the responsibilities of cousins, grandparents and grandchildren, aunts and uncles and nieces and nephews, and so forth.

Given the disagreement as to whether the nuclear family should take precedence over the extended family and the dearth of information in Scripture concerning the extended family, we need to look at what Scripture *does* say about the nuclear family. In both the Old and the New Testaments the nuclear family has a clear identity and a specific set of responsibilities. Its distinctiveness from the extended family can be seen in Genesis 2:24: "A man will leave his father and mother and be united to his wife." And though the extended family and the tribe are prominent in the Old Testament, even here it is the nuclear family that is responsible for child rearing. In Deuteronomy 6:6–7 we read: "These commandments that I give you today are to be upon your hearts. Impress them on your children. Talk about them when you sit at home and when you walk along the road, when you lie down and when you get up."

The New Testament also affirms the distinctiveness of the nuclear family, even setting it apart from the church. This fact should not be overlooked, despite the fact that there are some who blur the distinction between the nuclear family and the church. Paul refuses to relegate to the church those responsibilities that belong to the nuclear family. Paul charges the parents, not the church, with the responsibility for nurturing children. And, as stated above, when Paul touches on the care of widows, he says this is first the duty of the family. He expects the church to care for widows only when there are no children to do so (1 Tim. 5:3–4).

Martin Luther lamented over the lack of emphasis on the family in his day. He explained that it was in part the result of the priority given to both monastic life and the institutional church. He accused the church leaders of his day of misunderstanding the glory of family living because of the "counter-glory" given to monastic life.[32] We see that the church can even become a competitor of the family.

FAMILY FUNCTIONS AND THE CHURCH

That God created the family for society and that it must be maintained becomes even more important when we look closely at the relationship of the church and the home. Ted Ward calls the family the "unitary structural building-block of the church, a vital linkage between the community of the redeemed and the offspring of that community."[33] The home does this by developing the capacities of children for loving relationships so that they may function properly in the life of the church.

The home also provides experiences that will help children understand concepts of God and His church. Many scriptural ideas are taught by using terms taken from family life. For example, were children to be raised in government institutions, apart from their father, the analogy of God as Father would be lost. In addition, many other biblical concepts, such as the doctrine of the church, can be understood only in terms of family experience.

While few would deny that the church has an important part to play in the nurture of children, it can nonetheless be stated that the family is the primary agent for developing a child's awareness of God. Though it is conceivable that a communal arrangement, such as some of the Christian communes in the United States today, could be an effective nurturing body, such a structure is not biblical. It is in the home that children experience relationships and the spiritual sustenance that shape their awareness of God.[34] It is true, as I will explain in chapter 6, that the kind of interaction that takes place in both the church and the home should be similar; that is, love and honesty should be the hallmarks of relationships in both places. However, this does not mean that either can or should replace the other. If they maintain both their similarities and their differences, they will complement one another and thus fulfill their strategic function in God's design for family life.

Summary

Challenges to the existence of the nuclear family may increase in our postindustrial age; it is difficult to make a prediction here with any degree of certainty. Many aspects of nuclear-family life have changed and there will be more changes in the future; but the Christian has solid and extensive theological warrant for maintaining the place and function the nuclear family has in our society.

PART THREE

THE
FAMILY-CHURCH
FAMILY

5

Family Ministry
in the
Church's Life

At its heart family-life ministry is related to the nature of the church, not merely to its work. Family-life ministry is not a mere appendage to the church's organization. Like missions, it must be integrated into the church's life. Family renewal requires church renewal.

While all contemporary social institutions hinder the development of quality family life to some degree, it is the church that holds the most promise for fostering it. The church alone brings the whole family together into one fellowship of persons of various ages and circumstances. To what other place or meeting does the family regularly drive together? Important growth for all ages happens at church. In the context of the church, individuals of all stages of development find support and encouragement as, along with others, they endure and negotiate the stress involved in advancement from one stage to another.

But even the local church has been blamed for contributing to the family's plight. The substance of the accusation is usually a complaint about time. The church program, by its time demands, competes with the family. Moreover, when family members go to church, they often find themselves separated from one another. For these reasons many church leaders resist family-life education because they see it as another bundle of programs that compete for people's leisure time.

The problem is not one of time, however, but of dichotomy. Church life, in reality, is more distinct from family life than it should be. The church thus involves people in activities that are so distinct from family life that these activities contribute very little to the family. The present institutional form of the church is at fault. Complaints about this form of the church center around its nature.

The Nature of the Church and of Family Ministry

Ideally, it would seem that people could best train for family life in their own families. But that would require solid Christian homes to begin with, and there aren't enough of those. The difficulty is that problematic families perpetuate themselves in a vicious downward spiral. This is why the church's role is so crucial. People can train for Christian family life in a church life that is familylike.

But the past century has given birth to an institutional form of the church that lacks family dynamics. The church has become, first of all, a task-centered institution. This is true, in particular, among evangelical churches where corporate evangelism has tended to dominate the purpose of the church.

The result is, as in other task-oriented institutions, that relationships are viewed in the light of the job to be done. Each individual is noted and needed for his or her place in the corporate structure. The church's concern for maintaining relationships among Christians is often reduced to making certain people know their responsibilities (job description) and function with limited discord with others (work management).

Resulting relationships are superficial in this form of the church. It is not that good relationships for getting a job done are unimportant, but their quality is determined by the corporate task. In this approach to the church, the important thing is that interpersonal relationships not become a hindrance to the church's fulfillment of its task. Webber observes that "the congregation remains a collection of individuals, determined to avoid conflict and maintain pleasant but largely innocuous relationships."[1] Instead of familylike relationships, the church is marked by institutional kinds. Consequently, the individual is little more trained for family life at the church than he is at work or at school.

The age-group structure of the church also competes with the family. Growing out of the last century, this approach is characterized by a proliferation of programs. Since these programs rarely involve

75

the whole family and demand time and energy of church leaders, the family is adversely affected. This agency approach is really a substitute for family nurture, thus diminishing the importance of the family.

THE NATURE OF THE CHURCH AS FAMILY

That the church should be familylike is a major focus of those who talk of its renewal. "Christian community probably comes closest of any community to the family of childhood," writes renewal spokesperson Elizabeth O'Connor, "and all the unassimilated hurts and unresolved problems of that family come to light again in the context of the new 'family of faith.'"[2] George Webber urges: "In a family brothers speak the truth in love. This necessary family relationship is relevant for a missionary congregation."[3]

But we cannot take for granted what the church as family of God should be like. Such a crucial matter needs a careful exegetical foundation.

We could legitimately start by itemizing all of the characteristics of the New Testament church that are familylike. We could list the images, the descriptions, and the exhortations and then compare these with the biblical characteristics of the family. For example, Paul's command to speak the truth in love could be submitted as evidence that the church should be familylike. Yet, this conclusion is a bit indirect, since Paul does not base this command on the familylike nature of the church. Rather, he refers to the figure of the body: "Speak truthfully . . . for we are all members of one body," he reasons (Eph. 4:25).

We are on more solid ground if we first limit ourselves to those specific characteristics that are extracted from the figure of the family.

In theological discussions the family is among the various metaphors used of the church (such as branches, body, sheep, etc.). This is established by the fact that the church is called family or household of God several times. In addition, many familial terms are used of the church. It is surprising, then, to find that the church is rarely designated "family" in the New Testament. Ephesians 3:15 speaks of the "whole family in heaven and on earth," but that this refers to the church is by no means certain. Paul clearly calls the church "God's household" in 1 Timothy 3:15, but the Greek word *oikos,* when used as a metaphor, refers more to the temple than to the family.[4] Yet, it is clear elsewhere that in the household of God (the church) all are brothers and sisters and that the family theme prevails (Philem. 16).

Drawing on New Testament statements that actually compare church and family, we can see exactly how the church is to be familylike. However, it must be remembered that many of the statements regarding the family, particularly those related to brotherhood, are grounded in the Old Testament. Thus, the New Testament statements are not taken directly from the then-contemporary view of family life, but arise from the Old Testament pattern of presenting Israel as a brotherhood.[5] Nevertheless, even if it is done in this indirect way, the family connection to the church is still present.

Order and Responsibility

The church is to have in it order and responsibility, just as a family has. Perhaps this truth shows up most clearly in Paul's require-ment that an elder be able to "manage his own family well" if he is to "take care of God's church" (1 Tim. 3:4–5). James and John capitalize on the family motif more than any other New Testament writers.

And in this connection, they both emphasize duty. Both include physical care for the needy brother or sister in Christ as a duty (James 2:15–16; 1 John 3:17). Paul also mentions this obligation in a pas-sage intended to distinguish between a mere neighbor and a member of the family of God (Gal. 6:10).

That the apostle Paul thinks of the church as family is clearly im-plied in a number of his remarks. It is most obvious in 2 Corinthians 12:14, where he compares his relationship to the church at Corinth as that of a father to his children: "I do not seek what is yours, but you; for children are not responsible to save up for their parents, but par-ents for their children" (NASB). John cites responsibility in the realm of moral duty: "If anyone sees his brother commit a sin . . . he should pray and God will give him life" (1 John 5:16).

Family order is used primarily to depict the relationship between God and the church. Peter commands compliance with God's will "as obedient children" (1 Peter 1:14). And neither Paul nor John hesitates to utilize the father-child metaphor. John makes an appeal for obedi-ence to his admonitions to his "dear children" (1 John 2:1). Paul bases some of his authority on the fact that he is the Corinthian Christians' father (1 Cor. 4:15).

Though order and responsibility are most clearly expressed in the parent-child and brother-sister realms, Paul also draws on the husband-wife order. He compares Christ and the church with hus-band and wife (Eph. 5:22–33), saying, "For the husband is the head of the wife as Christ is the head of the church. . . . Now as the church submits to Christ, so also wives should submit to their husbands in everything" (vv. 23–24). The emphasis of this passage is not on the responsibility within the family as much as it is on love, another quality that is to be in the church as family.

77

The Family-Church Family

Love

Love within the family motif is emphasized far more than order is. The comparison between love in the family and Christ's love for the church reaches an unmatched intensity in Ephesians 5, where Christ's love for the church as His wife is expressed in these tender and unselfish terms: "Just as Christ loved the church and gave himself up for her to make her holy, cleansing her by the washing with water through the word" (vv. 25–26).

It is John who stresses most that family love characterize church life. Being offspring of the same heavenly Father makes us brothers and sisters, whose love for one another is to reflect the love of Jesus for us (1 John 3:15–18; 5:1–2). The use of the phrases *brotherly love* and *brotherly kindness* often places the metaphor of the concept of *brother* within church life.

Paul brings even the maternal image to his relationship with believers in the church in a striking way. He stresses the loving aspect of his connection with the Thessalonian church rather than the authoritarian one. "But we were gentle among you, like a mother caring for her little children. We loved you so much that we were delighted to share with you not only the gospel of God but our lives as well, because you had become so dear to us" (1 Thess. 2:7–8).

One major question about this love involves the matter of closeness. Does love imply the presence of intimacy?

The answer to this question is, in part, determined by one's definition of intimacy. Critics of the institutional church note, especially, that its communication channels are not very deep. Many leaders who uphold the institutional form of the church point to the formal expression of love in the church through its deacons' poor fund, missionary budget, and evangelistic activity. Members discharge their family responsibilities to one another without fostering closeness.

But the New Testament image of the church goes beyond these expressions of love. Brotherliness, as we have seen, extends to sharing material things and showing moral concern. Those two features alone would suggest an involvement in one another's lives that goes beyond institutional relationships. Also, a special, warm relationship is revealed through the statement about the erring church member: "Warn him as a brother," writes Paul (2 Thess. 3:15).

Taking their concept of brotherhood from the Old Testament, the New Testament writers found a warm and loyal relationship there. Proverbs describes a brother as one who is present in adversity and who "sticks close" (Prov. 17:17; 18:24).

But we get nearest the contemporary concepts of intimacy when we look at the special features of relationships described in the New

Testament, though they are not directly joined to the family figure. Christians are urged to "speak truthfully" (Eph. 4:25) and "confess [their] sins to each other" (James 5:16). They are to "carry each other's burdens" (Gal. 6:2) (related to moral faults and failures) and even to "greet one another with a holy kiss" (Rom. 16:16), a physical expression of endearment. Besides such features, their church life included feasting together and often meeting together in someone's home. We are hard-pressed to defend a system in which a church member slips into a pew to sit beside people whose names he or she does not even know.

Gathering these bits and pieces of exegesis, we can construct some solid conclusions in regard to the familial nature of the church.

First, the church as family does include order and a corporate responsibility of the members for one another. Being a family does not negate organization. In fact, the family is viewed as a managed organization itself. Loving as brothers can be less personal in its expression. The collection gathered from the Gentile churches at the request of the apostle Paul was for believers in Jerusalem that these Gentiles had never met. That collection was an expression of the universal brotherly relationship of believers.

Second, there is clearly a kindly, personal relating in the church. A corporate, superficial expression of love and responsibility cannot possibly qualify for the intimate expressions of the church family seen in the New Testament. All of the close, dynamic aspects of family life are to be found in the church body: cherishing, caring, encouraging, rebuking, confessing, repenting, confronting, forgiving, expressing kindness, and communicating honestly. Critics of the contemporary church are correct when they maintain that we must recapture the deeper aspects of interpersonal relationships.

Third, church life and family life are closely interrelated in New Testament experience. The dynamic relationship between the two is so obvious that it appears to be taken for granted by the New Testament writers.

6

Family Ministry in the Church's Educational Program

Along with its institutional form, the church's educational process is under attack. With respect to family ministry, education in the church is too distinct from Christian education in the home. Larry Richards, a major evangelical educator, summarizes the differences between family education and church education as follows:[1]

HOME	CHURCH
1. Nonformal teaching/learning	1. Formal teaching/learning
2. Frequent personal contacts	2. Infrequent personal contacts
3. Less structured communication flow	3. Structured (often one-way) communication flow
4. Daily time/contact	4. Limited time/contact
5. Regular observation of behavior in varied life settings	5. Limited observation of behavior
6. Much opportunity for exchange of feelings, values, data, etc.	6. Little opportunity for exchange of feelings, values, data, etc.

These contrasting educational styles affect the family in a number of ways. First, to the chagrin of those most heavily involved in these concerns, the ability to teach at church does not always transfer to the home environment. Trained in formal, structured methods of teaching, pastors and church workers are not necessarily equipped to communicate Christian truth in nonformal, intimate exchanges in their own homes. Add to this the tension between family demands and church demands made on church leaders, and they become parents who are not exemplary family leaders. This causes them, in turn, to be less effective in their positions in the church.

Second, Christian education in the home has been devalued. Church education has been based on "schoolization," an attempt to communicate the faith through the educational insights gleaned from the North American educational enterprise. The home process of education is a socialization, which has been a major subject of research in anthropology and sociology. Only in recent years have religious educators turned to socialization as being the most potent for Christian education. The traditional church educational programs emphasized activities in the classroom and the club program, ignoring in large part the important place of the nonformal, intense interaction of the home.

The third result logically follows: the home is styled after the church. Instead of the church patterning itself after the more nonformal process of the home, the family has tended to pattern itself after the formal process of the church. Textbooks have been printed for study in the home, and the Christian faith has frequently been communicated as orthodox truth to be known instead of living truth to be experienced. Having served zealously in the agency era of the church, I believe Richards's statement is accurate:

> Years of treating Scripture as "classroom content" has left most believers unable to relate Scripture to their own feelings, attitudes, and values. For parents this creates a deep sense of inadequacy to relate God's Word to daily life experiences of their children, and a dependence on *formal* teaching even in the home.[2]

The Christian family's power to nurture and its desire for intimacy among its members are among the forces pressing for change in the church's educational strategy. The disagreement among those who discuss change in the church as well as the frustration of those who attempt such change should cause us to study this issue carefully.

Richards calls for both church and home to gain expertise in the socialization process of Christian education, which he calls a holistic viewpoint. The transformation of believers into those who are Christlike cannot be accomplished through educational technologies focused on a single dimension, such as the belief system taught in Sunday school. "Whole person transformation takes place in the context of intimate, loving personal relationships, and where Christian living is modeled by maturing Christians. It will require openness in communication on multiple levels of sharing beliefs, personal knowledge, convictions and feelings."[3] By mirroring each other, the church and the family will more adequately accomplish the nurture task that is the responsibility of both.

Richards addresses the most prominent matter in contemporary Christian education philosophy. The issue he raises is too crucial to be ignored here, but it is also too large for us to fully explore it, much less to resolve it.

Clearly, two dominant systems of education in the church are currently in use. The "schoolization" approach is a structured educational program consistent with the prevailing institutional form of the church. The socialization approach depends more on the home process of education than on the school process and fosters a familylike process in the church, and this calls for radical structural changes in the church program.

Both of these church educational systems bloom today, and both are rooted in theology. Both have promise and problems as well. "Schoolization" is attractive because it fits well the evangelicals' desire to transmit truth. The institution of the church can control the imparting of biblical concepts through a systematic, carefully designed program. The "schoolization" approach allows for modification of methodology to fit contemporary understanding of teaching and learning, but it does not require a radical change of the church's structure.

Keeping Christian education primarily within the church structure also gives primacy to the church, a theological consideration. In addition, keeping the program primarily within the church structure does not risk handing the church's educational task to the family, which "enjoys diminishing influence."[4] "How might nurturing find a place in our society of tiny nuclear families, unwed, divorced, deceased and estranged parents?"[5]

But the schoolization approach also has a weakness. By-passing the family will continue to result in neglecting it. Unless the church and the home are joined together in some sort of symbiotic union to form the total educational strategy, family life will suffer.

The socialization approach also has both strengths and weaknesses. Socialization is strong as an educational philosophy because it is grounded in some educational principles that have solid theological support. The science of anthropology confirms the prominent place of the home and other primary groups in forming the life of the individual. In the field of religious education C. Ellis Nelson, Wayne R. Rood, and John H. Westerhoff have strongly defended the socialization strategy.[6] Larry Richards provides an evangelical foundation for socialization in his *Theology of Christian Education.*[7] Anthropological information can be found in numerous places—for example, Edward Zigler and Irvin L. Child's *Socialization and Personality Development* is an impressive, short discussion.[8]

Those who support socialization appeal to the apostle Paul's treatment of church life as education. Particularly in his epistles to the Ephesians and the Colossians Paul links the community life of the church to individual growth.

In socialization it is not the classroom or the teacher that needs to be modified, prepared, updated, and readied for the Christian development of the church's youth. Since the matrix of the process of Christian development is the combination of home life and church life, the quality of life in both of these must be overhauled. The chain of events goes like this: for children to be nurtured, the home life must be Christlike; for the home life to be Christlike, the church community life must be Christlike; for the church community life to be Christlike the adults must be resocialized.

Of course, such an approach requires more than adult classes or sermons; it means a restructuring of Christian education as we know it. Socialization cannot appeal to a schoolization process to initiate the changes demanded. Thus, the Achilles heel of this approach, according to many, is the structured changes that would have to take place in the home and in the church. Westerhoff speaks forthrightly of the demands that socialization places on Christian education:

> We cannot nurture (socialize) persons into an understanding and way of life we do not hold and exemplify. . . . The cost of that discipleship is obviously great, for it requires not only educational programs for children but new efforts at the resocialization of adults through institutional change. And that means a new reformation in the church.[9]

The Christian education dilemma today is so severe because the choices to be made are so radical. Innovations no longer revolve around incorporating new agencies or installing new chalkboards or expensive videotape equipment. The cost and effort go beyond the energy and time expended in drawing up a new organizational chart or inaugurating a new teacher-training program. We can continue to involve ourselves in such matters, attempting to bring change through our programed efforts. However, in the meantime lack of love and intimate communication will continue to erode our home and church experience. Individuals will continue in their isolation from one another in their experiences of life, allowing for little mutual support and modeling of behavior to take place. And we will continue to demonstrate an unwillingness to truly relate God's truth to our lives and to each other.

Yet, to take the socialization approach will be costly and precarious. Some of us will have to be changed before the church itself can be changed. And we will have to remodel our home lives, something nurturing theorists have called "a painful process."[10] Transforming both the church and the home may be such an ambitious option that it is in reality no option at all.

On the other hand, we may not have such a difficult choice after all. I get the impression that most of the evangelical churches that have wrestled with the questions of renewal have finally settled for both the structure and the nurture approaches. In fact, this is recommended to us as a philosophy in a recent appraisal of North American religious education. "The decision may be," Piveteau asserts, "not to choose one over or against the other but to use the two—precisely and specifically for their differences." He continues:

> Conceive the structuring approach as a model of education having for its symbol the father. He sets and administers laws, principles, goals, norms; he evaluates, adjudges, and accords merit, reward, punishment.
>
> Conceive now the nurturing approach as a model of education having for its symbol the mother. She is welcoming, reassuring, comforting; she nourishes and fosters growth.
>
> As father and mother are singularly and jointly useful and necessary to the child, so also may be the two approaches as conceived. Moreover, the child even as adult finds himself during the course of life recurring to his parents, if not in the flesh then in the figure. So too in the course of life's term, and not merely in school years, may the person now benefit from the one approach, now from the other. Thus, at one time and another for one need and another, we provide one approach and another.[11]

Thus, it may be correct to conclude that the biblical pattern of nurture does not support the exclusive utilization of auditorium or classroom models. These paradigms cannot contain in themselves the rich, nurturing congregational life Paul describes in Ephesians 4:15–16:

> Speaking the truth in love, we will in all things grow up into him who is the Head, that is, Christ. From him the whole body, joined and held together by every supporting ligament, grows and builds itself up in love, as each part does its work.

Yet auditorium and classroom models, which are rather impersonal, may legitimately comprise part of the education experience. And they may even be modified somewhat to support the socialization viewpoint. Although we cannot do much actual living together in the auditorium-oriented worship service, we can make it a point to talk more about real, everyday living in these meetings. Pastors can share their life's struggles and experiences along with their exposition of Scripture. Testimonies and sharing times can be incorporated into the services of the larger body so that our inner worlds and private struggles are made public. Thus we will, in a sense, participate together more than otherwise, and the examples of each will be shared by all.

Thus, the overhaul will not extend to all of the church's life, but just to some of it. We can modify those experiences that are quite formal in order to make them more nurturing. Even James Michael Lee, who calls for a structural approach to religious education, includes these kinds of changes. In addition, we can incorporate educational forms that are patterned after the socialization approach. We need not dismantle our congregational structures and rebuild them into small house churches in order to reap the benefits of a nurturing approach that will strengthen family life. Instead we can construct periodic intergenerational experiences within the church educational structure and we can even form Sunday evening or weekday house groups or neighborhood groups to supplement the large Sunday-morning group. These groups will provide the informal, personalized, in-depth sharing that will furnish both a model for individual families and conditions for individual maturing. In this way the body of Christ can maintain some of the task-oriented benefits of the institutional congregation while capitalizing on the socialization aspects of the small, intimate groups.

7

Home/Church
Symbiosis:
A Proposal

What has emerged from the theoretical and theological discussions of the preceding two chapters is that a particular kind of church program may cause home life to be neglected or even damaged. No matter which educational strategy and church form is chosen, the fact that God has established the family makes it imperative that the pattern of education we choose preserve and foster family life. The family needs more than sermons and classes on the home.

Accomplishing its part in the tasks of family nurture and the development of Christian family life will place some demands on the church that will require more than applying cosmetic touches here and there. This chapter is an attempt to be systematic and practical in approaching these changes.

STEP ONE: ANALYZE FAMILY NEEDS

In a sense this section is the heart of the matter, the core of this book. Considering the theology of the church and the family along with the contemporary situation of both, what does the family need from the church?

The Family Needs Identity in the Total Church Life

By the word *total* I am referring to what many social scientists identify as the impact of the total institution as community. Robert Worley has defended well the proposition that the total life of the church is a vast and powerful communication system:

> The church as an organization is a collective entity that has a personality, character, or climate of its own. The character or climate of that organization influences to a great degree the commitment people give to the church and what they actually receive, hear and understand of the church's faith, life and message. . . . The church organization as organization teaches. The total church is an alive, teeming source of information.[1]

Truth is broadcast not just in sermons and lectures but in what the church does and how it does it. No activity is neutral or without consequence in the church system. In other words, Christian education is the total activity of the church because the total activity of the church is Christian education.

Thus, if the church program offers only theological, content-centered lessons and sermons devoid of any relationship to life, the church is teaching that truth is important only for the mind but not for one's lifestyle. This will happen no matter how much teachers and preachers exhort people to become doers of the Word and not hearers only. If the church budget reveals no interest in the poor, not any number of sermons or lessons on sharing will overcome the message of the budget.

Apply that theory to the church's teaching about the family, and the task is equally clear, but no less difficult to implement. The church as a whole will need to be saying something positive about the family. If the church is built around its institutional and numerical growth, demanding from its members so much time and energy that home life suffers, it will broadcast a negative message about the home that no Mother's Day sermon can overcome. Expressing family-life ministry in this larger context will require the following: selecting church leaders who hold that the family is to be in a position of priority and who relate in a Christlike manner in both the home and the church; planning the budget with expressions of Christian values in mind; planning the program of the church so it does not compete with the family but rather involves it in church life; developing the church's evangelistic thrust so that whole families are reached, not split up; providing services and fellowship for singles, divorced, widowed, single parents, and others who need the church as "family"; recognizing the family unit in announcements and printed messages; building the church's Christian-education program so that it is integrated with the home instead of being a separate program, sufficient in itself. While it is true that some children without Christian parents will be part of the church's constituency, such children will be considered the exception rather than the rule in most church situations. In general, children and youth programs will be constructed to cooperate with, not replace the home.

The Family Needs Exposure to Models

Because parental models are not enough, the congregation can be a source of other Christlike models for youth and children. There will need to be provision for open, intimate relationships between such models and the youth and children. In addition, these relationships will have to be developed in a great variety of experiences. Children, youth, and adults together will need to be exposed to the "whole range of human experiences," as Larry Richards so rightly asserts.[2] Church life will be constructed to allow for intergenerational learning, serving, playing, worshiping, struggling, praying, and living in as many ways as feasible.

The Family Needs Training in Relating as Christians

Knowing how to relate in the institutional form of the church will not be enough. Though both the family and the church are organizations and consist of ordered life, they are also more than this. Family members will need a place to be involved in the whole spectrum of New Testament interpersonal dynamics that are part of the life of the church: such as, caring, sharing, rebuking, encouraging, confessing, and forgiving.

The Family Needs Realism

An idealistic church so out of touch with reality that it fails to acknowledge the struggles that are inherent in contemporary life is dysfunctional as far as the family is concerned. Pretending all is well, hiding our strivings and our failures from one another produces pressure, guilt, and little change. Certainly, ideals should not be surrendered. But a certain realism should be incorporated into the verbal messages and the interaction within the body. Bringing people into small groups will generate the emotional and social proximity necessary to dispel a hypocritical covering of weaknesses. But an openness to this kind of sharing is indispensable. A reluctance to be exposed precludes involvement in this kind of group, and such reluctance only serves to foster the larger, more comfortable, formal group teaching and worship experiences that are our hiding places.

The Family Needs Support

The social sciences have made us increasingly aware of the role of the group in the development and renewal of individuals. And biblical exegesis has made us conscious of the Holy Spirit's transformation of individuals by means of the collective life of the church. Since behavioral change within the family unit is perhaps the most difficult of all, the congregation has a dominant role in providing the support base for effecting such change. This support base will take a number of forms.

The sharing described in the preceding section will be one form of support. Our self-imposed privacy, a sort of insistence that home problems should not be exposed outside the doors of the home, is a hindrance to growth. Once family members realize they are not alone in their perplexities and problems, they will gain courage to appropriate God's grace in overcoming them. Such realization will reduce the loneliness, isolation, and discouragement that come from feeling that one's problems are unique.

Interfamily units close enough to know each other's crises and temporary setbacks will also occasion actual burden-bearing when it is most needed. The church family, then, takes on the support functions of the extended family. Proverbs 27:10 seems prophetic for our times: "Better is a neighbor nearby than a brother far away."

Church life so constructed allows families to share their strengths as well as their weaknesses and problems. In family cluster groups, as in other aspects of congregational life, individual families can offer suggestions and examples that contain solutions for other people.

Families Require Church-Family Experiences

The widowed, the divorced, single parents, children of broken homes, and singles need a familylike church life, just as complete families do. Certainly the traditional church can provide for such persons, as Britton Wood has shown in his excellent description of single-adult ministry in a large-church setting.[3] Many of the needs of single adults can be met in a vibrant singles department. However, those who are not part of a nuclear family also seek intergenerational experiences within the warm family climate present in less traditional churches. These people are the widowed and the orphaned so apparent in New Testament consciousness. There will be an important place for them in the family kind of church.

STEP TWO: FORMULATE OBJECTIVES FOR FAMILY MINISTRY

Comprehensive objectives, stated in behavioral terms, will provide direction for planning and shaping the family-life program. The following objectives are stated for individuals as well as for family units.

The Family-Church Family

Adults

- That husbands and wives be able to explain biblical concepts of marriage, family, love, sex, roles, and Christian standards
- That adults possess and continually improve their skills of problem solving, flexibility, communication, conflict management, and praying with others
- That adults be able to state and practice principles related to mental and emotional health
- That adults be able to discover resources in cassettes, books, and conversation to apply to their particular problems and questions
- That parents possess skills and information in regard to discipling, teaching, and providing sex education and values training for their children
- That singles, single parents, the widowed, and the divorced be able to explain biblical concepts related to their situations
- That parents be able to discuss ways to relate to their youth and explain the characteristics of youth
- That adults be able to discuss information and apply biblical data when handling special family problems such as divorce, death, and other crises

Youth

- That youth be able to explain biblical concepts of marriage, family, love, sex, roles, and Christian standards for the family
- That youth possess some initial skills in problem solving, flexibility, communication, conflict management, and praying with others
- That youth be able to explain biblical standards, goals, and information related to friendship, dating, engagement, and mate selection
- That youth be able to discuss adolescent experiences and explain ways to relate properly to parents during adolescence

Children

- That children be able to state biblical concepts related to family, sex and marriage, and their own roles in the family
- That children begin to develop skills of problem solving, flexibility, communication, praying with others, and conflict management

All

- That all demonstrate an appreciation for God as the Creator of family life

- That all accept their roles in life
- That all demonstrate an appreciation of family life and the Christian values related to family life

Intergenerational and Family-Unit Experiences

- That each family member and single person have intergenerational Christian fellowship on a weekly basis
- That in particular each single person, single parent, and child of a single parent experience intergenerational Christian fellowship
- That each family member and single person have periodic intergenerational learning and worship experiences, both formal and informal

STEP THREE: DETERMINE PRINCIPLES

The actual principles of church programing will depend, in part, on the existing form and circumstances of the local church. These principles will arise out of a convergence of theological dictates, educational insights, and family members' needs.

1. Family life concepts are best communicated by the church's total expression of family relationships and values. This is a restatement of the major emphasis of chapter 5. Family ministry will require structural change in many churches. Excellent guides for developing the relational life of the church are now available.[4]

Since our church life has taken on a cultural form, it is appropriate for us to appeal to current administrative resources, particularly those relating to the management of change. When it comes to structural innovation, we should be familiar with the principles of organizational change and development. The gaining of particular expertise is increasingly made possible through the studies of organizational development by the National Training Laboratories. Organizational development has been applied to business and schools and has promise of church application.[5]

2. Family-life education can be built into existing programs and can be an ongoing ministry. The problem of time demand can be partially solved by inserting family-life themes and activities into the existing program. Offering special family-life electives for the Sunday school hour is a simple procedure. Ongoing instruction for all age groups ought to be part of the regular Sunday school curriculum. Intergenerational events can periodically replace Sunday evening services or Sunday school teaching. Even a Sunday morning service could be transformed into a genuine interfamily event from time to time.

3. Family life should not be hindered by the life of the church, since home and church, both of God's design, should not be competitive.

4. Christian education should be carried out in both the home and the church with an integrated program and plan. A later chapter will be devoted to the philosophy and practice of this.

5. Provision should be made for children who have no Christian parents; but evangelistic programs for children should not be made without an adequate evangelistic ministry aimed at their parents. It is quite axiomatic that a family-life emphasis gives priority to adult education and evangelism.

6. Family-life emphasis should include singles, with every effort being made to protect them from feeling left out.

7. Intergenerational experiences can be intentionally designed, but the total church program should provide for regular informal interaction between generations. I have included this principle to prevent us from thinking that a periodic, special interfamily experience is enough to accomplish the kind of support the family needs.

8. Laymen should be enlisted for various phases of family-life ministry; teaching and training programs should be transferable. The transferable concept merely means that courses and training be conducted in such a way that the gifted recipient of the training might be able to impart to others the knowledge and training gained. If courses are so designed, we will increase the reservoir of qualified teachers and leaders needed for the vast enterprise ahead of us. Relationship courses, such as Gary Collins's *How to Be a People Helper,* are creatively designed in this way.[6]

9. New family-life programs might be initiated on a voluntary basis. Because of the multifaceted threat involved in many of the family-life programs, it is best not to force or cajole people into them. Offering them to those who are ready to respond will reduce the criticisms and resistance, making future changes more probable.

10. Attempts at influencing the family should give priority to the training of fathers for their role. Theoretically, the biblical injunctions regarding the father's place in the home suggest that he is the primary route to changing home life. Yet, the fact that the North American mother is highly influential makes it imperative that our training not be exclusively directed at fathers. Whole-family training is very beneficial.

11. The church life and program should communicate and be built on the concept that the parents are responsible for the child's nurture (Deut. 6; Eph. 6:4). Though Christian education is a cooperative task of both church and home, no church educational program

should communicate to the parents, "We will do it for you."

12. The teaching and training ministry of the whole church body should be related to family life. Just as the New Testament epistles touch on the home when it is appropriate, the preaching and teaching within the present-day church should do the same. Doctrine and practical teaching should speak to contemporary life, including family-life situations.

STEP FOUR: MOVE IN THREE PROGRAM DIRECTIONS

There are three dominant directions within the family-life ministry movement. First of all, there is the attempt to educate parents and train husbands, wives, children, and youth for participation in family living. I would call this *family-life education.* Every resource of the church has been enlisted for this task: books, articles, sermons, periodicals, conferences, Sunday school classes, counseling, etc. Family-life education is most visible in the adult Christian-education thrust, in which much attention has been given to marital and parental roles.

A direction similar to this, but quite distinct, is *family nurture.* In the broad sense, family nurture refers to the total child-rearing experience. Parents who are maturing Christians play a major part in the Christian-education enterprise through their total interaction with their children. In the narrow sense, family nurture refers to centering Christian teaching in the home. The family rather than the church is viewed as the primary agency of Christian nurture. More than any other strategy, this calls for major changes in the churches, which for centuries have considered themselves to be the center of the discipling process. The family-nurture approach has had its day in the past and is now enjoying a renewed emphasis in evangelical Christian education.

A third, more recent family-ministry strategy insists on some changes in the congregational lifestyle. This strategy has two aims. A humpty-dumpty-type project aimed at putting the family together again, it is both an interfamily movement and an intrafamily one. Church leaders are attempting to structure programs that will bring nuclear families together for worship, recreation, and learning. These programs attempt to reverse the practice of splitting the family as soon as they enter the church doors. Also, these leaders want to bring family units into touch with other families in meaningful, intergenerational contact. A term I have reserved for this strategy is *family-unit ministries.*

All three of these programs are essential to the family church. No church could conduct all of the many options that are possible within these programs; but those in leadership will have to be sensitive to God's leading in determining their church's situation and their families' needs as the church moves toward family-life ministry in these three major areas.

PART FOUR

FAMILY-LIFE EDUCATION THEMES

Marital Dynamics
and Roles

In my counseling, I frequently find couples who need answers that are already readily available to them. A visit to a library or bookstore could lead them to numerous books or at least a number of chapters dealing with their specific problems. Also, in a given year several seminars or conferences will have dealt with their situation. But, surprisingly, they are completely unaware that help is so close at hand. They have stumbled along in their ignorance, sometimes for decades, until finally deciding that something must be done.

The marriage-enrichment and family-enrichment movements have achieved a lusty stature in just a few years. Yet this is almost unnoticed by the public and by large segments of the professional community.[1] These movements incorporate a storehouse of knowledge gained in the past two decades from the fields of theology, communication, human sexuality, conflict resolution, human psychology, family sociology, small-group dynamics, and affective education.

Evangelicals acquainted with this reservoir of knowledge have rejected some portions and have incorporated other parts. Those of us who seek to integrate biblical principles with modern concepts and practices appeal to societies' changes as a basis. Contemporary problems need contemporary answers. Chapters 8 and 9, dealing with the intellectual substance or content of family-life education, are admittedly an integration of biblical and contemporary ideas. The limitation of space permits my being only suggestive; so each section will be followed by a list of choice books in that subject area.

Marital Dynamics

If couples were told they would live in a box for the rest of their lives, they would be full of questions about its location, its exact size, the facilities available, etc. Yet, many persons today fail in marriage because they entered it without knowing what it was all about in the first place.[2] We have already determined that marriage is a becoming "one flesh," and that this is a total experience. Therefore, one of the major tasks of marriage education is to provide couples with the necessary motivation and tools to be "one."

We are aware that oneness will require open communication. Drawing from the humanistic psychology of Abraham Maslow, authors like John Powell have been picturing the potential of intimacy through communication. We are not yet fully aware of the many complexities and intricate dimensions present in the relationship of two individuals, but it is clear that we have been researching this domain as never before. Books and articles from the pens of evangelicals reveal their participation in this exploration. And in the process we have begun to uncover and look at some biblical texts we have been partially ignoring. We are departing from the mechanical, institutional, impersonal marital relationships of the past.

Sharing Feelings

One of the major marks of the new form of communication is its emphasis on the sharing of feelings. This emphasis promotes a willingness to disclose oneself, represented by a variety of terms: vulnerability, openness, transparency, etc. Early proponents of this open approach were psychologist Carl Rogers and prominent Swiss counselor and medical doctor Paul Tournier.[3]

Self-disclosure is threatening and can even be traumatic. It needs careful definition. Equating it with psychological nakedness is a mistake. Honesty does not require complete disclosure. Hazen Werner warns those who would try to lose their own individuality and aloneness completely.[4] This we cannot fully do, since life has some experiences we cannot share with others. Nor should self-disclosure be confused with impulsiveness. One can be spontaneously genuine

97

without being annoying and one becomes annoying to others if he is always going from the lung to the tongue in the name of authenticity. Paul writes that we should say those things that will edify (Eph. 4:29). For this reason Lawrence Crabb wisely advises husbands and wives to sometimes keep their feelings to themselves:

> If we asked people to define an intimate relationship, most in our feeling-oriented culture would suggest that an intimate relationship is one in which they can share everything they feel. . . . There are times in relationships built around mutual ministry in which one part will choose *not* to share certain feelings . . . because holding in his feelings furthers the purposes of God. . . . A depressed husband should simply push his depression on the back burner when his wife is boiling from the pressure of three kids and a dirty house.[5]

Yet true self-disclosure is the most basic and simple route to intimacy for Christians who truly love one another. Paul commands believers to "speak the truth in love," and to "put off falsehood" (Eph. 4:15, 25). Paul was given to sharing much about his feelings and his thoughts in reconciling himself with his brethren and maintaining his relationships with them. "He is difficult to comprehend," A. T. Robertson concluded regarding Paul, "not because he conceals himself but because he reveals so much about himself."[6]

The marital intimacy described in the Song of Songs, or Song of Solomon, is replete with expressions of feelings and self-disclosure.[7] It occurs sometimes in explicit statements such as the following: "You have stolen my heart with one glance of your eyes" (4:9). Often in the Bible feelings are expressed in similes or metaphors. Earlier in this same passage the lover says to his beloved, "Your hair is like a flock of goats descending from Mount Gilead" (4:1). He may here be describing his emotions as much as he is picturing his lover. By comparing her hair to a flock of goats, he tells of the refreshed and restful feelings he experiences when he looks at her; it is similar to how he feels when he looks at a flock of goats at the end of a day.

Although verbalizing one's feelings can be selfish when it is done merely to ventilate or manipulate, it can also be a profound expression of love. John Powell explains that such intimate sharing is an act of love because it includes an entrusting and an accepting of the most personal gift one has to offer or receive, the inner soul.[8]

SUGGESTED READING

Clinebell, Charlotte H., and Clinebell, Howard J. *The Intimate Marriage.* New York: Harper, 1970.

Powell, John. *The Secret of Staying in Love.* Niles, Ill.: Argus, 1974.

Small, Dwight H. *After You've Said I Do.* Old Tappan, N.J.: Revell, 1968.

Wright, H. Norman. *Communication: Key to Your Marriage.* Rev. ed. Glendale, Calif.: Regal, 1979.

Handling Conflict

Conflict results from building oneness out of two. It is to be expected and is not always the result of sin. Marriage is like two individual streams of water cascading gleefully down the mountainside, now joining in a frenzied, noisy, bubbling, swirling current. Conflict can be avoided by the two persons withdrawing from each other, but it cannot be successfully solved that way. And the closer the two get, the more potential there is for conflict. Dwight Small says that it's like two porcupines sleeping together. In fact, communication is relatively easy when there is little conflict. For this reason engaged couples are lulled into thinking they have no communication problems. But the true test of communicating is exercising it when in conflict. Resolving the conflicts openly will deepen the relationship. Leaving them unresolved or using manipulative maneuvers only separates people.

Conflict management will require some restraint, first of all. Avoid the negative ways of handling conflicts. Instead of facing the issue at hand, many couples allow nagging, blaming, and criticizing to become habitual. Public sarcasm and joking often result from inner feelings about undiscussed conflicts. Instead of using these methods, Jesus calls for open confrontation between Christians in such situations. "Go and show him his fault, just between the two of you," He urges (Matt. 18:15). Obstacles within the relationship should be discussed with sensitivity and openness. Since we would rather "flee than fight," according to Fromm, open discussion is not easily achieved.

Once discussion takes place, the couple will discover that there are a number of options for solving the issue. Sometimes, one person submits to the other. But not always. At times, acceptance of bothersome behavior will be the final decision. Tolerance and forbearance sometimes have to be substituted for the other's changing the habit or personality trait. Sometimes the couple can compromise in a fashion that shows mutual respect.

SUGGESTED READING

Augsburger, David. *Caring Enough to Confront.* Glendale, Calif.: Regal, 1973.
Bach, George. *The Intimate Enemy.* New York: Morrow, 1969.
Small, Dwight H. *After You've Said I Do.* Old Tappan, N.J.: Revell, 1968.

Handling Feelings

If we flee from conflict, we may ignore our negative feelings. Yet a negative surge of feeling that is built up through months and years finally creates explosions in relationships. The sensible approach to a problem is to recognize one's negative feeling. Admitting that we have such a feeling is the place to start. But we do not always do so. In the name of being a good Christian or a good spouse, we can easily deny that we really are angry or jealous. "Good wives don't get jealous," the Christian woman says to herself. This denial can lead to repression, whereby the feeling may build up in the subconscious. Repressed, unrecognized, unresolved anger results in millions of marital fights and even thousands of murders each year.

The honest, confessional spirit of the New Testament forbids our fooling ourselves about ourselves. When angry or jealous, a Christian, above all, should be able to face himself and admit that whatever is going on inside him is really there. Once the feeling is recognized, he should seek to analyze it to identify its nature and to uncover its cause. Not being used to doing this, many of us will find this difficult to do.

It's tough at times to know whether one is angry, jealous, or just disappointed. Yet, to know the exact feelings in a certain situation may be very important. If a wife refuses her husband's sexual advances, it will be crucial both to him and her to know what he is feeling at the moment. This search for one's feelings is not a surrender to them. It's just the opposite. Ignoring one's feelings may be the easiest way to succumb to their influence.

The recognition of a particular feeling will make possible the next step—control. In part, the New Testament answer to hostile feelings is the control of the indwelling Holy Spirit (Eph. 4:30–31). There are times when He will keep the feeling from occurring; but apparently He also works to control the negative actions, even though the hostility is not curbed. Thus Paul says, "In your anger do not sin" (Eph. 4:26).

The third step is crucial: verbalize your feeling. Admitting your feeling honestly to your partner as well as to yourself is a healthy route to dealing with both the feeling and whatever caused it. Once this is done, you can both work together on managing the feeling and solving the problem. When my wife said recently, "Chuck, I'm angry with you," I actually responded with excitement: "That's wonderful, let's sit down and discuss it." For us, this directness was a sign of the maturing of our relationship.

SUGGESTED READING

Lesson, L. Richard. *Love and Marriage and Trading Stamps.* Niles, Ill.: Argus, 1971.
Wahlroos, Sven. *Family Communication.* New York: New American Library, 1976.
Wright, Norman. *The Christian's Use of Emotional Power.* Old Tappan, N.J.: Revell, 1974.

Realizing What the Foundation Is

Marriage is a personal contract. It is based on commitment. That fact has very practical implications for marriage. It shatters, first of all, the popular notion that marriage is based on romantic love. Couples often marry according to feeling; if the feeling leaves, the basis of their union is taken away. Being an emotion, romantic love cannot provide a firm foundation for marriage. It too easily wanes and fluctuates. In addition, it is too idealistic. After marriage, each partner must face the other on a realistic basis, seeing the faults and differences previously overlooked. Commitment must take the couple through the stressful ordeal of facing the truth. Saying that romance is not the basis of marriage is not the same as saying it is unimportant. It is important; it is just inadequate by itself.

Commitment, not romance, will provide a foundation for building a true love. Love includes an acceptance that is realistic, as Gibson Winter has so graphically described:

> Acceptance in marriage is the power to love someone and receive him in the very moment that we realize how far he falls short of our hopes. It is love between two people who see clearly that they do not measure up to one another's dreams. Acceptance is loving the real person to whom one is married. Acceptance is giving up dreams for reality.[9]

In this sense mature love comes after marriage. Romance may bring a couple to marriage, but commitment keeps the two together while a reservoir of rewarding experiences produces a satisfying, realistic attachment. Couples who don't understand this process often panic when the romantic feeling fades.

SUGGESTED READING

MacDonald, Gordon. *Magnificent Marriage.* Wheaton, Ill.: Tyndale, 1976.
Ramsey, Paul. *One Flesh.* Grove Booklet on Ethics, No. 8. Bramcote Notts: Grove Books, 1975.
Timmons, Tim. *Maximum Marriage.* Old Tappan, N.J.: Revell, 1976.

MARITAL ROLES

Perplexity is the most appropriate term to describe North American thinking about roles in marriage. "Men are having a more difficult time defining precisely what their role is," reports a *Newsweek* article.[10] *Confusion* is the article's most prominent word. Theoretically, it's not difficult to outline the various approaches to roles. The Scanzonis list four structural types.[11] In the *enforced authority* type the wife is the property of the husband, who may bring her to obedience through beatings if he chooses. It is an owner-property relationship. In the *traditional head-complement* arrangement the wife is submissive, she is supportive of her husband, and she is a homemaker. In the *companionship* type the wife is allowed to pursue a career. This may involve the husband in household duties, but the husband's career takes precedence over the wife's. The husband, too, usually has the last word in decisions. Most recent to appear is the *egalitarian* form. Here both the wife and husband have careers, share household duties, and have equal power in decision making.

Historically it is not too difficult to trace these four forms in North America. Probably the first type never did appear here in true form because it belonged mostly to medieval life. In the Colonies, religion promoted mutual love and respect that mellowed the husband-wife relationship. On the frontier, the rugged life of challenge and conquest developed a greater equality between the sexes. But the traditional arrangement prevailed in North America, particularly in Puritan New England and in the patriarchal South. By the time of the Civil War or mid-nineteenth-century America, the husband's headship was not a result of compulsion but of mutual love and respect.[12]

At this time Alexis de Tocqueville, the French observer of American life, wrote, "The father exercises no other power than that which is granted to the affection and experience of his age; his orders would perhaps be disobeyed, but his advice is for the most part authoritative." A companionship type of marriage was already emerging.[13] Democracy had worked its way into the American family, even among Christians. By 1946 the American Lutheran Church expressed what is the general evangelical viewpoint today:

> The husband is to be the head of the household, the wife to be submissive to her husband. Each of these relationships carries with it the overtone "as to the Lord," for the husband is not tyrant over his wife nor does the wife meekly grovel before her husband. The teaching emphasizes the importance of orderly human relations, in which, for the sake of good order there must and can be only one head, the husband. The church has not taken a stand against "the democratic family," which does not imply indiscriminate equally divided authority.[14]

Recently the traditional and the companionship forms have been challenged as being unbiblical and impractical. Supporting a change to egalitarian marriage, Letha Scanzoni and Nancy Hardesty were the earliest evangelicals to lay down this challenge.[15] Evangelical theologian Paul Jewett gave a lift to the egalitarian movement through his exposition of roles in *Man as Male and Female.*[16] A practical, complete guide to a fully egalitarian marriage is now made available by Herbert J. and Fern Miles.[17]

102

Egalitarian arguments against a special order in the home take three forms. First, the egalitarians assert that there is a mandate for equality among all Christians. Paul insists that "there is neither . . . male nor female, for you are all one in Christ Jesus" (Gal. 3:28). This equality, the egalitarians maintain, means equal power in a marriage. Equality precludes any difference in roles.

In the second argument it is asserted that all Old Testament references to submission-headship are a result of the fall of man, not the creative order. Such references arise from chapter 3 of Genesis, not chapter 2. According to this view, many of the New Testament references to marriage are related to this old view of the husband-wife affiliation originating in Genesis 3 and are now done away in Christ.

They insist, in the third place, that all of the New Testament references to headship can be explained as adaptation to the culture or hangovers of pre-Christian Jewish thought. In the case of Ephesians 5, where Paul declares that wives should submit to their husbands, egalitarians point to the revolutionary character of the passage. Paul calls for mutual submission of all believers in verse 21, thus nullifying any distinct submission of wives to their husbands. And Paul urges men to love their wives as Christ loves the church, which cancels out any ordained management order. In the case of 1 Corinthians 11:3–12, where the husband's and wife's roles are related to the differences between man and woman found in Genesis 2, Jewett dismisses these thoughts as old rabbinical views still lodged in Paul's mind and thus not normative for Christians today.

Those who hold to a companionship type of marriage, in which there are some differences between husband's and wife's roles, cite several references in Scripture pertaining to this type: 1 Corinthians 11:3–12; Ephesians 5:22–33; Titus 2:4; 1 Peter 3:1–7. Those arguing for this position insist that what is called for is not an order of privilege but of function. And that function is quite balanced. "At no time did this headship mean unlimited rule," a denominational statement points out. "At no time as a Christian could he dictate that his wife must do the work, while he enjoyed the wages. . . . At no time could he exercise violence upon her person. His wish is not to prevail in an arbitrary manner in the household."[18] Headship directed by Christlike love is drastically tempered. Calvin characterized it as being gentle and liberal.[19] It is recognized that even Peter's example of appropriate submission, Sarah, opposed Abraham and won her rights from him on several occasions.

That these principles are hangovers from rabbinic times, based on the Fall, or are concessions to culture, is rejected by those who support role definitions. Paul gives theological root to the roles by

103

appealing to Genesis 2, which covers the time prior to the Fall. Roles are based on the woman's derivation from the man and her being created for the man (1 Cor. 11:3–9). Were Paul adopting the cultural views of his day, he would not have appealed to Scripture to support them. It is possible to see a consent to slavery in his writings, but he never offers theological support for the practice as he does for order in marriage. And to accept Jewett's explanation that Paul is presenting outmoded rabbinical ideas would place one outside evangelical principles of biblical interpretation and understanding of biblical authority.

That there can be a God-given arrangement for marriage and still be equality between the partners is also easily maintained. Peter urges husbands to consider their wives as "heirs together of the grace of life" (1 Peter 3:7 KJV), just as Paul acknowledges that there is equality in Christians' relationships with one another in Christ. But equality need not cancel difference and order. Even in the Trinity, where there is equality among the three persons in the Godhead, Christ is in functional subordination to the Father. Paul points to this as an example: "The head of every man is Christ, and the head of the woman is man, and the head of Christ is God" (1 Cor. 11:3).

The balanced tenor of biblical data and the confusing tone of contemporary life suggest that we should avoid two extremes when teaching about roles. We would do well to resist making too little of roles, including the temptation to be silent because of possible controversy. Role guidelines, stated generally in Scripture, can provide stability even though their application in modern society is not always immediately clear. We will continue to need realistic dialogue between individuals and couples to satisfactorily work out the biblical arrangement today.

On the other hand, we should also be careful not to make too much of roles. To suggest that legalistic compliance with God's order for marriage is the final answer to all family adjustments and conflicts is unbiblical and too simplistic. Family members are to relate to one another as persons, not as parts in an organization. Patience, understanding, forbearance, unselfishness—these are to be the final words in family relationships. The bottom line of the New Testament is love, not compliance.

SUGGESTED READING

Andrews, Gini. *Your Half of the Apple.* Grand Rapids: Zondervan, 1972.
Boldrey, Richard, and Boldrey, Joyce. *Chauvinist or Feminist?: Paul's View of Women.* Grand Rapids: Baker, 1976.
Elliot, Elisabeth. *Let Me Be a Woman.* Wheaton, Ill.: Tyndale, 1976.

Hardesty, Nancy, and Scanzoni, Letha. *All We're Meant to Be.* Waco: Word, 1974.

Liftin, A. Duane. "A Biblical View of Marital Roles: Seeking a Balance." *Bibliotheca Sacra* (Oct.–Dec. 1976).

MacDonald, Gordon. *Magnificent Marriage.* Wheaton, Ill.: Tyndale, 1976.

⑨

Marital Sex, Dating, Engagement

MARITAL SEX

As with marital roles, either too little or too much can be made of marital sex. Its importance is overstressed when it constitutes the major definition of intimacy, which is not reducible to sexual intercourse. "Human encounter is not the same as sexual encounter," Thomas Oden reminds us.[1] In fact, sexual encounter may even diminish intimacy, since the quest for sexual satisfaction by itself becomes manipulative and defeats its own deepest intention. Oden charges that equating sexual closeness with interpersonal encounter has yielded untold misery in our culture. The entanglement of bodies without the intermingling of souls constitutes the major misuse of sex.

Thinking of sex as being trivial and unimportant, if not downright bad, is the other extreme. Sex is not everything—only about 10 percent of a good marriage, according to some psychologists. But sex is extremely powerful and prominent in marriage. Thus, it is about 90 percent of the problem in a bad marriage. Because sex is a private matter, only marriage counselors and researchers are fully aware of the extent of sexual difficulties in marriages. Masters and Johnson

106

estimate that more than four out of five marriages need help in this area.[2] Physical causes of difficulty are minimal; the main causes of sexual problems are in the mind and the emotions. And of these two, probably improper attitude, not incorrect information, is the major cause of sex problems. At this point our biblical faith can have the biggest impact. Religion, in general, promotes a better sex life because it creates a better attitude. Several large surveys have confirmed this conclusion.[3]

Lectures and discussions within the context of the church body is one way to shape attitudes. Emphasizing realistically the biblical stance will be another. Drawing inferences from God's purpose of sex in marriage provides an effective means of communication.

Procreation

Sex is for procreation. In the first chapter of Genesis male and female were told to reproduce, revealing a basic purpose of their sexuality. "Sex is good," Billy Graham once said, "without it none of us would be here."

Identity

Sex in marriage strengthens identity; therefore, sex should be fulfilling. Each of the first two chapters of Genesis maintains that maleness and femaleness is a major aspect of being created in the image of God.[4] Sex is not the most important aspect of personal identity. Being a child of God is the Christian's greatest feature of identity. Nonetheless, sex is a major ingredient. Within marriage, sexual fulfillment will enhance the person's feeling of manhood or womanhood, creating a healthy view of himself or herself. If the sexual interaction is frustrated, the identity of the person will be challenged and distorted. Of course, it is possible for the frustrated person to compensate and cope. But it is, first of all, sensible to seek knowledge, and even therapy, to help with problems related to impotency and orgasm failure. And those facing less serious struggles than these can learn ways to cultivate and enrich their sexual life.

The curriculum on this subject should include material on helping individuals accept each other's sexuality. Couples can err in rejecting each other's advances in an unkind way. Or else a partner can be repulsed needlessly and harshly because of the variety he or she wishes to initiate in foreplay and intercourse. Such rejection can be felt deeply, since it deals with such a deep-seated identity factor. Rejection can take a nonphysical form as well. Jokes, criticism, and sarcastic remarks can repudiate the other's sexuality. Married persons should be encouraged to maintain an unconditional acceptance of their partner's sexuality within biblical guidelines and to be patient with each other's likes and dislikes.

Asserting one's own sexuality is the other side of the needed affirmation of identity. Being the right kind of partner can make the other feel good about his or her sexuality. Differences of outlook may exist. It is said that man seeks love to get sex and a woman seeks sex to get love. This may not be universally true, but it could constitute a general guideline. A woman may need to cultivate her ability to be erotic, since her husband's focus may be on the gratification of his sexual desires. On the other hand, the man needs to cultivate his ability to be romantic. James Dobson's survey proved that romance is one of a woman's greatest needs.[5] The husband's manliness should be asserted on her terms; and her womanliness on his. Both should be asserted, of course, within Christian terms of personhood.

Oneness

Sex in marriage is to produce oneness; therefore, sex should be enriching. Becoming one flesh is an intimate form of communion. Sexual intercourse is a unique form of communication, as Elton Trueblood affirms:

> One of the most significant things to say about sexual intercourse is that it provides husbands and wives with a language which cannot be matched by words or by any other act whatsoever. Love needs language for its adequate expression and sex has its own syntax.[6]

Couples will be advised to ask themselves what they are communicating. A positive attitude in sexual intercourse can be communicating, "I love you; I need you; I like you; I enjoy revealing myself to you; I thrill over your revelation to me; I like all of you." On the other hand, a negative attitude and experience may be saying, "I don't like you; I don't respect all of you; I don't like revealing myself to you; I don't care about you; I take you for granted; I think you are strange." Out of the sexual experience either a poisonous brew of ill feeling or a refreshing stream of new life can flow steadily into the marital reservoir.

Pleasure

Sex in marriage is for pleasure. The sensual, pleasurable content of sex has been attacked by Christians from early church times. Mostly due to the influence of Platonic philosophy, whose followers viewed the body as the sinful habitation of the pure spirit, Augustine and others before him propagated a negative view of passion. For Augustine the sexual act was innocent in marriage, but the passion that accompanied sex was sinful.[7] Even Calvin warned against having too much variation in sex. He warned that marriage should "be recalled to measure and modesty so as not to wallow in extreme lewdness."[8] Pietists tended to view *eros* as something to be ashamed of because it competed with the believer's continuous Christ-consciousness.[9] But church history does not always reveal such a negative attitude. Luther said that God laughs and rejoices when married people get along well together. Luther saw sex as being the bond of marriage.[10] He called attention to Genesis 26:8, which describes Isaac's caressing of Rebekah, his wife, and said that the Holy Spirit recorded the incident in order to show that married sex is beautiful.[11] The misunderstood Puritans maintained a reverent attitude toward physical love, as displayed by Milton's famous apostrophe to wedded love:

> Hail wedded love . . .
> Far be it that I should write thee sin or blame,
> Or think thee unbefitting holiest place,
> Perpetual fountain of domestic sweets,
> Whose bed is undefiled and chaste pronounced.[12]

Biblical passages that confirm the pleasure and beauty of sexual embrace have been cited again and again throughout history. None is more affirming than Proverbs 5:15–20, where the husband is urged to be intoxicated always with his wife's love: "May her breasts satisfy you always," the writer says (v. 19). No biblical example is more expressive of the variety in sexual enjoyment than the Song of Solomon. Whatever its purpose and literary form, among the Jews this song was clearly used as an expression of married love.[13]

Cultivation of sexual enjoyment can assume three forms. Couples can avoid boredom by changing the surroundings. Periodic weekends away as well as different occasions or different places at home can enhance the experience. Variety in technique will also prevent the expression of sex from becoming matter-of-fact. In their manuals evangelicals Tim LaHaye and Ed Wheat have given popular expression to the rightness of agreed-upon variations in marital sex that are not harmful, such as mutual fondling and oral-genital expression. Having variation in the total set of circumstances can be most rewarding. Practicing other forms of intimacy during the physical act enriches the total context and meaning of sex itself. Reading love poems or prose aloud to each other and communicating in writing can be done as a prelude or accompaniment to sexual intercourse.

A Preventive

Sex in marriage prevents immorality; thus, sexual satisfaction should be given to each other freely. In one of the most important

New Testament passages on sex Paul affirms this truth for a very practical purpose: "Since there is so much immorality, each man should have his own wife, and each woman her own husband" (1 Cor. 7:2). Temptation to commit sexual sin was so prevalent in cosmopolitan Corinth that Paul urged Christians to marry one another to deal with the problem. Furthermore, he encouraged free expression of sex within marriage "so that Satan will not tempt you because of your lack of self-control" (v. 5). Because giving the pleasure of sex to one's mate is an obligation, sex is not to be withheld except by mutual consent, and then only for a limited time. Sex is not a favor that a partner has the right to withhold; it is not to be a weapon to dominate the other person nor a reward for good behavior. One is obliged to offer sexual pleasure freely to his or her partner because each has authority over the other's body, said Paul. It is wrong to improperly accuse one's partner of being oversexed. Neither should an unbalance of need and desire call for stoic, ascetic discipline for the one with the greatest appetite. Couples with unbalance can manage their differences in loving accommodation, the nonaroused one providing release for the other from time to time in various ways.

SUGGESTED READING

Eichenlaub, John E. *The Marriage Art.* New York: Dell, 1969.

Greeley, Andrew. *Sexual Intimacy.* Chicago: Thomas Moore Association, 1978.

Guernsey, Dennis. *Thoroughly Married.* Waco: Word, 1977.

LaHaye, Tim, and LaHaye, Beverly. *The Act of Marriage.* Grand Rapids: Zondervan, 1976.

McCarthy, Barry W.; Ryan, Mary; and Johnson, Fred A. *Sexual Awareness.* New York: Boyd & Fraser, 1975.

Wheat, Ed, and Wheat, Gaye. *Intended for Pleasure.* Old Tappan, N.J.: Revell, 1977.

DATING AND ENGAGEMENT

Since Scripture should dominate all of life, teaching about dating and engagement should be part of family-life education. This is especially true because such knowledge is so crucial to marital success. The greatest problem with American marriage may be American courtship. Though there are distinct moral and spiritual guidelines for courtship in Scripture, there are few practical ones given. The Old Testament patriarchal process, by which parents selected partners, cannot be normative for today, though there is a principle to be found in that method. Children should be sensitive to parental opinions. During New Testament times in Rome marriage was the choice of the individuals. What Scriptures does yield, however, is that (1) a person should seek a husband or a wife and the process is not to be left to chance (Gen. 24; 1 Cor. 7). (2) A Christian should seek God's will in this matter. But God's will concerning marriage to a certain person must be decided on sound reasons as well as circumstantial direction and feeling.

Scripture provides mostly spiritual qualifications to keep in mind in the selection of a mate. The Christian is to marry only another Christian (1 Cor. 7:39; 2 Cor. 6:14). Romantic love is possible before marriage (as in the case of Jacob, Gen. 29:20), but it is not always present (as in the case of Isaac, Gen. 24:67). Selection will need to be made after a successful courtship and after sound judgment based on the best cultural criteria has been made.

Youth will need to be taught the practice of proper courtship in the schools and in our church education. Courtship instruction should include information about stages and goals. There are four stages, each narrower than the preceding stage.

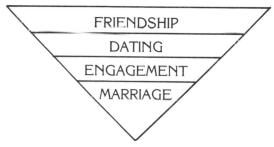

Once goals are attached to each stage, teen-agers can see that dating is not regulated by arbitrary parental or biblical rules but by a sensible approach to selecting a mate. And this selection process begins during the *friendship stage,* which includes these goals. Young people should seek to cultivate many friendships with those of the other sex; in this way youths get a chance to learn about themselves and the characteristics of others. Social contacts with a number of persons can help a young person realize there are a variety of personalities available. Another goal for the friendship stage is to develop qualitative relationships. Such relationships will help the person more easily be a friend to one's future wife or husband. He or she will also learn appropriate ways of relating to the opposite sex outside marriage. Unwholesome and flirtatious relating may harm the person after marriage as well as hinder the success of the selection process. An old saying reminds us, "Everybody's sweetheart is nobody's wife."

Goals should be kept in mind also during the *dating stage.* In our society this stage contains a number of objectives. It is most advisable to date widely and qualitatively, as this will give the same benefits for the person as he receives in the friendship stage. In addition, one will have a greater certainty about the final choice if he or she has known many possible partners. This is the stage to formulate and confirm moral standards in regard to male-female relationships. And it is a time for a person to formulate a list of qualities he or she desires in a future mate. One will wrestle with the answers to three questions: What do I need? What do I want? What can I get? The answers are not always the same. Somewhere a compromise, and then a decision, will need to be made.

Courtship may then pass to another stage called "going steady." It is a stage above dating and a stage below engagement. Other forms of commitment may also be sandwiched between these two stages, depending on one's subculture. Among college youth the act of "pinning" may be a definite preengagement stage.

The *engagement stage* has some crucial objectives:

(1) Intimacy. That the relationship should become more intimate than it was previously is usually accepted. Just how intimate is quite a controversial subject. Premarital intercourse is obviously forbidden, though in Scripture it is not dealt with as harshly as adultery is. Though many psychologists advocate it as practically advisable, the weight of research and judgment falls on abstaining. Going too far in intimacy creates many problems, since this stage is not the final one. Engagements are made to be broken. Estimates of the proportion of engagements broken run as high as 50 percent.[14] Physical intimacy prior to marriage can make an advisable separation difficult and painful to carry out and leave the participants guilt-ridden. Sometimes people carry their guilt feelings into marriage, causing sexual dysfunction. Mistrust can be fostered when one partner is suspicious of a mate who has broken moral standards prior to marriage.

(2) Learning. The engagement period is a ripe time for learning about intimate relationships and marriage. Through reading and group or private premarital counseling, couples can arm themselves with information.

(3) Communicating. Communication before marriage should be easier than afterwards, when the pressures increase. Engagement offers a chance for developing and testing the couple's communication skills.

(4) Deciding. Once the couple is engaged, others will look on them differently than before. The vantage point from which each views the other will also change. Out of this unique perspective the final decision will emerge. In *The Dating Game* Herbert J. Miles offers the best summary of the basis for that decision from a Christian perspective. When one or both are in doubt, the most favorable ally is

time. Sometimes postponement of the marriage will eventually bring the needed confirmation, but many times the relationship will fade and eventually be terminated. The American Institution of Family Relations declares that the best marriages are those that take place after the two have known each other for at least two years and have been engaged for several months.

SUGGESTED READING

Miles, Herbert J. *The Dating Game.* Grand Rapids: Zondervan, 1975.
Rosner, Stanley, and Hobe, Laura. *The Marriage Gap.* New York: McKay, 1974.
Wright, H. Norman. *Premarital Counseling.* Chicago: Moody, 1977.

10

Concepts of
Christian Parenting

Mention children, and many parents will think of Psalm 127:3: "Children are a gift of the Lord." Still others may think of trouble and feel pain. Catherine Brown states the case realistically: "As all parents and non-parents know, life with children can be hell."[1] Because of this, many parents wish they had had no children.

Many parents feel guilty and uncertain. Haim Ginott notes this as a special feature of today's parents: "Whatever grandfather did was done with authority; whatever we do is done with hesitation. Even when in error, grandfather acted with certainty. Even when in the right, we act with doubt."[2] Parents badly need assurance about their parenting practices. Giving them that assurance may be the greatest contribution of the parent training that is available. Speaking of participants in these courses, Brown observes, "The change that excites them most is that they no longer spend so much time vacillating between suicide and murder. They find themselves able to love, even enjoy, both their kids and themselves."[3]

But experts in the field often don't provide the needed confidence. And personal feelings of being a failure as a parent himself often

114

render a pastor reluctant to speak with conviction about parenting principles. A lecturer once had a talk entitled "Ten Commandments for Parents." But after having his first child, so the story goes, he changed the title to "Seven Principles for Parents." After having two more children, he modified his speech again, entitling the talk "Three Suggestions for Parents." And when his children were in their teens, he quit lecturing altogether.

Modern controversy surrounding modes of parenting also erodes the confidence of parents. Sometimes the credibility of a researcher or a teacher who is confident of his or her own viewpoint is destroyed because of the contradictions of other researchers or teachers. Even Christian experts are not unified on basic issues, such as spanking. One book seems to say that all parents need to do Is love their child, while in the same year another book appears calling for a more rigid discipline.

Inconclusiveness in theory is producing contradictions in practical application. Theorists are not yet agreed on explanations regarding the forces that shape a child. And evangelicals do not agree on a sound theology of child rearing. This confusion results in the spreading of a variety of ideas on parenting in a given church or community. Closest friends will not always agree on what is best. Their judgment will depend on their church affiliation, their own parents' practices, or the wisdom they have gained from the latest seminar they attended.

Our task is to search for some common biblical and practical guidelines that will make parents more comfortable with their role. Parents will need to be taught theory that is consistent with their faith; and they will need training in skills. Theory will be the major theme of this discussion. Chapter 13 will deal with the description and development of parental skills.

AREAS OF AGREEMENT

Scanning the fields of learning, theory, developmental psychology, and parenting theories, we see that there is surprising agreement about many things. By integrating these concepts with biblical principles, we can lay out some foundational guidelines for contemporary parenting.

Good Parenting Does Not Require Perfection

A parent can assume that he can be a responsible, successful parent without being perfect. Faith in Christ strikes at the root of the problems of being a parent because forgiveness and love, not obedience and perfection, constitute faith's bottom line. Realistically, the home will be a place of conflict, sadness, tension, hurt, and sinfulness.

115

Parents will have to deal with chronic, trivial problems without the benefit of the wisdom of Solomon. Parents will face reluctance to do homework, sibling fighting, bad table manners, disobedience, communication breakdowns, etc. Parents will be distressed—sometimes shouting, or criticizing, or exploding, or wondering how they can manage their child's sinfulness without being able to control their own. Continually repenting of their failures, they will go from one crisis to another, uncertain about their ability to cope.

The Christian knows that the task will not require sinlessness. He understands that the dynamics of Christian relationships are built around forgiveness, grace, forbearance, understanding, and love. These dynamics work. A parent or a child may explode from time to time, but the parent can ask for forgiveness or offer it. An example of these dynamics of parenting is not to be found in a psychology book. Rather, such an example is discovered in the biblical picture of God the Father. He is the ultimate parental model. The dynamics that God exemplifies to us are these: caring, responding, disciplining, respecting, knowing, and forgiving. Myron R. Chartier develops a view of parenting along these lines.[4]

The nonrequirement of perfection offers the parent hope that he or she can somehow manage what sometimes looks like an impossible task. Awareness of this lends realism to the task, too, since parents often think they are the only ones who struggle and worry so much, and it should make them more comfortable with their role. They believe that ultimately their success will not depend on any particular skill or management technique but on their own personal growth and development in God's grace.

Parental Power Is Limited

Parents are responsible for their children's behavior, but the influence of parents is limited. Virtually all authorities are agreed on this. Some parenting experts see the child as being basically good, but they don't see him as being independent. Parents can't divorce their child. They must face the parenting task.

The necessity of managing one's children is so clearly stated in Scripture that the principle doesn't require much exposition. The obligation to honor one's parents is one of the Ten Commandments. Many verses in the Proverbs relate the importance of childhood training to later life (e.g., 22:6). The necessity for parents to guide their children well is a general New Testament concept (Eph. 6:4). Being successful at controlling them is necessary for one to be a church official (1 Tim. 3:4–5).

Yet the implications of this responsibility can be too strongly stated. Proverbs 22:6, which reads, "Train a child in the way he should go and when he is old, he will not depart from it," has received a variety of interpretations. This verse is even used as a text to confirm treating a child according to his nature and personality since the phrase "in the way he should go" can be translated accurately as "in his own way." But this proverb, like other proverbs, is a general statement of truth, not an absolute promise in every individual case. This verse does not teach environmental determinism, as if no other force can undermine parental training. If no other force could work against it, parents could be held responsible for their grown children's sins, but they are not. Even the Old Testament law recognized the possible rebellion of youth, despite parental effort; and the rebellious youth, not the parents, was stoned to death (Deut. 21:18–21).

Overemphasizing the influence of parents has led to the indiscriminate heaping of guilt on their heads. In sermon and in print the weeping David is blamed for Absalom's political revolution, despite the fact that God vindicated David through Absalom's judgment and defeat. The general, prevailing idea that parents are always the major cause for their grown offspring's behavior has created an insensitivity to the grieving parents' plight, and we have handed them blame when they needed our support.

Good Parenting Is Good Relating

Good parenting requires the building of warm relationships. The leaders of most parent workshops would agree with William Glasser's idea that the home should include warm, honest, affectionate relationships. Some see these relationships as an end; Glasser views them as a means to an end. Any helping relationship needs to be warm, honest, and affectionate, he maintains.[5] And parenting is a helping relationship. That discipline and love are not mutually exclusive is obvious from the biblical viewpoint: "The Lord disciplines those he loves" (Heb. 12:6). God's love, as a model, is not expressed in stern, cool, authoritarian discipline; His relationship with His children is expressed warmly, intimately, and forgivingly.

Good Parenting Produces a Healthy Self-Concept

Good parenting will result in the child's feeling of worth. What the child ultimately thinks about himself is a basic concern of the parenting process. All modern theorists agree with this statement. As a child grows into adulthood, a good feeling about himself becomes a basis for good action. William Glasser stresses this truth in a program called Parent Involvement Program. Parents too often ignore or punish children when the children have failed and are upset with

117

themselves. Glasser thinks that the feeling of failure is a cause of a child's misbehavior. Therefore, to improve his or her conduct, the child must improve his or her self-concept. Even behaviorists emphasize that their techniques should help children feel good about life and themselves. Behaviorist techniques are not manipulative devices to get the child to conform to the parent's arbitrary wishes but should help the child be comfortable with himself or herself.

As believers in the Bible, we should have no quarrel with this statement. Basic to all of people's conduct with others is the fact that all are made in the image of God and that all are of great worth. Parents should avoid cursing their children as well as any other person made in the image of God (James 3:9). The tenderness and kindhearted approach of the Christian in general should be the approach of the parent in particular (Eph. 4:31–32). Love believes in and hopes for another (1 Cor. 13:7). Paul speaks even more directly to this point in his instructions to parents. He warns parents to consider the inner life of their children when nurturing them. Do not drive the child to anger (Eph. 6:4) nor to exasperation (Col. 3:21), he cautions. Measures that push a child to anger or depression ignore the inner life, the sense of personal worth, and the right to life. Parenting should impart self-respect to the child.

Good Parenting Produces Self-Discipline

Good parenting should result in inner control. While there is some difference of opinion over the use of outer constraints, there is none when the matter of inner control is concerned. The child is to be handled so that eventually he will become responsibly independent of the parents and be able to function in society on his own. For this to be accomplished, parents must build eventual detachment into the disciplining process. They will need to attach certain consequences to certain kinds of behavior in order to shape the child. But they will also need to make the child aware of the fact that improper behavior produces all kinds of negative consequences for others as well as for the child. The more the punishment and reward conform to real life punishment and reward, the easier the transition from the dependent to the independent life will be. Misbehavior will be seen by the child as more than merely a matter between self and parents; behavior will need to be viewed as being related to others, to God, and to the child's own well-being. Thus, a prominent national program like Parent Effectiveness Training is geared to teaching children to solve their own problems with a view to making them independent. Glasser's PIP program proposes to cause children to see the results of their behavior. A behavior-modification approach in a seminar called "Re-

118

sponsible Parent" trains parents how to support children in changing their behavior.

All of these approaches are biblically supported. Paul urges parents to bring the child up in the nurture and admonition of the Lord. The test for good parenting is not merely to control by any means. Methods used to control children should be in conformity to God's methods and to ethical principles, not merely to the arbitrary whims of the parents. Otherwise, the necessary ingredients for later self-discipline will be lacking.

Good Parenting Develops Sensitivity

Good parenting should lead to the development of empathy in the child's personality. A large measure of internal self-discipline results from learning to respect others. This demands awareness of the way one's behavior affects others, along with an understanding of personal rights. Teaching children that they have no rights will give them little basis for understanding about the rights of others. Brutally forcing children to comply may make them ethically irresponsible. Glasser has been commended by Christians for his strong emphasis on human responsibility. He insists that we avoid a Freudian approach to delinquency, by which a child's misbehavior is blamed on early childhood experiences over which the child had no control. Delinquents should be made to feel responsible for their actions, Glasser demands. Thomas Gordon, with his Parent Effectiveness Training, seeks to train parents to share their feelings with their children in order to help the children know how their behavior affects others internally. This is an important parental function. Telling children that their loud talking is making you feel nervous helps build their awareness of others and responsibility to them.

That we have biblical warrant for this training seems clear enough from our Lord's view of ethics. Certainly He viewed one's love of God as a major means of control of conduct. But love for one's neighbor as oneself also regulates one's actions. Children should be guided to see this fact.

Parenting Includes Power

Parents possess a certain power. Parental power is basic to all of the major national parent programs but one. William Glasser works toward equalizing the power between parent and child; the child, with the parent's backing and assistance, evaluates and changes her or his own behavior. But Glasser does affirm parental power. Rudolph Dreikurs's parent-training program, based on the book *Children: The Challenge,* stresses power as a fact of life, a drive we are born with. Of

119

course the parent must use this power to direct the child's behavior into socially useful channels.[6] And behavior-modification advocates build on the use of power. Thomas Gordon radically departs from the others, believing that a parent can and should give up the use of power. In his Parent Effectiveness Training (PET) he teaches that power is destructive and that in any situation, through conversation and compromise, everyone can win.

For this reason the biblical approach is distinct from that of PET. While growing up, the child is to be taught to respect parental authority within God's order (Eph. 6:1). This parental power is modified, however. It is limited and governed by the framework of God's values and standards. Thus, parents are reminded to bring up children according to Christian nurture, not according to their own whims. Behavior-modification approaches lack standards. Mastering the techniques of these approaches gives a parent unusual power over the child without any protective guidelines for its exercise. For the Christian, parental power is to be exercised toward biblical ends and is to be harnessed by kindness and love. Thus, the Christian can more easily validate parental power as being part of God's order because that power is protected from misuse.

Parenting Utilizes Behavioral Modification

Parenting through using certain consequences for certain behavior is effective. One does not have to be a behaviorist to know the results of an action will influence whether or not the action will be repeated. This idea was around long before B. F. Skinner's animal research demonstrated it to be so. One critic of Skinner put it well: he said that Skinner had spent millions of dollars on research to tell us what we already knew—that if you pay a man to work, he will, and if you stop paying him, he'll stop working.

The role of consequences in shaping behavior is well grounded in scriptural teaching. Numerous proverbs speak of regulating behavior through punishment (Prov. 13:24; 19:18; 23:13). The New Testament confirms God's use of consequences to guide us (Heb. 12:5–7). But there are differences between scriptural learning theory and behaviorism. The Christian parent can use the guidelines of behaviorism, but not exclusively.

AREAS OF CHRISTIAN CONCERN

The Sinful Nature and Parenting

Parents should consider the sinful nature of their child. It is over the matter of the nature of the child that the Christian clashes most

120

with current parent-training programs. Thomas Gordon and other humanists believe that the child really wants to do the right thing. The child misbehaves only because he is legitimately trying to satisfy personal needs. In doing so, however, the child comes into conflict with others who are only trying to satisfy their needs as well. Thus, the child who arrives late to dinner is catering to his own needs and, at the same time, hindering the fulfillment of other people's needs. Thus, Gordon recommends discussing this clash and coming to some compromise.

Glasser places more stress on human responsibility than does Gordon but still sees self-fulfillment as man's basic drive. Behaviorists take a neutral attitude toward man's nature, refusing to define acts as being either morally good or bad. Since they deny human will, they view all action as being conditioned by outer circumstances. Thus, for example, being a good driver is not to be classified as morally good behavior since the driver was only conditioned to be so, something he or she is not responsible for.

Christians identify misbehavior as a result of sin within the individual and society. Humanists see man as being basically good and they ignore evil as it is presented in Scripture.

Understanding Misbehavior

Saying that misbehavior is sin is theologically correct, but it is also too general. It does not deal with the actual reason for misbehavior specifically enough to be used as a base for nurturing practices.

Dealing with misbehavior requires careful understanding of its cause. Psychologists are not agreed on its cause but they offer some insight. Gordon says that misbehavior results when a person tries to meet his own needs and, in the process, his actions constitute an obstacle to someone else meeting his desires. Parents also call such actions misbehavior. When a child's screaming disturbs the parent's reading, for instance, it is misconduct. But PET advocates tell parents to discard the word *misbehavior* since it is only motivated behavior. PET is relativistic; according to its doctrine, conduct is forged out of legitimate individual expression in a democratic context.

In Glasser's system, conduct is considered misconduct when it is neither helpful for society nor for the individual. Rather, the conduct is prompted by the desire to succeed. "People who engage in *irresponsible behavior,* Glasser's catch-all term for everything from schizophrenia to neglect of chores, see themselves as failures," notes Brown.[7] Dreikurs views misbehavior in terms of goals that children are seeking to achieve in relation to their parents. When children want attention, power, respect, or a sense of adequacy, they may misbehave. Because of Dreikurs's Freudian base, he does not believe children ever misbehave for reasons unrelated to their parents.[8]

If we think our way through the above descriptions, it is by no means clear that these explanations of misbehavior are entirely unbiblical simply because the authors refuse to use the word *sin.* Two matters are in question.

The first matter has to do with the definition of sin. To understand naughtiness, we must first understand the nature of sin. What is the evil tendency that causes children to misbehave? But there is another issue. What is misbehavior? Is every incidence of naughtiness sin? Is it a sin not to eat green beans?

In regard to the first matter, conservative scholars have never been fully agreed. Is sin equal to selfishness, as Augustus Strong suggests? Or is Calvin right in calling sin pride? Or is the heart of sin rebellion, as some biblical words suggest? Take Gordon's explanation of misbehavior. All people, including children, are pursuing the satisfaction of their needs. This is legitimate, he maintains. However, when this pursuit brings one into conflict with someone else, it is termed misbehavior. Thus, when a child who is talking loudly (fulfilling his need to enjoy excitement) interferes with a parent's reading (fulfilling the need for some diversion), the child is being naughty in parental terms.

We can agree with Gordon, at least in part. The quest to satisfy one's needs is not always wrong. Sometimes parents need to talk with the child and negotiate a conflicting situation. Speaking biblically though, the quest to satisfy one's needs is not always right either. Sometimes a person is extremely self-centered in trying to reach his goals, disregarding others. Also, man tends to disregard his need for God. People seek satisfaction for their needs from the wrong source and in the wrong way. Thus, in a clash between persons, not everyone can have his own way. Gordon wants us to teach the child to align himself with others, using only conversation and compromise in the process. But Christian parents seek to train the child to comply with God's Word, and this calls for discipline. Thus, Gordon's analysis is partly true and helpful; but it is also misleading.

Glasser's approach may also be instructive. People misbehave because they are made to feel like failures, he asserts. When other people begin to have confidence in them, they will begin to improve their behavior and their self-concept. Glasser's approach can explain man's sinfulness. In this case it is the social nature of sin that is obvious. The self-centered lack of respect for others prompts misbehavior. At times the individual seeks recognition in the wrong way. The motivation for self-fulfillment need not be seen as wrong per se, but the means of attaining it are sometimes perverted and wrong.

Also, society itself is sinful, often preventing the self-fulfillment of people and condemning them needlessly as failures.

The theological problem of the nature of man revolves around two facts about man: Humans are created in the image of God and yet are depraved by sin. However, total depravity does not cancel entirely the creative work of God in man's nature (James 3:9). Thus, it is not always immediately clear whether an act is motivated by the created impulse or the sinful perversion. Is seeking to fulfill one's needs sin? Or is the manner of seeking their fulfillment wrong? Is self-fulfillment wrong? Or does sin lie in the direction self-fulfillment takes?

Whatever form a Christian system of psychology takes, of some matters we are sure enough so that we can construct a view of child training that includes the concept of sin. First, self-fulfillment or satisfaction of one's needs is basic to human life and should not be considered the essence of man's sinfulness. Jesus promised abundant living for believers, and Paul said that God would supply all of the believer's needs. God is not opposed to life; He created it. Therefore, we can assume that some of the acts of children are expressions of creativeness even though they come in conflict with the parent's desires. The two-year-old who wipes his peanut-butter-and-jelly-laden fingers across the kitchen wall may merely be expressing his created self, not the sinful Adam, even though he had been warned against doing so. A preschool child learns about the world through touch. His impulse is legitimate.

But the Christian also knows that a child will at times act in a self-centered way or in a manner that is morally and ethically wrong. And the child may also have a tendency to rebel against God and her or his parents. Concerning this biblical understanding, Christian psychologist James Dobson strongly warns parents to make certain that the young child is not allowed to control the parent.[9]

Thus, the Christian parent should approach an instance of misbehavior with a number of questions in mind. Is the misbehavior contrary to God's revealed standards and values? Parents who tend to see all misconduct as being sin may jump too quickly to this conclusion. Much naughtiness and resistance from children may constitute a conflict with other peoples' wishes but may not constitute a sin. When a child forgets momentarily and noisily and spontaneously bursts into a room, he or she may not be rebelling or sinning. It may be true that the child has broken the parent's command not to run in the house, but the running may not be a manifestation of a rebellious nature, just a childish one.

Is the misbehavior a quest for legitimate fulfillment? At the time the behavior may bother the parent, but it should be handled with respect for the child's right to live. When a child is talking loudly in the kitchen while the mother is talking on the phone, the situation should be handled so that the child is not exasperated. By explaining that excited talking is not bad in itself and by explaining how it is conflicting with the parent's right to talk on the phone, the mother can suggest that the child continue his conversation in his own room. Thomas Gordon's suggestions at this point are quite good, since they convey a proper respect for the child.

Is the misbehavior sometimes possibly a result of the parent's sinful reactions? Psychologists who study discipline are discovering how misconduct is linked to a pattern of interaction with others. Sometimes the teacher or the parent can contribute to the problem. Parents, too, are sinful. Not all misbehavior is entirely the fault of the child. A parent might prompt sassy remarks from the child by giving disrespectful orders to the child.

A parent, in his or her view of childhood conduct, will need some specific answers to these questions about the nature of children. It is not enough to build a philosophy of discipline on some general statement about the sinfulness of man.

Use of Punishment in Parenting

The question about the role of punishment does not draw a unified answer from the experts. The advocates of the principles of PET present a thoroughly positive approach, believing that all problems can be handled by talking them through, except in emergencies. When the toddler is headed for a busy street, for instance, there is no time to talk. Glasser recommends praise, not punishment, since punishment will cause physical and mental pain, which will interfere with the parent's helping relationships to the child. But Glasser does suggest the use of reasonable negative consequences, such as withholding privileges until the chores are done. Behavior-modification advocates do recommend some forms of punishment, such as deprivation. Yet they usually refrain from endorsing spanking.

That Scripture advocates punishment for the purpose of maintaining control is quite clear. Physical spanking is advocated in Proverbs. It is true that we might have some basis to question its normalcy for all periods of time since the instruction concerning spanking is within the Old Testament context, the period of the Mosaic law. But since the Book of Hebrews places "chastisement" in the heavenly Father's repertoire of child-training techniques, its use is validated for Christian parents and may well include spanking (Heb. 12:5–13).

But these biblical occurrences do not call for a stern, authoritarian, punitive control that lacks warmth and kindness. Studies show that children subjected to such an atmosphere have emotional problems. Exclusive use of punishment, particularly in a cool or negative atmosphere, is the wrong manifestation of parental power. Parents in our society may tend to be punishment-oriented; it is part of our culture. This orientation spills over into other negative forms of punishment, particularly psychological whippings and dressing-downs, prompted by the parent's outburst of anger and resentment.[10] We get trapped in negatives. We maintain control, but the environment is neither warm nor pleasant.

The use of physical punishment from time to time is no substitute for positive words or acts. In the struggle of immature children to grow up, they need encouragement. And it may take many positive remarks to overcome a few impulsive, critical ones. Thus, the positive, reinforcing approach of the behaviorists can prove to be a suitable practice for Christian parents. Good long-range results come from the use of praise. Encouragement can build the child's self-esteem while improving his behavior. Most parents find it difficult to praise a child for doing only a little better than previously or for only partially complying with an order. After a seminar on behavior modification, one parent said, "I found it hard to praise a child for small decreases in behavior you think should never occur at all, partly because it sounds so silly. But I am learning to say, 'Gee, Dan, I don't think you've bitten Michael in two whole days—that's great,' and 'Look at that: you asked for an apple and you ate almost half of it all up!'"[11] Such remarks are not out of keeping with a biblical understanding of childhood. The parent must analyze the motives and nature of the child's behavior to determine what response should be made to a given action.

Building the Child's Awareness of God in Parenting

Parenting includes building the child's awareness of God. This proposition introduces us to the greatest difference between the secular and the Christian system of child education. Though some of the secular-based programs operate in churches, they are not concerned with orienting a child to God. Yet they do not interfere with the parents' passing on values, including religious ones, to their children.

The moral and ethical system of the Christian is based on man's relationship to God. Christian nurture should call attention to that fact. "Bring them up in the training and instruction of the Lord," says Paul (Eph. 6:4). Teaching, counseling, and reproving should be God-related. Humanistically based programs are built around man's relationship to man.

As alluded to earlier, however, this God-orientation does not exclude a man-to-man consideration. Humanistic parent-training programs have some worthwhile suggestions for training children to relate morally to others, even though God is not part of the systems. Children need to learn how to respect the feelings of others, something that is emphasized by PET. PET also teaches the skills of listening and problem solving—skills that orient children to loving their neighbor as themselves. William Glasser's responsibility-based approach is also helpful here. Parents are in a position to help children see the consequences of their behavior for themselves and for others. Certainly the Christian adds God to the nurturing process, but he must not ignore the good ideas of others who do not reckon with God in their systems.

SUGGESTED READING

Biller, Henry, and Meredith, Dennis. *Father Power.* Garden City, N.Y.: Anchor, 1975.

Brandt, Henry, and Landrum, Phil. *I Want to Enjoy My Children.* Grand Rapids: Zondervan, 1975.

Drescher, John M. *Seven Things Children Need.* Scottdale, Pa.: Herald, 1976.

Dobson, James. *Dare to Discipline.* Wheaton, Ill.: Tyndale, 1970.

_____. *Hide or Seek.* Old Tappan, N.J.: Revell, 1974.

Ginott, Haim G. *Between Parent and Child.* New York: Macmillan, 1965.

_____. *Between Parent and Teenager.* New York: Macmillan, 1969.

Kesler, Jay. *Too Big to Spank.* Glendale, Calif.: Regal, 1979.

Skoglund, Elizabeth. *You Can Be Your Own Child's Counselor.* Glendale, Calif.: Regal, 1978.

Wright, Norman, and Johnson, Rex. *Communication: Key to Your Teens.* Irvine, Calif.: Harvest House, 1978. (Teacher's Guide: *Building Positive Parent-Teen Relationships*)

11

Family
Matters

Somehow problems and crises hit us on the blind side. Life seems to bring those for which we are least prepared. We feel this way because we can never be fully prepared for novel experiences. But family-life education can provide some preventive education, along with remedial counseling and support when they are necessary. Scripture can be brought to bear on life's crises in the regular Christian-education program. In addition, special teaching and training can be offered in preparing family members to face death, accidents, divorce, and other crises.

Inability to handle problems causes severe stress. Too often the Christian family delays action, hoping the problem will dissolve itself. Even prayer can become a form of delay and denial, a substitute for needed action. First of all, then, families need to be encouraged to face the problem or crisis head-on. Emotionally stunned, the immature person spends precious time asking, "How could this happen to me?" instead of asking, "How can I handle it?" Guilt also worms its way in with an insidious inner voice saying, "This shouldn't have happened to me." The temptation to deny the existence of a problem instead of admitting to its reality is destructively forceful, lulling a person into inactivity when activity is most needed.

Analysis of the problem should include not only seeking its cause but also its present consequences. Fallout from the problem affects different family members in different ways. Measures are needed to deal with the way a member's death or birth is affecting each other member, including the children. Good analysis will also uncover the one who has the problem. "Owning another's problem" is as wrong as it is frustrating. A wife needs to know that she cannot quit drinking for her husband and that her efforts to do this will fail. It is his problem. Parents should not accept for themselves the child's struggle with math. Both youth and adults are often only too happy to give the responsibility for solving their problems to someone else. That is part of the difficulty. People must help the problem bearer to see that the challenge to solve the problem belongs to him. Once that is established, other people can offer help when it is asked for and give support when it is needed. Parents of young children, for example, can create conditions for the child's success in math, but the parents cannot succeed for the child. Intense emotional outbursts and inner disappointment accompany any attempt to own someone else's problem.

Having analyzed the problem, the individual can be encouraged to see possible solutions. This calls for creative thinking; therefore, any child training that stimulates creativity will improve problem-solving skills. A course of action can be prayerfully chosen and attempted. Though trusting God in the situation, the individual is still prepared for the possible failure of his approach, knowing that the Lord will enable him to discover other solutions. He knows he must not be afraid to fail. Praise and thanksgiving to God will follow success, with the knowledge that it is He who saves us from all troubles (Ps. 34:6).

SUGGESTED READING

Ahlem, Lloyd H. *How To Cope With Crisis and Change.* Glendale, Calif.: Regal, 1978.
Gage, Joy P. *When Parents Cry.* Denver: Accent, 1980.
Kooiman, Gladys. *When Death Takes a Father.* Grand Rapids: Baker, 1975.
Neuhaus, Robert, and Neuhaus, Ruby. *Family Crises.* Columbus, Ohio: Merrill, 1974.
Pincus, Lily. *Death and the Family.* New York: Random, 1976.
Smetzer, David. *The Dynamics of Grief.* Nashville: Abingdon, 1970.

PLANNING

Christian psychologist Jack Pease maintains that planning is the major route to Christian growth. Particularly is this true in the area of family life, where it may even be used least. A prominent feature of his family-life course is that it includes several sessions on how to plan. He suggests that couples have a weekend together away from home several times a year.

The skills used in good planning are basic to business administration. After evaluation, the husband and wife determine their objectives, then seek means to put these into their routine schedule. In addition, they plan ahead of time for special events like conferences, study programs, vacations, etc. Monthly and weekly planning sessions will also be necessary in order to put principles of Scripture into practice. Otherwise, strong family-life teaching can produce an unbearable guilt; or else the teaching prompts people to reject suggestions as being idealistic and unworkable.

MANAGING FINANCES

Larry Burkett states that in over 70 percent of the marriages that fail the primary symptom of failure is finances.[1] This is overstatement, perhaps, but counselors agree that in our credit-ridden and materialistic economy the love of money is indeed the root of much marital evil. A nationwide survey disclosed that when it comes to the cause of fighting between husbands and wives, nothing else even comes close to money.[2] It may not be enough to preach and teach Christian values if our Christian education programs do not help people relate those values to practical financial matters. We Christians need faith to give some of our income to God but wisdom to know how to handle the rest. This wisdom includes analyzing one's spending habits and discovering the basic problem behind the symptom of failure in the handling of money; sometimes the problem is ignorance in budgeting, at other times it is sheer covetousness. Skills for determining financial needs and goals and for managing through budgeting can be taught through suggested reading or elective courses.

SUGGESTED READING

Burkett, Larry. *What Husbands Wish Their Wives Knew About Money.* Wheaton, Ill.: Victor, 1977.
Foshee, George, Jr. *You Can Be Financially Free.* Old Tappan, N.J.: Revell, 1976.

ENRICHING RECREATION

Two important social trends make the enrichment of recreation an important theme. The growing amount of discretionary time, provided by our affluent society, gives added responsibility to people for the use of their leisure time. In addition, the capture of this time by the mass media of television, radio, and movies has proved to be damaging to people. Television not only separates family members, interfering with in-depth communication, but also robs them of time for more wholesome activities. Despite the fact that people have more time today than in past generations, they feel hard-pressed to do what they would like. Believers in Christ's body can serve one another by discovering principles for using leisure time as well as by seeking practical suggestions for family activities.

SUGGESTED READING

Edgren, Harry. *Fun for the Family.* Nashville: Abingdon, 1967.
Edwards, Vergne. *The Tired Adult's Guide to Backyard Fun With Kids.* New York: Association, 1965.
Eisenberg, Helen, and Eisenberg, Larry. *The Family Fun Book.* New York: Association, 1953.
Rice, Wayne; Rydberg, Denny; and Yaconelli, Mike. *Fun 'N Games.* Grand Rapids: Zondervan, 1977.

HANDLING SEX EDUCATION

Sex Education in the Home

Until recent times, sex education was ignored or else relegated to sharing biological facts through books or through showing the child the sexual habits of pets and other animals. Freud uncovered childhood sexuality, making it clear that the attitudes and inner feelings toward sex are framed early in the child's experiences. Sex education begins when the mother first holds her newborn infant. In the warmth and comfort of the mother's arms the child experiences human love through touching, which provides the basis for later exchanges of sexual affection. Should those early sensate experiences be excluded or be negative, the child's sexual capacities and outlook may be greatly harmed.

Sex education is far more than just transmitting facts. It includes the ways the child is cared for, talked to, and held and touched by both parents. It also includes the way sex-related concepts are discussed in those early years. Parent's attitudes are conveyed unconsciously in a myriad of verbal and nonverbal interchanges. Any parental embarrassment connected with repeating words like *penis, vagina,* or *intercourse* helps to build an unfavorable inner attitude toward sex in the child. The parent's comfort with his or her own body as well as with the child's body and its functions will favorably influence the child's view of and acceptance of sex.

The child's attitude toward sex is also developed through exposure

130

to the parents' love relationship between themselves. Howard and Jeanne Hendricks have said it well: "Parents are stamping a permanent tattoo on their children in terms of marriage readiness."[3] Though the child never really witnesses the explicit sexual relationship of his parents, he will nonetheless see and hear much to color his image of sex in marriage. The child will catch their warm glances directed at one another; their casual, lingering touches; the occasional hug; and the excited, passionate kiss and embrace at the airport or doorway celebrating the return of a loved one. The absence of such visible manifestations of love may distort the child's attitude, contributing to his or her being a very passive, unaffectionate mate later on. For this reason Charlie Shedd maintains that the best thing a father can do for his children is to love their mother.[4] The impact of these informal channels of love makes the right sexual training of parents a prerequisite to the right sexual education of their children. Biblical concepts of sex must first shape adult minds, hearts, and practices before parents can teach these concepts to their children.

Parents can also be intentional in their sex education. They can deliberately make use of everyday experiences as well as special experiences. The arrival of a new baby in the home or the neighborhood can be used to teach the anatomy of the human body and the reproduction process. Exposing children to animals is a proven sex-education experience but it is not a substitute for frank talk about human sexuality. Parents can respond to television scenes in a way that conveys a positive stance to the beautiful aspects of sexuality while affirming the reality of high morals and biblical guidelines in this area. The same is true of parental response to sex words the child brings home. By the parents' explanation and emotional reaction the child will learn to distinguish between an unacceptable word and a perfectly acceptable act or part of the body. An imprudent parent may denounce something good when deploring a bad word.

Another guideline that reflects common sense for mothers and fathers is for them to respond honestly to their children's sex-related questions. The answers should be true and simply given, including whatever is necessary to satisfy the child's curiosity. Words used to describe the body and the sex act should be factual and acceptable. Speaking in general terms to avoid specific instruction will only make the child suspicious, cautious, and curious. It is better to answer, "The baby comes into the world through the vagina, an opening in the mother's body," than to merely respond, "God brings babies into the world." To envelop factual terms in loving phrases is most acceptable. While stating that the father's sperm enters the mother's body during intercourse, it can also be explained that this occurs during a very private, loving, and pleasurable experience that married people enjoy.

Sometime before puberty some explicit instruction should be imparted to children. James Dobson says that sex education should be over by the age of twelve. Prior to puberty the child is much more objective about such intimate matters than he or she is later and is able to discuss them without embarrassment with the parents. After puberty the subject becomes emotionally laden.

Parents can take the emotional edge off the explicit discussion through the use of a good book for preadolescents. Reading it aloud together and discussing matters in depth as they arise is probably the least threatening way for child and parent to handle the subject. Perhaps the parent who is more comfortable in taking this task should be the one to do so, while the other stands by to respond to questions so that communication lines are open with both parents.

If books on sex were used earlier than the age of eleven and twelve, it would make this special prepuberty training easier. For this reason a number of good sets of books have been prepared, supplying information to children at the various stages of childhood. An effective method is to assign books for reading. One parent can then administer a simple, multiple-choice or true-false test to the child; and the testing period can be turned into an occasion of discussion.

The method for conveying information should conform to the fact that children need to see that their parents are willing to talk about these things. Merely purchasing a book and giving it to the child without any plan for discussion may show a concern on the part of the parent, but it also may reveal the parent's reluctance to talk with the child. Besides, if the parent doesn't discuss the book, he or she will not have assurrance that the book was read, let alone understood.

Sex Education in the Church

It is obvious that the most important role of the church in sex education is the training of parents. Marriage-enrichment programs will help the most. Special courses on parenting and sex education will also contribute.

How and what the church teaches directly to children and youth about sex is an issue subject to debate. Some parents object to explicit sex teaching in the Sunday school or in club programs, particularly since it may be handled by persons untrained for the task. Yet, the church program can legitimately include sex education and marriage preparation for youth. Pastors can deal with this subject in the normal course of biblical exposition, since the Bible frequently touches on this area. Special sermons and lectures can focus on Christian values and practices related to sex.

Pastors and church leaders can build bridgeheads to youth during special Sunday-school talks or youth gatherings. A special series will open communication lines as well as convey the biblical stance. Theologians and other visiting lecturers could be enlisted to speak to children and youth at special times. This might be especially appropriate during a family-life conference.

Sex education is especially the task of the church and the home because at heart sex education is substantially a matter of morals and attitudes, not biological facts. If it is left to public-school classrooms and peer conversations, deviance from Christian values and principles is likely to occur.

SUGGESTED READING

Books for Parents and Church Leaders

Child Study Association. *What to Tell Your Child About Sex.* Rev. ed. New York: Dutton, 1968.

Grant, Wilson W. *From Parent to Child About Sex.* Grand Rapids: Zondervan, 1973.

Harty, Robert, and Harty, Adnelle. *Made to Grow.* Nashville: Broadman, 1973.

Scanzoni, Letha. *Sex Is a Parent Affair.* Glendale, Calif.: Regal, 1973.

Voland, Arlene S.; Weiss, Caroline; and Talman, Judith. *Sex Education for Today's Child.* New York: Association, 1977.

Books for Children

Dobson, James. *Preparing for Adolescence.* Santa Ana, Calif.: Vision House, 1979.

Frey, Marguerite Kay. *I Wonder, I Wonder.* St. Louis: Concordia, 1967.

Gruenberg, Sidonie M. *The Wonderful Story of How You Were Born.* New York: Doubleday, 1952.

Hummel, Ruth. *Wonderfully Made.* St. Louis: Concordia, 1967.

Taylor, Kenneth N. *Almost Twelve.* Wheaton, Ill.: Tyndale, 1968.

Books for Teens

Bueltmann, A. J. *Take the High Road.* St. Louis: Concordia, 1967.

Lester, Andrew. *Sex is More Than a Word.* Nashville: Broadman, 1973.

Richards, Larry. *How Far I Can Go.* Grand Rapids: Zondervan, 1980.

Scanzoni, Letha. *Sex and the Single Eye.* Grand Rapids: Zondervan, 1968.

Trobisch, Walter. *I Loved a Girl.* New York: Harper, 1965.

Trobisch, Walter, and Trobisch, Ingrid. *My Beautiful Feeling.* Downers Grove, Ill.: InterVarsity, 1977.

Witt, Homer. *Life Can Be Sexual.* St. Louis: Concordia, 1967.

PART FIVE

FAMILY-LIFE EDUCATION

12

Marriage
Enrichment

Current pessimism about the family's condition holds out little hope for family change. Psychologists who work daily with family entanglements seem to be the most cynical, perhaps with good cause. Christian psychologist Lawrence Crabb frets, "The unhappy truth is that people seem quite capable of enduring our well-researched, attractively packaged, and skillfully managed family-education programs without really changing very much."[1] Getting at the root problem of man's sinfulness is our only hope, he contends. In a moment of candor, Bruce Narramore spoke of his postconference feeling. After a weekend of speaking on marriage and the family, he pondered whether or not he had merely entertained and inspired people who would remain very much the same within the walls of their homes.

Changes in family life require changes in individual behavior. And the resistance to change in one's behavior is tenacious because the actions of people are made of whole cloth. Herbert Otto notes the tendency "for two people who spend much time together to become enmeshed and frozen in deeply ingrained habits of interaction."[2] This creates a form of living together that becomes routine, a pattern almost totally lacking in dynamic components, with an unconscious drive to keep things the way they are.

Thus, family-life education is primarily in the affective realm. Changes are required in attitudes, values, emotions, and spiritual perspective. Modifications in the affective domain do not exclude needed changes in the cognitive area. Times of knowing will many times amount to times of changing. Sometimes a wrong attitude is due to ignorance; acquiring knowledge can thus transform the inner perspective and change the attitude. This is especially true when the message is authoritative, as it is in Scripture. But even scriptural knowledge does not always produce change. Right doctrine does not always produce right living. Thus, James reminds us that it is possible to know the right thing to do and not do it (James 4:17).

Family-life enrichment demands an affective educational system and it should include the biblical patterns of exhortation, discussion, rebuke, reproof, and support. It will also be characterized by an experiential approach, in which contrived and actual experiences are utilized to facilitate change.

Marriage Enrichment and Marriage Encounter

Scores of novel marriage-enrichment programs, based on affective education, are now sweeping North America. A few years ago Herbert Otto estimated that over 800,000 couples had attended such marriage-renewal sessions.[3]

Their timeliness is due, no doubt, to their novelty of both purpose and approach. The varieties of religious and secular labs and retreats all have a common goal—to enrich the marriage and, through it, the family experience.

The excitement of the participants rather than high-powered publicity promotes the sessions. "This is the first time in twenty-three years of marriage that my husband has opened up to me," reported an excited, red-headed mother of five.[4] Don L. shared this: "I became aware of the impact of love, and that the deep, personal love you share as a couple should be reflected out to others."[5] "Since that weekend we have felt closer to each other and to God than we did at any time in all the thirty-one years of our marriage," was the joint statement of another couple.[6]

Marriage-encounter programs are sponsored by a variety of religious and secular groups. Some, like the Gestaltists, who see marriage as a system, seek to make couples aware of the ways to function within the system.[7] Those with transactional analysis as a base focus on development of communication skills. The Catholic form of marriage encounter claims to combine sound psychology, spiritual values, and practical technique for reviving the relationship between husband and wife.[8] Catholic marriage encounter stresses the need for family intimacy but includes the development of love for God and for others. Jewish marriage encounter proposes to strengthen oneness.

In general, these groups have set sail by the winds of the intimacy quest blowing across the land. They foster, as well as are fostered by, the newer understanding of marriage. What David Mace observes is no doubt true: "Enduring dyadic intimacy has been a basic human quest throughout the entire span of recorded history."[9] Yet, modern life has provided the context for a new surge in that search, making marriage-encounter groups so timely. "Modern life tends to eliminate from interhuman relations all character of intimacy, of personality," contends one advocate of marriage encounter.[10] The majority of conversations are impersonal. "Now the profound desire of the human heart is to obtain a direct, personal communication. If this desire is not reached, the result is sadness, melancholy, anguish, neurosis."[11] Enrichment leaders speak of people being half-married or spiritually divorced in the modern, impersonal context. Just plain and simple distractions are credited as a cause for these problems: "Though marriage has a tremendous richness, most people never achieve this— not because of bad will, but because of so many distractions."[12] Our closeness of bodies but remoteness of souls is blamed on the technological society's concept of marriage. Referring to the time factor in the success of the marriage-enrichment movement, Dr. John Nolan said,

> Husband and wife are so straitjacketed into occupational roles and the need to be productive in these roles. The emphasis is on the marriage partnership, rather than on the marriage relationship. Thus, the human pulse of the marriage is diminished; it is that pulse that these renewal efforts want to get beating again.[13]

The methods the advocates of marriage-encounter groups use are often misunderstood, primarily because of the name *encounter* attached to the primary movement. Marriage encounter is not a group encounter. It is something that takes place solely between husband and wife.[14] The public expression of feelings is rare in the movement, and even in those groups that employ group participation, the privacy of the marriage relationship is generally maintained.

Nor is marriage encounter a therapy experience. As marriage enrichment is an educational venture, those in charge of promotion encourage couples with severe problems to stay away, offering the experience for those who are batting .300 to increase to .350 or .400. No attempt is made to personally counsel each couple that attends sessions.

Apart from encounter groups conducted by professional psychologists, the general marriage-encounter pattern is quite simple. Group fellowship is maintained through shared meals and some superficial group discussion and casual conversation in order to provide a warm context for the sessions. Lectures are given to explain concepts and dynamics of marriage. For example, couples are urged to consider the sharing of feelings as being both right and healthy. A priest or a minister may lay down the theological or religious basis for this concept. Afterward, a lead couple shares something of their experience that is related to the subject at hand. Couples are then given exercises to perform to induce change in attitude and interaction. While there is a growing number of tests and exercises for use in these groups, the most prominent one uses questions and writing. Questions such as the following are designed to produce intimate sharing:

- Why have I come here?
- What do I intend to get from it?
- What have been the happiest moments in our relationship?
- What three times have I felt most united with you?
- What are my reasons for wanting to go on living?[15]

The writing and subsequent sharing are unique. After receiving a question, each person is given ten minutes to write an answer in the form of a love letter to his or her spouse. The couples are then dismissed to their rooms to read aloud and talk for a while. They then return for another question or two. And so the weekend goes— lectures on various aspects of communication followed by questions, writing, sharing, and the final time of group sharing. It is at this point that married people are saying such things as "We've been introduced to a whole new way to live."[16] Later, many buy new wedding rings to symbolize the beginning of their "real marriage" at the encounter.

That which is unique and emotionally acclaimed is usually controversial. Marriage encounter is. Some outside the movement dismiss it as a fad. Many participants are quite unimpressed, stating that a weekend at a motel or resort would have been more memorable. Such couples are not always critical of the objectives; they merely feel that their relationship didn't need a marriage-encounter weekend.[17]

Having slipped into this country from Spain about ten years ago, the Catholic version of marriage encounter has become a national phenomenon since the early seventies. During the summer of 1977 twenty thousand "encountees" spoke glowingly of their experiences at Los Angeles during the first international convention. In trendy Orange County alone about two hundred couples are "encountered" every month.

Catholics have encouraged authorized offshoots of the program, now labeled Jewish, Episcopalian, and Lutheran. Evangelical marriage encounters are also successful. And adoption of marriage-enrichment exercises and techniques is common.

Despite criticisms, there is good reason for evangelicals to utilize marriage-enrichment features. First, rightly understood, the goals are biblical. Theologically, marriage is not a mere mechanical, institutional arrangement. Marriage is a dynamic, intimate relationship, a oneness built on the couple's relationship to God. However, the relational emphasis is sometimes backed by "relational theology." Del and Trudy Vander Haar are wrong, from the evangelical point of view, when they write, "There is a new understanding that God is primarily concerned, not with doctrines or dogma, but with people and their relationship to each other."[18] Doctrine is of primary concern because truth provides a basis for fellowship. And so John writes, "We proclaim to you what we have seen and heard, so that you also may have fellowship with us" (1 John 1:3). Marriage enrichment does not require a relational theology but a proper theology of relationships. And evangelical theology should demand a total trust, openness, and commitment between husbands and wives that is no less than that found in any other theology.

Whether the love between husband and wife will spill over into the rest of the family and the community is another question. I know of no research that has been done on this. But it would seem theoretically and theologically right to say that a husband and wife loving each other deeply will greatly benefit the rest of the family.

As for the techniques used in marriage enrichment, there should be no controversy here. Those involved in evangelical Christian education are becoming more and more conscious of the importance of affective education. We cannot expect couples to change merely because they have heard a sermon or even have understood a passage of Scripture. While God's Word is a power of renewal, the Word is not the only means of grace. And the dilemmas in our modern context make it imperative that the body of Christ practice and promote experiences based on biblical values and principles. Otherwise, the credibility gap caused by the discrepancy between ideals proclaimed and ideals practiced will grow even larger than it is now. And poor preaching is not always the problem. Incorporating truth into life is the issue. One of the most prominent and internationally known marital experts today, David Mace, put the matter clearly: "The average American couples are no more able to make use of our present knowledge of marital interaction than is the Indian peasant farmer to draw on the resources of agricultural science."[19] Tests, exercises, dyad communication techniques, discussions, couple and small-group worship, and other experiences are not a replacement but are rather a supplement to the study and proclamation of Scripture.

For these reasons, I believe marriage-enrichment programs should and will become a regular part of the evangelical curriculum of family-life education.

DESIGN FOR A MARRIAGE-ENRICHMENT EXPERIENCE

Whether a marriage enrichment experience takes place during a weekend, a series of elective sessions, or even one special "couple's night," marriage enrichment necessarily involves a number of objectives. Goals are rather total in scope, embracing the individual, the couple, the church, the world community, and God. Self-understanding is a major objective, particularly since the nature of marriage makes one's marriage partner a unique mirror for beholding oneself. Such self-understanding contributes to the second goal— discovery of the marriage relationship. Couples are guided into an understanding of their own marriages in the light of biblical ideals and the experience of others. The third goal is related to the second goal but is distinct from it. It is the renewed discovery of one's marital partner. Essentially this is the major *encounter* in most enrichment programs. Where superficial communication has previously hindered a genuine, accepting self-disclosure, the couple's experience in this domain is often revolutionary.

These objectives are spiritual as well as relational. Through Bible study, worship, and prayer the couples grow in their awareness of Christ's love as a basis for theirs. In addition, their ability to relate to God together is enhanced. Finally, the marriage-enrichment goals should go beyond the marriage to the family, the church, and the world. Loving expression within the home will be seen as a basis for loving ministry outside the home.

Though the methods of achieving these goals will accent personal "discovery," traditional methods are also used. Lectures on various marriage themes are in order and should provide a biblical pattern for guidelines. A lecture on intimacy, for example, can provide a solid basis for a sharing exercise that follows. Second, having one or two "lead" couples share their personal experiences can be a catalyst for sharing between couples and increased awareness of one for the other. The lead couple can explain practical guidelines for developing intimacy as well as share their struggles and experiences. Third, learning methods can include the distribution of brief essays, of chapters in books, of a one-page definition, or other forms of direct content input. Couples can read together or separately and then dis-

141

cuss. Sometimes that discussion can be done in groups. Most distinct and central to marriage enrichment is the fourth methodology—couple-discovery experiences, including tests, exercises, questionnaires, nonverbal interaction, etc.

While the first three of the above methodologies are important, the fourth is crucial for accomplishing the highly personalized goals of the program. And because discovery is the key, discovery techniques are essential.

Sometimes the discovery techniques lead to knowledge: a husband learns about his wife's dreams or ideas of marriage. These techniques usually also facilitate experiencing; for example, the couple learns to experience what it is like to share feelings they never before had expressed verbally. Thus, they will actually experience affirmation, acceptance, sharing, intimacy, and love. In past marriage education we have talked about these, but the new marriage programs emphasize actually experiencing them.

Experiences to Develop Oneness

We turn next to a discussion of the experiences and learning that are necessary to gain true marital oneness and of the ways to produce these experiences. Following is an extensive list of recommended possible experiences. From among these it would not be difficult to construct a marriage-enrichment weekend, a ten-week course, or even an evening session.

Sharing backgrounds. Those who stress this technique do so on the basis that "knowingness" is important to understanding and accepting. Enjoyable games are used to establish rapport between the couples when group interaction is important to the success of the sessions. Or else couples participate in communication games with each other. Games involve sharing things like a memory from age six, the greatest event that happened in the sixth grade, a religious experience of the teen years, or the time when one felt he or she had become a man or a woman. Many of the exercises in James Kilgore's book *Try Marriage Before Divorce* are appropriate for this type of sharing.[20]

Sharing feelings. Sharing of significant meaning and feelings is one of the deepest forms of intimacy. It is the touching of the inmost selves of two human beings that the Clinebells maintain is the "foundation of all other forms of intimacy."[21] The leaders of Marriage Encounter prompt this sharing through their "ten-and-ten" approach. For ten minutes the husband and wife individually write an answer to a question. Then, for another ten minutes they read their answers and discuss them. The questions in this approach can relate to personal life, such as "When do you feel the most secure?" or to the couple's relationship, such as "When do you feel the most secure in your relationship?" Questions can cover the range of human emotions, such as "How do you feel when you are rejected?" "How do you react when you fail?" and "What feeling is most difficult to talk about?" A list of open-ended statements can prompt openness in sharing feelings.

- I usually handle frustration by . . .
- When I feel rejected, I . . .
- Right now I am feeling . . .
- When I meet new people, I feel . . .
- The situation that makes me feel anxious is . . .
- I need support of others most when I feel . . . (If a married couple is doing this exercise, use this statement instead: I need your support most when I feel . . .)
- At a social gathering I feel most uncomfortable when . . .
- I feel very comfortable when . . .
- When I am alone, I feel . . .
- When I don't like myself, I feel . . .
- What I am most afraid to talk about is . . .
- The feeling I find most difficult to talk about is . . .
- Right now I feel . . .

Sharing desires and wishes. Ability to tell the other person what one hopes for in the relationship is basic to communication. Yet because of fear of rejection it is difficult to share one's desires. Unstated wants and needs in a relationship form a divisive dynamic. Based on a systems view of marriage, Bud and Bea Van Eck foster one's "being intentional."[22] If couples do not tell one another what their needs and wants are, they may resort to nonverbal means of expression; and those expressions, in turn, are often overlooked or misunderstood by the other partner. Bringing these desires into the open facilitates the function of the marital give-and-take system. To discover their patterns of communication, as well as their needs in this area, the couples can first list five nonverbal behaviors they have observed in their spouses. These behaviors are then shared by a husband or wife with his or her partner by acting them out or by stating them. Then there follows a discussion of the power and the pace of these actions in their relationship, as well as of the need or the desire being expressed. After this, each partner can write down and then communicate to the spouse three or four wants.

A simple tool for achieving this is a wish list. Wives and husbands write down what they wish their mates would do and would not do. The latter are told that they are not necessarily bound to comply with their spouse's wishes but that an open and trusting relationship should include such sharing. According to one leader who uses this approach, the wishes are sometimes quite simple: "I wish you would stay at the table until I finish eating"; or "I wish you would do more just for yourself."[23]

Sharing images of love. Closely related to the sharing of desires is the sharing of forms of love. Often mates are unaware of the way they are saying "I love you" to each other. Their different backgrounds and personalities have endowed them with varying concepts of love's expressions, out of which two things result. One partner may miss the other's signals of love because they are not in his or her terms. He may value gift giving as a major expression of love, while she may not. Irrelevant expression of love is the other result of partners having different concepts of love's expressions. Not understanding why his message fails to get through, the husband continues to offer his irrelevant expressions while accusing his wife of not understanding how much he loves her.

To share knowledge about ways of expressing love, couples are asked to formulate two lists. The first list is "Five ways I express love to my spouse." The items are numbered according to importance. "Five ways I believe my spouse is saying 'I love you' to me" comprises the second list, the items being numbered according to frequency of occurrence or perceived importance. Ideas are compared and dialogue follows. Knowing each other's concepts can help bring expressions of love into line with each partner's expectations, as well as provide newer appreciation of one another's acts of love.

Sharing ideas about sexuality. The confirming of one's sexual identity, which is basic to marriage, takes two forms—accepting and asserting. He accepts her femininity while asserting his masculinity. She makes him feel like a man by accepting his maleness as well as by asserting her femaleness.

Crucial to such accepting and asserting is one's concept of sexuality. If a husband believes vulnerability is not masculine, he will try to maintain that posture with his wife, rarely revealing any of his weaknesses. This can cause trouble if her concept of maleness involves his sharing areas of weakness where she can help and support. Dissatisfaction is generated because each is accepting and asserting on his or her own terms of masculinity and femininity.

Discussing such terms can help immensely. Formulating and comparing lists is a simple means of getting at this subject. Each is asked to list five concepts of true manhood and five of true womanhood. Comparison of the lists may bring surprises that will merit discussion and change.

Affirming each other. Focusing on positive relationships is usually done early in the enrichment sessions. A "revolving dialogue" is used by Herman Green.[24] Each person is asked to write down what he or she loves about his or her mate in terms of behavior, looks, and being. The "revolving dialogue" that follows is an attempt to prompt thorough understanding. The first person makes a statement. The second person either agrees with the impression or clarifies the statement and then expresses his feeling about the statement. Couples are encouraged to sit with knee-to-knee, hand-to-hand, and eye-to-eye contact during the exchange.

Affirmation can be centered on events or expectations related to the past, present, or future. Telling each other about the three most meaningful experiences together fosters appreciation of one another. Frequent opportunities for affirmation can be created by open-ended statements, such as "I want to tell you I love you in a very special way because . . ."

Looking at their integration. In order to provide more appreciation for and understanding of their relationship, couples can be encouraged to see the way they look together as a unit. They concentrate on seeing the way they have integrated and on what they have become as a couple. This is particularly urged by those who see marriage as a system, the understanding of which creates better functioning. A verbal integration exercise can make a husband and wife think about themselves as a couple. After each person writes down five characteristics about himself or herself, the couples are asked to combine the two sets. Or else they are asked to give a nonverbal expression of their marriage, perhaps by doing a living sculpture or drawing a picture. If these things are done in a group, other couples can react to the sculpture or picture, giving each performing couple knowledge of the way he and she are perceived as a couple.

Evaluating and building trust. Expressions of and feelings of mistrust greatly interfere with closeness. Wayne Oates suggests that trusting is more important to each mate than verbal expressions of love. Healthy couples can be encouraged to explore their trust levels though leaders should be aware of the sensitive nature of this process. A nonverbal expression, "the trust walk," has been used for many years with groups and couples. A blindfolded person is led by his partner on a five-minute walk. The roles are then reversed for another walk. Afterward, the spouses discuss (1) when each trusts the other and why, (2) when one of them mistrusts the other and why, and (3) what each can do to improve the feeling and expressions of trust. Or else trust can be explored through a series of statements. For example,

- I feel you trust me most when . . .
- I feel you trust me least when . . .
- When you trust me, I feel . . .
- Whenever I think you don't trust me, I feel . . .
- Some reasons behind our mistrust are . . .
- You communicate mistrust by . . .
- You communicate trust by . . .
- I think I can improve your trust of me by . . .
- I think you can improve my trust of you by . . .

Evaluating and understanding intimacy. Besides biblical exposition related to intimacy, couples can be helped to think about ideals in this area through dailogue. The Clinebell's dimensions of intimacy can be distributed as a guide to the couples' discussion. These authors describe the following as constituting the many strings of the instrument of intimacy: sexual intimacy, emotional intimacy, intellectual intimacy, aesthetic intimacy, creative intimacy, work intimacy, crisis intimacy, commitment intimacy, and spiritual intimacy.[25]

Sharing negative feelings. A backlog of undiscussed conflicts and ill feeling, the proverbial sleeping dogs, destroys intimacy. Carefully developed maneuvers and manipulation replace honesty and understanding. Skills related to verbalizing hostile feelings can be taught. After the leader explains that negative feelings should be stated accurately by the mate while he or she is in control, and without judgment, couples are asked to identify from a list accurate statements of feeling. For example:

- I feel bad when you tear me apart like that.
- I feel you are always putting me down.
- You have all the right answers, don't you?
- Well, I'm sorry I'm not a superperson too.
- I feel rejected when you say that.

The last expression is the best since it is an honest expression of one's feeling without putting the other person on the defensive. None of the expressions but the first and the last even state what the feeling is; the rest are judgmental remarks that arise from the feeling. A complete exercise can be found in David Johnson's book *Reaching Out.*[26]

Another popular approach to the development of this skill is used by family-enrichment programs based on transactional analysis. The use of *I* rather than *you* statements in order to communicate the feelings that are going on beneath the surface is encouraged. Instead of saying, "You are inconsiderate," the partner is taught to say "I feel left out when you act like that."

Identifying feelings. The modern stress on feelings in the marriage relationship should not be misunderstood as a surrender to emotion. Rather, the opposite is intended. Currents of emotion need to be understood and identified lest they carry us off in the wrong direction. Thus, each of the partners needs to learn to understand his or her own and the spouse's feelings. Worksheets, in which a partner practices identifying the feeling behind one or more statements of her or his spouse, can help in this process.

For example, a worksheet for wives might include a statement by the husband such as the following: "Why do you say it's my fault? You didn't do anything to help!" One of the statements of the wife on a worksheet for husbands might be: "Sure, just roll over and go to sleep as if nothing had happened!" Behind each statement on their spouse's worksheet the husbands and wives write what, in their opinion, their mate is feeling when she or he makes this statement.[27]

Handling conflict. Some enrichment programs avoid dealing directly with conflict; instead, they prompt positive expressions of intimacy and allow conflict to arise naturally. Some programs encourage couples to grapple with conflict but always within a loving, positive context. For instance, after a half hour of exercises containing open-ended statements that share positive feelings, a statement can be used to prompt discussion of conflict: "There is something about our marriage that has been bothering me for a long time; it's. . . ." Of course, conflict exercises are sensitive and should be preceded by teaching about biblical conflict management.

Exercises should focus on helping the couple to understand the ways they have been handling conflict and the ways they might improve their handling of it. They can often identify their past patterns from a list like this:

- I always yield.
- I always fight to win.
- I nag.
- I avoid discussing it.
- I simmer in silence.
- I always seek to compromise.
- I make public statements of sarcasm or insult.

A list of "fight guidelines" can be distributed to help couples establish their own pattern for dealing with conflicts that arise.

- Don't harbor ill feelings for more than a day without discussing them. "Do not let the sun go down while you are still angry" (Eph. 4:26).
- Stick to the subject. Don't bring up other problems.

- Don't misuse a third party, getting this person to side with you and confiding in him or her and not in your spouse.
- Don't bring up past history; deal in the present.
- Avoid name-calling and insults.
- Share feelings without judging the other person.
- Hold hands while quarreling.
- Talk about the problem behind your "outbursts" later, when you are in control of your emotions.

Planning together. Planning experiences are not difficult to formulate; they can be patterned after a management process, which begins with evaluation. Evaluation exercises include any of those mentioned previously. In addition, questionnaires and tests can be constructed to review the marriage relationship. At the end of the chapter are two examples: a "Growing Guide" and a "Husband's Role" worksheet.

The second step involves goal setting. A guide for goal setting should include answering questions like the following:

1. What areas of your relationship are most in need of improvement?
2. What area is of the highest priority right now?
3. What area can be improved easily?
4. What area will take the most time to be improved?
5. What areas of improvement would you establish as being short-range goals (taking several months)?
6. What areas of improvement would you establish as being long-range goals (taking a year or more)?

Developing a specific improvement program, the last step in planning, can be facilitated by the following suggested guidelines.

1. Choose the most important long-range goal: state it in terms of the place you would like to be in your relationship a year or two from now.
2. Determine what things you would need to do to reach that goal (reading, getting counseling, practicing, experiencing, discussing, deciding, etc.).
3. Determine the actual order of the steps it will take to reach your goal. For example:
   a. First, read a book together on this subject.
   b. Take a course related to the subject.
   c. Begin to discuss weekly how to improve in this area.
4. Determine which of these steps or activities can be put into

your regular schedule—such as scheduling Tuesday evenings to go out together to work on a certain area.
5. Determine which of these steps will need special, monthly, or annual scheduling.

Sharing differences. Consciously looking at differences can enable partners to better understand themselves, their mates, and the ways each relates to the other. Actual tests like the Taylor-Johnson Temperament Analysis can help couples come to grips with their dissimilarities of temperament more objectively and understand how these differences affect their relationship.[28] Though it would require personal counseling for each couple, it is possible to use this approach at a retreat or within a seminar or course.

A more simplified approach is to ask couples to write about and discuss the perceived differences of their personalities and the differences they make.

Evaluating Communication

While all of the above exercises promote communication, some are designed specifically to evaluate and improve this dynamic. A questionnaire called the *Marital Communication Inventory* distributed by Family Life Publications is a useful educational tool.[29] Or you may use communication games. For example, using building blocks or Tinkertoys, spouses sit back to back on the floor. One leads by building something and verbally communicates directions to the other, who builds a model according to instruction. The one following the instructions must be silent. This rule makes the exercise a hilarious test of the ability to give and receive verbal messages.

A foursome dialogue is used by the Vander Haars. Two couples decide to participate in this together. The first husband and wife to converse select a real issue that faces them. They discuss it together for five minutes while the other couple observes the interaction of the first couple. The observing couple then gives feedback on various aspects: who initiates conversation; who checks out what he or she thought he or she heard; who looks for alternate solutions, etc. The process is then reversed and repeated.

Sharing about the sexual relationship. The subject of sex will probably come up. Questions in this area can be expressed in an affirmation exercise such as the following one: What is the thing I do for you sensually that you appreciate the most? Or a more explicit appraisal can be accomplished through tests like Herbert Otto's *The Love Life Development Test,*[30] or the *Sex Attitudes Survey and Profile* of Family Life Publications.[31]

Sharing spiritually. As is true in other areas of marriage, each couple will be unique in their abilities and problems in the matter of relating jointly to God. Imbalance in spiritual maturity is a major contributing factor to problems at this point. But other factors are influential, communication ability being one of them. Some individuals are unable to pray aloud with a spouse, though they are able to pray individually. Part of the problem of such individuals is the inability to be vulnerable before someone else. Therefore, exercises in spiritual sharing could help couples with problems in other areas. A simple pattern for those unaccustomed to relating to God together is to ask them to share ideas on a problem, and then, while they face each other and hold hands, pray silently about the matter. They then do the same with another issue, and then another, until every issue has been dealt with.

Exercises in inductive study of Scripture can be distributed for private use. Such exercises can induce questions to be asked related to discovering the meaning and applying of Scripture. For example, after studying the subject of the fruit of the Spirit, the partners may be asked to share what fruit of the Spirit they see most prominently in each other. Then, what quality each would like to see more of in himself or herself.

Thanksgiving and praise exercises can lend a positive note: to ask "What was the greatest evidence of God's presence in your life today?" prompts an answer that becomes a prelude to prayer. Praying between the reading of verses from a psalm prompts expressions of worship that otherwise might not so easily come to mind.

Principles and Hazards of Marriage-enrichment Programs

Those familiar with the helpfulness of marriage-enrichment programs are also aware of the hazards. Such programs use teaching methods that can be misunderstood. And such programs aim at in-depth spiritual and personal changes that can prompt resistance and resentment. But the implementation of these programs can have a powerful, positive effect if established guidelines are followed.

Promote marriage-enrichment programs on a voluntary basis. Whereas sermons and teaching on marriage and the family can be included in any church program, in-depth marriage encounters should not be forced on couples. Such experiences can be incorporated into the church program as special events—a special weekend, a course, or an evening just for couples who really want to do something different. A Sunday evening or the Sunday school hour can be used for a participatory exercise if there is enough flexibility so that couples can choose the level of communication that fits them best.

Promotion should make it clear that the sessions are for growth, not correction. People with serious marital problems could expect too much. And couples with either good or bad marriages will not want their attendance at such an activity to be a signal of marital struggle. Some may even suspect that this is really therapy in disguise.

Promotion should also aim at dispelling notions that produce threat or opposition. A pioneer in family development, David Mace, counsels that we must deal with resistance. He writes: "The sober truth is that married couples desperately want to have loving relationships but fanatically resist attempts to enable them to get what they want."[32]

In our culture certain roadblocks to a loving relationship exist in the form of myths. The first one is the myth of naturalism that by following one's instincts, anyone can make a marriage work. Mace characterizes this myth as an "unexamined prejudice that persists in the face of all evidence to the contrary."[33]

The second roadblock is "privatism." It says, "Marriage is a very private, very personal matter. Whatever you do, don't ever talk to anyone else about what goes on inside your marriage." When kept within reasonable bounds, this approach makes sense. But it also constitutes a marital taboo that does much harm. It shuts married couples up in little boxes, where in their fumbling ignorance they destroy the very things they most desire. It prevents their obtaining the help they badly need.

Cynicism is the third roadblock. Boisterous jokes and snide remarks prevade many discussions of marriage. Despite our prizing the concept of a happy marriage, this lack of serious discussion about marriage makes people feel that it is an overrated institution.

The body of Christ, by its biblical message and positive marital programs, can be the foremost destroyer of these myths.

Plan for biblical and God-centered experiences. Many of the marriage-encounter and marriage-enrichment programs have a secular or a nonevangelical base. But the evangelical can allow God and His Word to dominate a program even if a sizeable percentage of its sessions are experiential. Lectures relating the Bible to current issues, presentations and testimonies about a personal relationship to Christ, inductive study of Scripture, and group Bible study can inject God's truth into the program. And throughout the sessions the theological basis of the family can be laid so that it is said clearly that one must be open to the Savior and His love.

Use groups wisely. While some marriage-development programs use group encounter, most do not. Close and intimate group interaction usually requires professional leadership. Because many are suspicious of sensitivity groups and because of the strong sense of "privatism" in regard to marriage, group experiences should avoid in-depth sharing of family problems. Certain feedback activities, by which the group helps the partners understand each other, might be employed, but these activities must be handled carefully. Some opportunity for insight into other couples' relationships might also help couples admit that there are problem areas in their relationship. Positive sharing can be encouraged, as well as general discussion of struggles. A warm, enthusiastic group context should be built as a support for each couple's own encounter, not as a substitute for it.

Utilize couples as leaders or contributors. Modeling is a prominent feature of many groups. Lead couples may share their struggles and successes in areas under discussion. This sharing can be part of a lecture on an aspect of marriage or it can follow such a lecture. Before husbands and wives are sent to complete an exercise or answer a question, a couple can demonstrate the process. Their candor before the group can have a dramatic effect, not only clarifying the exercise but also stimulating openness between the partners.

Be realistic. One of the most frequent criticisms of marriage encounter is that its leaders tend to exaggerate. Hyperbole easily replaces realistic statements about the joys of intimacy. Susan Middaugh noted this tendency in her encounter experience:

> I got the same feeling [about exaggeration] the next day, when Sal and Rita [lead couple] told how desolate and lonely they felt one afternoon at home. Sal was working on business; Rita was cleaning. They were together but separated by responsibilities. To me, this scene is a part of everyday life. But Sal and Rita made it sound extraordinary. If hyperbole is used so casually, what words are left over to distinguish those rare moments of grief and joy from the mundane?[34]

Caution against exclusiveness. In a desire to promote future sessions, we often send people home to tell others what they have missed. This too easily separates people into the haves and the have-nots. For this reason some leaders are warning that Marriage Encounter is becoming an "exclusive club."[35] Couples who have not participated are made to feel that their marriages are inferior, that they could not possibly in any other way gain what is available at the retreat or through the course.

Produce some follow-up approaches. As a movement Marriage Encounter has a twofold follow-up. A monthly group meeting for those who "encountered" is one form of follow-up. Here concepts previously given at the weekend retreat are reviewed; then discussion between partners and between couples is fostered. For couples at home there is the ten-and-ten tool mentioned earlier. This method gets both spouses to express their feelings on a chosen theme in a written note (ten minutes of writing), which is then exchanged and shared as the take-off point for their daily dialogue (ten minutes of talking).

Advanced courses and retreats are also part of a follow-up approach. Thus Bud and Bea Van Eck have developed their Phase II Marriage Enrichment Lab.[36]

However the follow-up is handled, some carry-over exercises, suggestions, or programs can help the couple build and develop what was initiated in the retreat.

Beware of legalistic approaches. Closely related to the danger mentioned above is the danger of legalism. Effective, man-made methodology too easily becomes a set of absolutes. The ten-and-ten method advocated by the New York branch of the Marriage Encounter movement has generated a wave of controversy. When presenting this daily exercise, these leaders insist that it is not optional—a couple must agree to commit themselves to the daily assignment, or they are not really "making" the encounter. When asked if there are other ways for maintaining intimate communication, a leader explains: "The main source of strength for the couple is the dialogue. The writings technique is the only way a couple can be sure of setting aside some time each day for dialogue. The ten-and-ten is compulsory; it is absolutely not negotiable."[37]

An enthusiastic reaction by couples to the novel approaches of the movement can stimulate leaders to place all of their trust in a proven methodology rather than in the Holy Spirit. But when the trust is not misplaced and the objectives are biblical, the marriage-enrichment techniques merit widespread use among evangelicals. Perhaps this movement will be a temporary one, as so many North American remedial and educational movements have been. Yet it has been caused by the changes that have taken place in marriage—smaller families, the separation of sexual intercourse from procreation made possible by contraceptives, and the tripling of the life expectancy of both men and women. The result of these changes has been an inevitable revolution in the way in which people attempt to cope with life.[38] An institutional marriage, in which an emotional union is ignored and which, is held together by rules and roles, fits neither modern times nor biblical tenets. It is a necessity that marriage be marked by multifaceted intimacy and by satisfaction. Marital-enrichment programs are in the middle of this revolution, helping couples emerge out of their traditional, cool, contractlike entrapments into timely, warm, personal relationships.

153

SUGGESTED READING

Augsberger, David. *Caring Enough to Confront*. Glendale, Calif.: Regal, 1973.

Bird, Lois. *How to Be a Happily Married Mistress*. Garden City, N.Y.: Doubleday, 1970.

———. *How to Make Your Wife Your Mistress*. New York: Doubleday, 1972.

Clinebell, Charlotte H., and Clinebell, Howard J. *The Intimate Marriage*. New York: Harper & Row, 1970.

Eichenlaub, John, E. *The Marriage Art*. New York: Dell, 1969.

Gaulk, Earle H. *You Can Have a Family Where Everybody Wins*. St. Louis: Concordia, 1977.

Glickman, S. Craig. *A Song for Lovers*. Downers Grove, Ill.: InterVarsity, 1976.

LaHaye, Tim, and LaHaye, Beverly. *The Act of Marriage*. Grand Rapids: Zondervan, 1976.

Popenoe, Paul. *Marriage Is What You Make It*. New York: Macmillan, 1950.

Powell, John. *The Secret of Staying in Love*. Niles, Ill.: Argus, 1974.

Small, Dwight H. *After You've Said I Do*. Old Tappan, N.J.: Revell, 1968.

Wright, H. Norman. *The Christian's Use of Emotional Power*. Old Tappan, N.J.: Revell, 1974.

———. *Communication: Key to Your Marriage*. Glendale, Calif.: Regal, 1979.

13

Parent Training: A Model

The number of parent-training programs is growing by leaps and bounds. The largest secular-based program, Parent Effectiveness Training, has trained over 8,000 instructors and 250,000 parents. The Bill Gothard Seminars, evangelical lectures on home life, have attracted hundreds of thousands of people. Curriculum for parenting courses for local schools and churches is offered by numerous publishers.

The vast variety of philosophies and methods of parent training creates difficult choices for church leaders. The best option open to them is to create their own parent-training program. A program like this has the advantage of continuing over a period of weeks instead of only a brief weekend or a series of evenings. Local church seminars and courses can provide the necessary time to consider subjects in depth as well as provide practice, experience, and group support.

FEATURES OF PARENT TRAINING

We will take for granted that an evangelical program should be biblical. Certainly not all will come up with the same approach, yet the

155

training model will include grappling with biblical texts and raising theological questions. Merely bringing into the church contemporary psychological principles without scriptural references does not constitute an effective evangelical approach to preparing parents.

A second feature will be comprehensiveness. Too often the parenting task is reduced to following a few simple ideas or using a couple of clever techniques. Forcing the complex personalities, relationships, and problems in the home to yield to several simple principles or methods creates frustration. How often we hear words like these: "If you will only pray together"; "If the father will just lead"; "If you will praise the child"; and "If everyone will love." Certainly any one of these suggestions may be helpful for stable families; but for others who need more help, the insistence on such a simplistic approach can drive them to guilt and exasperation.

Third, parent training will need to include actual training. Lectures, and even discussions, will not be enough. Old habits will not easily give way to new patterns without some tools for evaluation and practice.

The following model for parent training attempts to bring all of these features together. It covers the range of parental skills needed as well as provides suggestions for the development of those skills.

BIBLICAL OBJECTIVES FOR CHILD REARING

We begin with parenting objectives. Biblical methods are best formulated in the light of biblical goals. What are parents really trying to do for their children? Keeping peace in the home and holding the family together are not sufficient as goals. Goals must be related to the child. When we look at goals in this way, three biblical goals of child rearing become clear.

Reverence for God is the first. "Bring them up in the training and instruction of the Lord," is the most significant New Testament injunction regarding this goal (Eph. 6:4). The purpose of child rearing, like the purpose of the commandments, is to develop love for God.

Second, parenting should produce respect for self in the child. Paul guards against severe or improper modes of discipline by urging parents to be careful of the child's inner attitude. Overbearing parenting may provoke the child to wrath, including perhaps self-hatred, or else may make the child "lose heart" (Col. 3:21 NASB), stifling self-expression and creating depression. It is theologically significant that Paul warns about methods employed by appealing to the results or ends of those methods.

Since the first objective relates to God, and the second to self, the third is quite obviously respect for others. Loving one's neighbor as oneself is part of the substance of the Old Testament and New Testament ethic. Built on regard for God's Word, morals and values training are also oriented around regard for others.

Any system that leaves out any one of these objectives is inadequate and even damaging. It is possible to develop persons who are oriented to God but who hate themselves and have little regard for others. Also, an unbalanced person can be related to others but have little respect for God.[1]

PARENT POWER

A parent-training program will be constructed around the avenues of influence a parent possesses. Calling this influence "parent power" is not a bad idea, since it calls attention to the fact that the parent does have something of substance to work with. This power can be broken down into five basic forms. All of these together comprise the sum total of the parent-child relationship, which is the realm in which the parent operates.

Modeling

Parental example is a major force in the child's life. Some learning theorists have documented the power of adult models.[2] We now have some new information about this old idea of being an example.

First, modeling does not call for perfection. A parent may project an unreal picture of himself in an effort to be a perfect example, thus hiding personal struggles and even marital conflicts. This projects an unrealistic and hypocritical example, which can cause disrespect or even rejection on the part of the child. Parents are to be maturing examples, not perfect ones. They should be real, modeling the dynamics of confession and humility so that the child will understand the way that imperfect Christians can live with respect for each other and with a forgiven relationship with God.

Second, a close, revealing relationship is best. Modeling is more effective when inner thoughts and feelings are shared than when they are kept to oneself. A child will learn morality and standards from parents who talk about their views of life and themselves.

Third, modeling requires, above all, personal development. It is not a dramatic show to be put on; it is a real-life demonstration that is often very subtle in its influence. The unsuspecting parent screams, "Don't yell in the house," not thinking about the way he or she is missing the essential ingredient needed to stop the child's shouting, which is that the parent must stop shouting first of all.

A fourth observation is simply this: modeling may not be enough. Values engineer Sidney Simon warns that parental models are insufficient of themselves, since modern children are exposed to so many other influential examples.[3] Parenting will require developing the child's internal knowledge and value structure in other ways. Also, children will need to be exposed in some depth to other Christian adults.

Control

Though not all parents exercise control, they do have an authority to control bestowed on them—not by their size but by society. Though there is considerably more discussion about and defense of children's rights today than previously, our culture supports parental rule. Also, the Scriptures urge parents to exercise control with care (Prov. 22:15; Eph. 6:4). This control is especially needed during the child's early years.

We are now discovering, though, that parents are not always able to exercise this control well. Their training will need to include both the understanding and the practice of the several ways to achieve this objective.

Control by consistent action. Actual physical control may need to accompany the parent's words when he or she deals with the very young child. Parents who depend on verbal control alone will soon recognize the powerlessness of the human voice. Parental discipline often fails at this point.

The mother nicely asks the toddler to put away his toys and then leaves without making certain he does so. He continues watching TV, ignoring her request. She returns to discover this disobedience and changes her tone. "Put your toys away," she commands a second time, now more sternly. But returning a third time, the mother discovers her child has not complied. Overflowing with frustration, she angrily shouts the child into submission; but the emotional scene is good for neither mother nor child. In effect, the mother has taught the child to respond only to shouting because she did not insist on obedience when she first spoke.

Control by natural consequences. Allowing natural results of happenings to shape a child's behavior is a kind of parental control, since the parent often has the power to intervene. Parents can even permit a child to go through a behavior they know will bring negative results. Shielding a child from serious physical harm is of course necessary. But allowing the child to use his money for a cheap toy that will easily break is a good form of discipline as long as the parent doesn't blame or ridicule the child later.

Sometimes the natural consequences of an action could be severe (such as being injured on a road that is off limits) or long range (such as failing in school work). Often a child can't detect the connection between his act and its consequences (such as eating foods that limit his energy). Parents can then produce some consequences for him, either good or bad ones.

Control by physical punishment. Clear-cut guidelines for spanking are laid down by one psychologist: (1) spank only when you are in control of yourself; (2) spank with a stick or an object that will not do harm, not with your hand; (3) spank only after an explanation; (4) spank only when all else fails; (5) spank in private; and (6) spank with ten swats (the child will feel five swats, but ten he or she will remember a lot longer).[4]

Control by negative consequences. The behavior-modification process includes other forms of punishment when they are appropriate: deprivation (no skateboard today), banishment (two minutes in the bathroom), and "overcorrection" (the child who spits on the floor scrubs the whole floor). Each of these must be used carefully, the parent keeping in mind concern for the child's self-esteem and his good relationship with others.

The authors of *Systematic Training for Effective Parenting* (STEP) suggest financial payment as an example of negative consequences. After children have failed to make their beds or to perform certain chores, they are required to pay a small sum (ten or twenty cents) to the family member who does the chore for them.[5] The good feature of this approach is that it is lifelike. As the child grows up, if he fails in his responsibility, someone else will have to bear it. Because the core ingredient of responsibility is recognizing the way one's actions affect others, this approach makes the child see that his failure causes extra work for others. When he must pay money for shirking work as a child, just as he would have to do in real life later, the consequences of shirking, which otherwise would be hidden from him, are made visible. Note, however, that the money is not subtracted from the child's allowance. If this is done, this is punishment rather than a payment, and this has a different impact on the child.

Control by verbal reproof. Loving rebuke is a scripturally sanctioned process. The rod and rebuke impart wisdom, says a proverb (Prov. 29:15). But care should be taken to reprove the child for misbehavior without damaging the child's sense of self-worth.

Control by reinforcement. Behaviorists such as Richard R. Abidin have constructed courses to teach behavior modification, built largely around encouraging remarks and other reinforcers.[6] Behavior modification would be unwise if it were used exclusively, but if it is used with other types of control and communication, it can be very effective, particularly with young children. It involves the following steps:

159

First, identify the behavior to be changed. Behavior is best changed in small bits and steps. Thus, we should be as specific as possible about the misconduct. This is difficult for those of us who generalize too much: "If the child jumps on the couch, he is unmanageable"; "If she doesn't put away the shampoo bottle, she is sloppy"; etc. Behavior modification calls for a specific goal—for example, getting the child to go to bed on time instead of getting the child to be on time in general.

Second, identify the positive behavior you wish to see. Usually we focus on the misconduct, getting the child to stop doing something. Rather, we are told, concentrate on what you want the child to do that is the opposite of the misbehavior. In other words, concentrate on getting the child to arrive on time for supper rather than focus on stopping his being late. The two objectives amount to the same thing, but the perspective of each is different.

Third, ignore the undesirable conduct. This is the toughest principle of all to carry out since most of us feel compelled to scold every time the child comes up short. But ignoring the specific misbehavior paves the way for the effectiveness of the next steps.

Catch the child being good is the fourth step. The proper behavior must be present sometime if it is to be developed. This will mean giving attention to the child, for example, when he or she arrives on time for supper. This turns the tables for the parent who notices the child primarily when she or he is out of step.

Finally, reinforce the desired behavior. A reinforcement is anything that will delight the child or give the child a good, confident feeling. If reinforcement follows the child's action, the action will tend to be repeated. That's the cardinal principle of behaviorism. A word of confidence is usually reinforcement enough. Not all behaviorists advocate giving material rewards. Activities can also be used as reinforcers: "Because you came to supper on time, you can chose your favorite game for the family to play tonight."

Reinforcements can be given even if the child has only partially achieved: "Well, great, you were only two minutes late tonight," or "You are really improving; you were on time four out of seven nights this week." Such statements communicate to the child that you don't consider his lateness a sinful pattern of rebellion but, rather an expression of immaturity he is overcoming.

Reinforcements in the form of pleasant activities can be promised for the purpose of promoting and developing a certain practice: "Make your bed first; then you can go outside." This is called the *Premack principle,* named for the man who stated it, or the *Grandma principle,* for the person who always seemed to practice it.

Some may criticize behavior modification for its use of praise that appeals to the child's ego. Yet a distinction should be made between pride-producing statements and confidence-building ones. Producers of the STEP parent-training sessions make this clear distinction and attempt to train parents to use the latter.[7] The commendation, "You played perfectly at the concert tonight; I'm proud of you," is a reinforcement, but it builds on the wrong base. It appeals to the child's pride, making him compare himself favorably with others. In addition, it will suggest that the parents' pride depends on perfection in the child, linking acceptance to excellence; such a commendation builds unrealistic standards within the child.

Instead, encouragement can be based on values that are not competitive—values that center on the child's contribution to others. The statement, "I really enjoyed hearing you play tonight; I know the others did too," puts the orientation in the right place. It focuses on others and gives the child a wholesome view of himself. To say, "I know God was pleased by your expression of kindness," relates our Lord to the reinforcement.

Praise comments are contrasted with confidence-building ones in the following ways. Praise statements emphasize external control, while confidence-building ones stress inner control; for example, "I think you are a great kid for winning that match" rather than "I know you really felt good about trying so hard." Praise statements provoke confidence in one's image while confidence-building ones inculcate satisfaction in one's actions. "I think you are a great pianist" (praise) instead of "You really seem to enjoy playing for yourself and others" (confidence building). By using confidence-building statements, Christian parents are emphasizing the values of cooperating, contributing, and living life as God intended. They thus avoid encouraging unhealthy competitive motivation that is based on pride.

Control with support. Attitude, not technique, is the most important ingredient of control. Studies show that two attitudes—being too permissive or overly restrictive—cause the most damage. In a recent project, researchers related each type of discipline to a child's self-respect and behavior. They concluded that the most effective pattern was the authoritative one.[8] The authoritative parent is compared to three other types: neglectful, permissive, and authoritarian. These four styles were measured in two areas: control and support.

The neglectful pattern offers little or no control or support. For example, "Work it out yourself, I'm busy." The permissive style is low in control but strong in support: "Well, you can stay up this time. . . . I know you like this program." Also less effective than the authoritative style was the authoritarian type, which consists of high control and low support. An example: "Rules are rules. You're late to dinner. To bed without eating!" Most effective of the four, the authoritative manner offers both control and support: "You're late again to dinner, tiger. . . . How can we work this out?"

Guernsey has written a simple test for parents to examine their own style of parenting.[9] This test can be found in Appendix 1 at the back of this book. It is an excellent tool for self-evaluation and group discussion.

Communication

While the section on control includes communication, this process deserves distinct treatment as an aspect of parental power.

Communicating feelings. Just as in the marriage union, self-disclosure is important in parent-child relationships. When parents share their feelings at appropriate moments, they are accomplishing a number of things.

First, parents help the child see the consequences of his or her actions. If the child's actions irritate the parent, the child needs to know that. When parents disclose their feelings of annoyance, children learn the result of their actions. Second, self-disclosure builds the parent's relationship with the child. Sharing inner feelings is a way of cementing a relationship. Saying, "I really feel good about being with you," draws parent and child together. Third, self-disclosure teaches the child about the real world. A parent who keeps all inward struggles to himself will hide from the child some important knowledge. The child will assume that dad and mom never had the same doubts, same inner temptations, or same unsettling dreams unless they share their doubts, temptations, and dreams. Knowing others have these same experiences will fortify the child's self-confidence. The child also benefits by learning to share his feelings, which is important for personal growth.

Simple guidelines and exercises can help a parent learn to verbalize feelings. Some of these are recommended for couples in the chapter on marriage enrichment. One simple guideline is to replace "you" statements with "I" statements. Instead of "You stop shouting, or I don't know what I'll do to you," try "I feel very nervous when you shout like that." An example is furnished by Kenneth G. Prunty, who has developed a training program for Church of God people patterned after Parent Effectiveness Training:

> Friends come over for a visit. Your two small children are playing in the kitchen and dining areas as they frequently do, but their joy, laughter and loudness in playing make it difficult for you and your friends to visit. Follow these steps in formulating and sending an "I" message.

162

Step 1: What I see and hear the children doing: They are playing and talking loudly and joyfully.

Step 2: The real effect: We cannot hear, and it is hard for us to carry on a conversation.

Step 3: The feeling: We want to be able to hear and talk, and are feeling upset because we cannot.[10]

Completing open-ended statements can also help establish the habit of exploring and expressing feelings. Parents can practice with one another with statements such as these:

- Whenever I feel frustrated, I . . .
- When I am alone, I feel . . .
- Something that makes me afraid is . . .
- Whenever I am upset, I feel like this inside . . .
- When someone disobeys me, I feel . . .
- Whenever someone disappoints me, I feel . . .

If the group includes both parents and children, adults could pair off with children for a twenty-minute sharing time, using a list like this. Exercises for sharing feelings, both positive and negative, are plentiful. Lyman Coleman's *Serendipity Books* are a major source of such exercises.[11] And *Reaching Out* by David Johnson can be adopted for family training.[12]

Communicate interest by listening. Listening is a form of power. If the parent fails to listen, it amounts to a damaging rejection. The parent's good listening prompts the child to think for himself and to build his self-respect and self-control. Thomas Gordon, founder of PET, teaches reflective listening. This form of listening helps children think through an issue for themselves. It is patterned after the non-directive counseling of Carl Rogers, who calls it paraphrasing.

In reflective listening a parent avoids a thoughtless reaction to the superficial aspects of a child's statement. When the child complains, "I don't know why Mrs. Craig gave me a *D* on that paper," the parent is often tempted to scold the child for complaining or to rise up in defense of the fairness of American education, surely including Mrs. Craig. A proverb says that "a fool finds no pleasure in understanding but delights in airing his own opinions" (Prov. 18:2). How often the parent plays the fool, offering no empathy and understanding little of the child's feelings or situation. Reflective listening can aid in both gaining understanding and conveying it.

PET teaches you, the parent, to repeat your child's statement in other words, to paraphrase it: "You don't see what Mrs. Craig saw about your paper that made her give you a *D*?" What you have done is to show a willingness to hear what your child has to say. You have also shown some concern without putting your finger either on Mrs. Craig or your child. In addition to all of that, your simple reflective statement gives your child a chance to think it through out loud. Gordon says the child will usually end up giving himself the advice you were about to give him in the first place.

The conversation is supposed to go like this. Child: "I'll bet she thought I didn't spend enough time on it. But how much time are you supposed to spend?" Parent: "You mean she expects you to spend a certain amount of time on it to get a higher grade?" Child: "I suppose that's so; I really did hurry it, didn't I?" Parent: "You don't think you really put out the effort?" Child: "No, she was probably right. Well, there are other papers." Sound idealistic? Perhaps. Certainly the Christian parent is entitled to offer some rebuke and some advice from time to time. But a very wise man once advised people first to listen: "He who answers before listening—that is his folly and his shame" (Prov. 18:13). Most parents will need a lot of practice in reflective listening before it is internalized.

Communicating God's Word. This is a prime aspect of parental influence, one that is most commended by Scripture. It is so central that Part Six in this book is devoted to this practice of family nurture. Preparing parents for this takes more than an annual sermon on family devotions. It demands some solid connections between church and home.

Interaction

Though the term *interaction* includes modeling, communication, and controlling, it embraces the total give-and-take in the household.

It refers, first of all, to the general atmosphere and life of the home. Dorothy Law Nolte describes in verse what takes place there:

> If a child lives with conflict, he learns to fight.
> If a child lives with fear, he learns to be apprehensive.
> If a child lives with pity, he learns to feel sorry for himself.
> If a child lives with ridicule, he learns to be shy.
> If a child lives with shame, he learns to feel guilty.
> If a child lives with encouragement, he learns to be confident.
> If a child lives with tolerance, he learns to be patient.
> If a child lives with praise, he learns to be appreciated.
> If a child lives with acceptance, he learns to love.[13]

Home interaction is so broad in scope that it requires no less than the personal development of the parents—their growth in grace and in the knowledge of our Lord. Thus the whole adult ministry is closely related to family ministry. But there are some areas of interaction in which parental training can be more specific.

Interact with understanding. The findings of developmental psychology should be made available to parents through library books and courses because home interaction should be based on understanding. An unknowing mother can stifle the child's zest for life by uninformed, unfair treatment. When a five-year-old lifts the skirt of another child, he is usually not displaying his sinful nature but rather his curious nature. The parents' reactions at such times are very important to the three goals of child rearing—the child's respect for himself or herself, for others, and for God.

Interact democratically in decision making. While it is biblical to teach children to live under authority, it is also right to teach them how to live in a democracy. Contemporary life demands that we be able to think through issues for ourselves and gain the moral and cooperative skills for successful living in a democratic society. Certainly life includes submission to Christ as Master, but not all issues are settled from a direct statement of Scripture.

For the answers to questions like "Shall we play Monopoly or Pay Day tonight?" and "Shall we endorse nuclear electric power?" the child must learn the process of give-and-take, giving due consideration to biblical principles and to other people. The child can't learn *that* in a home where all the answers are handed down by the father and mother. In fact, not allowing the child to hammer out rules and ethics in debate and interaction with others stifles his ability to think morally, according to developmentalist Jean Piaget.

Thus, parents can have some of their interaction on a democratic basis. A family council or meeting can serve the family well. A weekly or a periodic meeting of the family is called. There the family discusses matters such as vacations, recreation, relationships, home rules, standards, chores, etc. Care is taken not to permit problems to dominate these meetings, creating distasteful times of scolding and reproof. Decisions are made in a warm, businesslike manner that allows for arguing and free expression.

Interact in solving problems. Going through an acceptable approach to problems contributes to the child's later ability to manage. PET's problem-solving approach is quite commendable. When a Christian adds to this approach suggestions on how to know the will of God and insight on how to trust God's Spirit, the process is a solid one. There are five steps in this approach to solving problems.

First, identify the problem. Sometimes Christians retreat from problems instead of facing them squarely.

Second, analyze the problem prayerfully. We are justified in praying for insight, not just release. Problems are not dissolved by prayer; they are faced with prayer. God doesn't promise to take the challenge away. "With any trial he will give you a way out of it and the strength to *bear* it" (1 Cor. 10:13 JB, italics mine).

Insight in the case of family problems can be gained from asking this question: "Who 'owns' the problem?" If any family member takes another's problem for himself, successful overcoming of it will be hindered. Since a child's problem may cause problems for the parents, distinguishing between the child's and the parent's problem is important. If a child is failing a subject in school, that is the child's problem. The parent's difficulty is knowing how to live with and work with a child who is failing math. If the parent tries to "pass" the math course for the child, the parent becomes frustrated and the child becomes dependent.

The parental task is to help and support the child in solving his own problems and not to own the problem for the child. Families can be taught how to do this by giving them a case study and then analyzing it. In some situations the role of the parent may be to do nothing but stand by and pray; and the child is led to understand and accept this. In that case the parent is there to help but only if requested and only if the help is not in the form of solving the problem for the child.

Third, list all possible solutions. This requires some creative thinking.

Fourth, imagine all the possible consequences of each solution. This requires one to imagine the future on a cause-effect basis. Younger children do not have this ability. Therefore, when the parent helps the child think through possible courses of action and their results, the parent is aiding the child to develop his or her rational powers.

Finally, choose the best solution. This step requires some understanding of the ways that God leads us, such as through scriptural principles and circumstances. Our own inner feeling of peace regarding a course of action should also fit into place. Selecting the best solution demands adjustment to values and morals, since one's decision will affect others as well as oneself.

Leading a child through the problem-solving process need not exclude an order of authority in the home, where parents' decisions are final; but even when the parent hands down a decision, he or she should reveal to the child the process that led to the decision. The problems that are the child's alone to solve will provide many occasions for training in decision making for his or her future welfare. If children are not allowed to solve some of their problems alone, they are made unnecessarily and unhealthily dependent on the parents' authority instead of God's. Later, such children may be dangerously susceptible to blind dependence on some misguided political or demented religious leader.

Interact through recreation. Fun times of interacting can make their mark on children. Besides developing respect for their own mental health, recreation can build their relationships with the family. Recreation also induces communication by generating small talk that can lead to significant conversations.

Spending fun time together is not optional. Training in this area could include practical helps in planning wholesome family recreation and exposing parents to good books on recreation. The church can communicate recreational ideas during its church-sponsored intergenerational recreation and camping.

Creating Experiences

The fifth form of parental influence is the power to control the child's world of experiences. The parent's control here is not total, but it is substantial. Since so much learning results from interacting with life, the quality and type of experience will make a great impact. The parent can guide the child into situations both inside and outside the home. For example, reading missionary biographies can infect the child with hope and love for other people. And music lessons or sports participation can develop self-confidence. Such activities will shape the child's values, attitudes, and moral stance.

We can help parents be more systematic in directing the child's experiences. From my exposure to parents in training situations, I have often found that they are often unaware of the way to do this. It will take, first, an awareness of the values we wish to instill in the child.

One workshop guide to values training lists eight basic character traits and abilities related to maturity. These are: *affection*—the ability to love and care; *respect*—including both self-respect and the ability to respect others; *enlightenment*—referring to the skill of learning from others and from experience; *skill*—discovering and developing one's talents; *power*—participating in the making of decisions; *wealth*—a term used to describe the child's awareness of money as an instrument that should be respected and handled well; *wellbeing*—the attainment and maintenance of mental and physical health; and *rectitude*—an abiding sense of responsibility for one's attitudes and behavior.[14]

Drawing from Scripture, we can produce a list of Christian virtues that can be used in conjunction with these basic societal values. The list in 2 Peter 1:5-7 lends itself to drawing up a list of Christian virtues:

- Faith—trust in God
- Goodness—respect for virtue
- Knowledge—desiring to have wisdom and truth
- Self-control—self-discipline and the legitimacy of society's control
- Perseverance—enduring, finishing the job
- Godliness—being serious about God
- Brotherly kindness—respect and affection for others
- Love—sacrificing for others

Once parents are aware of the precise values they want to inculcate, they can explore the possible means of doing so. Listing the categories of life's experiences will reveal the many alternatives that are open to the parent:

- Exposure to examples
- In-depth relationships
- Reading
- Activities with nature and created life
- Large-group activities
- Small-group experiences
- Leadership experiences
- Serving experiences
- Decision-making experiences
- Responsibility-related experiences
- Skill-developing experiences
- Hobbies, sports, music, recreation, etc.

Parenting will require matching the child's experience to some value to be learned. Parents should understand that values are not merely taught by mere repetition of words or nagging rebukes. Rather, they are developed, that is, forged through interaction with life and interaction with other people.

For example, a couple might like to establish or develop rectitude, or responsibility, in their children. The parents would first define this value. They might define rectitude as follows: an abiding sense of responsibility for one's own attitudes and behavior. This quality would manifest itself in a dedication to truth, honesty, justice, fairness, and compassion.

The parents can then plan together to develop this value in their children. There are many areas that could be chosen for developing such responsibility. Here are some:

- Children are expected to obey rules that have been established and discussed in the home.

- Children are encouraged to establish their own rules and standards beyond those of the parents.
- Each family member is expected to do her or his chores, or duties, and these must be done consistently.
- Children can participate in family discussions of standards and rules and the reasons behind them.
- Children can participate in democratic family discussions of family practices.
- Children can be involved in programs and intergenerational events at church that give them in-depth exposure to adult models who practice responsible behavior.
- Children can be encouraged to read biographies and stories that show the value of acting responsibly.
- Children can be encouraged to participate in camping, sports, and other activities that show the need for personal discipline and cooperation with others.
- Children can be given the responsibility of caring for a pet or be encouraged to develop another hobby that builds responsibility.
- Children can be allowed to work out conflicts and thereby learn the importance of give and take, without the constant interference of an outside authority to settle disputes.
- Children can be involved in special occasions such as family get-togethers on holidays, dinner guests and parties in the home, etc., and thereby learn the importance of and practice of social skills and graces.

The above list is given for the purpose of developing one value. Parents can be taught to formulate lists of experiences for each of the values mentioned earlier in this section, and specific parent-training sessions can be devoted to this and the values developed can be discussed in other adult-education sessions.

THE BLAME-TRAIN OPTION

In our society, notes Thomas Gordon, parents are blamed, not trained. The church is in a strategic place to do something about this dilemma. The above model of parent training shows that we have plenty of agreement on some of the basics. And we have within our grasp some effective training tools to accomplish the job.

One of the most exciting aspects of this ministry is that it will benefit so many. Not only will children and future generations be helped, but present-day parental life will be enriched. Parenting skills are closely related to Christian-living skills. When learning how to communicate, to handle feelings, and to exercise parental influence,

169

parents are learning how to be mature Christians. Parent-development education is personal development. For that reason the task is as all-encompassing as it is imperative.

SUGGESTED READING

Dinkmeyer, Don, and McKay, Gary D. *Systematic Training for Effective Parenting.* Circle Pines, Minn.: American Guidance Service, 1976.

Gordon, Thomas. *Parent Effectiveness Training.* New York: Wyden, 1970.

Narramore, Bruce. *Help! I'm a Parent.* Grand Rapids: Zondervan, 1972. (Workbook: *A Guide to Child Rearing*)

————. *An Ounce of Prevention.* Grand Rapids: Zondervan, 1973.

14

Premarital
Counseling

Church leaders are in an enviable position from an educational viewpoint. The big moments and crises in people's lives—birth, marriage, sickness, and death—involve such leaders with people in an intimate way. When Christ's servants are sensitive to the opportunity, they can transform these experiences into occasions of unusual growth. The occasion of marrying people may qualify as the most unique opportunity of all, especially when premarital counseling has taken place. "This is a ministry for which I have no regrets," concludes one marriage expert. "I cannot say that about many things, but I have never wasted an hour in this form of ministry."[1]

This ministry has been given a number of different names, perhaps reflecting some question about its precise function. Called *premarital education* by some, they place the emphasis on the preparation aspect. With the term *premarital counseling* the stress is put on helping couples solve problems related to their premarriage experience, such as making the final decision or overcoming barriers in communication. The term *premarital conversations* portrays the informal nature of the sessions. Whatever the experience is called, it includes both counseling and education. It is a form of counseling that centers around the interpersonal relationships of a man and woman considering marriage, helping them evaluate their relationships and thoughts in view of their approaching marriage. This counseling also acquaints them with practical concepts related to building a happy marriage. It includes past, present, and future orientation.

Before viewing in more detail the functions of premarital counseling, it is necessary to establish its necessity and effectiveness. Writers in this field are enthusiastic and some times adamant in their recommendations. Thomas J. Schmidt insists, "A good rule of thumb for a pastor to follow in his own personal ministry is 'Never perform a marriage ceremony if you are unable to take the responsibility of helping the couple build a strong relationship in the marriage.'"[2] From a Christian standpoint pastors should view their task, not as performing weddings, but as building homes.

Psychologist Antonio Florio stresses the responsibility of pastors because of the strategic position of the clergy to operate on a preventive basis. He accuses many of failing because they either are not taking the time for premarital counseling or don't have the inclination or training to counsel as they should. "My plea to pastors is to recognize more fully their responsibilities in this area. They often deplore the rising tide of unhappy marriages and the soaring divorce rate, but if they stop and think about it, they may be a contributing factor."[3]

Such hard-line endorsement of premarital counseling should be backed by some evidence. Though extensive studies cannot be found, there is proof along three lines. First, there is the affirmation of married couples who have experienced it. Howard D. Vanderwell surveyed such couples to discover that 96 percent would recommend that other couples planning marriage take advantage of some premarital counseling service.[4] A research study of the premarital counseling programs of one thousand churches revealed that 90 percent of the couples responded positively to the mandatory sessions and encouraged their friends to go for counseling.[5]

The realistic appraisal of those responsible for marriage, the courts, might also confirm the importance of premarital counseling. Seeking to curb the divorce rate caused by early marriage, some courts are mandating premarital counseling as a prerequisite for minors who wish to obtain a marriage license.[6] James Peterson of the University of Southern California links three major causes of marriage failure to the lack of premarital counseling. These three causes are (1) improper choices in marriage partners, (2) unrealistic expectations on the part of potential partners when they enter marriage, and (3) inadequate preparation before marriage.[7] The occasion for all three of these could perhaps be eliminated or at least significantly reduced by adequate premarital counseling.

Available statistical evidence is also compelling. An extensive study in 1976 of over four hundred churches, representing twenty-five different denominations, showed the immense benefit of premarital counseling.[8]

Another study has uncovered an amazing phenomenon that could well be related to premarital counseling. Lt. Col. John Williams, a faculty member of the United States Air Force Academy in Colorado Springs, reported in his doctoral thesis that divorce among U.S. military officers is significantly lower than it is among the population as a whole. And among military officers, Air Force officers were found to have the lowest divorce rate, with the lowest of all found among officers graduating from the Air Force Academy. Between the years of 1959, when the first class graduated, and 1970 only twenty-one of the forty-five hundred Air Force Academy graduates (.005 percent) were divorced.

The statistics in the latter study may be explained, in part, by the high value placed on preparation for marriage indicated by the extensive premarital-counseling program at the Air Force Academy. Catholic chaplains spend eight to fourteen hours counseling with each couple; in addition, the program includes a weekend retreat, consisting of involvement with marriage counselors, gynecologists, and lawyers. The Protestant program consists of seminars on Sunday afternoons for three months and also includes a weekend retreat.[9]

While it is difficult to determine with precision the effectiveness of premarital education, its objectives suggest the potential. One purpose is to help the couple take some much-needed realism into their marriage. Entering marriage with blind idealism can be dangerous in that first eye-opening year of marriage. Entering marriage with cherished ideals, most couples are not prepared for the crises. As a counselor, you will never eliminate all idealistic notions (nor do you want to), but you can temper them with some conversation about the real problems of married life.

Second, in these sessions you can initiate communication where it may be lacking. In view of the obvious quest for intimacy today, we might expect couples to be equipped to communicate with each other. Yet they are not often ready to share positive matters effectually, let alone talk about problem areas. Because engaged couples tend to avoid the problems, you may be surprised to discover you have initiated communication about some things for the first time. Honest three-way conversation during the premarital counseling sessions can provoke much discussion regarding the couple's present experience and can enhance the probability of good future communication.

Not to be dismissed lightly is the information goal of premarital counseling. Lack of knowledge about married life is a hindrance for many. Helping the couples lay a theological foundation for family responsibilities is also of primary importance. But practical information at this preparatory time is especially strategic. Some experts claim that a high percentage of marriage failure involves financial causes. And often these tragedies are due more to ignorance of money management than lack of funds. Lack of knowledge in sexual relations is another cause of discord. The counselor must be sure that couples have an adequate working vocabulary for talking through bedroom problems. Husbands may be reluctant to talk about sex because they're embarrassed to use four-letter words that are the extent of their sexual lexicon. Adequate understanding and terminology is essential also for the couple's role in the sexual education of their children.

Rapport that is built with the couple is an important side benefit. Initiating counseling before marriage will swing the door wide open for marriage counseling if it is needed later. During premarital counseling, couples get accustomed to discussing their relationship with a third party, paving the way for their having less hesitancy to seek future counseling.

Because the deciding function is often preventive, it is frequently stressed as being the most important one in premarital counseling. Since an estimated 45 percent of engagements are broken, the possibility of preventing a poor match is a realistic one. In some cases the counselor will help the couple solve problems they might have failed to resolve on their own, thus preventing an unnecessary breakup. At other times during the interaction, it may be suggested that there be a postponement of marriage while the level of certainty is raised. And, of course, the premarital testing and interaction may enable either the couple or the counselor to decide that the relationship should be broken. Not always pleasant work, premarital counseling nevertheless deserves its reputation for being crisis counseling.

Another function relates, of course, to the prevention of future problems. Assimilating more than just information and insight related to areas of problem and conflict, couples gain problem-solving skills essential to their continued adjustment needed throughout marriage.

The potential of such a program means that it should become a regular part of the church's life. For this to happen, you will need to do more than make a premarital-counseling program a requirement for those who plan marriage. The awareness level of the whole congregation needs to be raised. Otherwise, couples will be coming to be married at the last minute, making it difficult or impossible to plan for the necessary four or five sessions. Without advanced awareness of what your requirements are in this matter, couples from your congregation will have a difficult time graciously accepting your refusal to preside at their weddings. Getting the backing of your church board is the place to begin. Then you can communicate regularly through oral and printed announcements. Both youth and adults will come to understand the necessity of notifying you of wedding plans months ahead of the date.

After a time, the best promoters of your sessions will be the enthusiastic couples who have benefited from them. But there are additional ways to advertise!

Some pastors conduct personal interviews with the youth of the congregation regularly, during which, among other things, the pastor informs the young people of the premarital counseling he offers. Sometimes pastors become involved in the preengagement stage of the couples' lives. By assisting them in the engagement decision, the pastor establishes rapport early in the relationship.

Promotional contact can also be made during annual lectures and discussions in the youth group or in Sunday school classes. By scheduling three or four sessions to discuss dating and marriage, the pastor can include mention of his counseling. By making known his program and policies, the pastor can soon anticipate that people will know (1) that premarital counseling is an essential prerequisite to marriage under his pastorate and that (2) his consent to give premarital counseling to a couple is no guarantee that he will perform the wedding, since making the decision of whether or not to marry will be one of the objectives of the counseling.

GUIDELINES FOR EFFECTIVE PREMARITAL-COUNSELING SESSIONS

We turn now to the actual sessions themselves. It is wise for you, the counselor, to tailor a program best fitted to you, as you follow some guidelines or principles. I will share what I consider to be essential guidelines for premarital counseling and then discuss briefly some of the more recent developments, such as group premarital counseling. An outline of a program that I have found to be effective can be found in Appendix 2; this program involves a counselor and one couple.

Whatever the actual program, premarital counseling should be premarital conversation. The objectives require discussion. Trained in the art of homiletics to communicate to many, pastors are sometimes unable to talk with a few. You may find two-way interaction threatening and difficult to initiate. In my first feeble attempt at premarital counseling I was anxious and unable to elicit conversation from the couple. Introducing the topic of sex relations, I asked if they had read any books on the subject. The young man said yes and the girl nodded slightly in agreement. When I scanned my mental computer for a question to approach the subject, I found nothing but a useless question: "Do you have any questions about sex you would like to ask?" Needless to say, after that clumsy, fear-ridden approach they didn't. In that awkward situation I passed by this critical area completely, apart from the mention of a few good books.

Since then I have discovered some effective tools to get beyond the couple's reticence and turn these sessions into dynamic times of interaction, while we still cover all the basics. An example of a tool easily secured and utilized is the *Marriage Expectation Inventory.* Have both the man and the woman complete a premarital questionnaire prior to the first session, and let them know you will not be lecturing on a subject but talking with them. This inexpensive marriage inventory prompts each to write his or her expectations in regard to the major family areas: love, money, sex, in-laws, religion, children, etc. After reviewing their answers, you can initiate discussion easily, even though you have had little previous contact with the couple. Further questions for your clarification of various points immediately establish a healthy rapport because the couple gets to talk about the subjects that matter most to them: their relationships, backgrounds, and expectations. Then you can begin to discuss discrepancies in expectations and the areas in which they will need to make adjustments. In addition, the written information can become a basis for determining compatibility and marriage readiness. Scripture and theological insights can often be inserted into a critical area of discussion, entering not as short, isolated, formal homilies, but as relevant messages from God. You are only a postage stamp away from scores of helpful interaction tools, some which will be discussed later, and many that are listed at the end of this chapter. Armed with these discussional, evaluative, and educational tests and inventories, you need not fear having a tense, pressure-cabin atmosphere or lecture-prone sessions.

Along with discussion, the premarital counseling should include content. Some counselors tend to downplay the informational aspect, and seem to emphasize the relational aspects of the counseling. But as the counseling is both spiritual and practical, it should be characterized by substantial information.

Two components of premarital counseling make it a choice educational opportunity. The anxiety level of the couple is one feature. Marriage failure being what it is today, we can expect that reality for couples entering marriage includes fear and uncertainty. And anxiety over the decision to wed is often accompanied by guilt about the past. In such cases the couple is ripe for learning about criteria for choosing a mate and about biblical passages related to decision making. Sometimes anxiety is related to the unknown, which can range from confusion about managing finances to ignorance about sexual matters. Information is needed and usually wanted.

Another motivating factor is their idealism. We can capitalize on this, urging them to prepare for the best, not the mediocre. I have always found couples to be in a state of readiness to learn in some, if not all, marriage areas.

To make the most of this learning moment, the counselor will include three features: (1) providing assignments, (2) utilizing tests, and (3) devising a plan.

Giving the couple assignments will give you some assurance that all important information will be provided, though not necessarily within the sessions themselves. In addition, if you know that both of them have completed the necessary study and reading, you will be able to proceed in a conversational way and not feel compelled to lecture. Assignments are either given in a prepared handout at the beginning of the premarital counseling series or presented at the end of each session as preparation for the next session. The form of assignments may vary, but usually they include (1) reading or listening to recorded material, (2) inductive Bible study, and (3) conversation-provoking exercises or inventories.

Recommended texts usually cover the areas of communication, such as Norman Wright's *Communication: Key to Your Marriage.* For ready reference on sexual matters the couple could not have a better book than *Intended for Pleasure,* written by Ed and Gaye Wheat, a Christian doctor and his wife who approach sex in a relational as well as a detailed, technical fashion. Their cassettes cover the same material and provide a good alternative for couples who are not used to reading or who need some variety in assignments. Adjustment in marriage is adequately handled in Paul Popenoe's *Marriage Is What You Make It.* Though published many years ago, it is still unmatched for offering a brief but profoundly practical chapter on each area of marriage. Scores of books are available, any combination of which will be chosen according to your viewpoint and the couple's needs. (See the Suggested Reading at the close of this chapter.)

Apart from reading material, assignments can take the form of study guides. Designed to guide the couple through appropriate biblical passages, some guides can be handed out by single pages prior to the appropriate session. Some study guides are oriented to other reading, to analysis of the individual, or to the relationship of the couple. Self-study can be most simply stimulated by including the *Handbook for Engaged Couples* as part of your program. Published by InterVarsity Fellowship, this guide can provide the basis for any discussion of the aspects of marriage. For couples who are not very familiar with biblical passages related to marriage, I commend the workbook entitled *Before You Say "I Do."*

Educational tests are similar to assignments but are geared toward learning through self-examination. The test itself can be either the actual means of learning or the means of motivating the couple to do further discussion or reading. One such test is the *Sex Knowledge Inventory, Form X* and *Form Y. Form X* deals with such technical subjects as anatomy, physiology, and contraception. *Form Y* is helpful in dealing with attitudes and broad areas of sexual knowledge. These are multiple-choice tests and are thus easily scored. They can be used as educational tools simply by having the person grade his own test and learn in the process. Or else you may grade them, and after discovering areas of weakness, you can offer information or suggest reading.

Another notable educational test is the *Marital Communications Inventory.* Responses given to forty-six items by each of the partners will determine the estimation of each one concerning this aspect of marriage and will provide some data for comparison of views. Like the sex-knowledge inventory, the communications inventory is published by Family Life Publications and can be used for self-learning or as a basis for discussion in the sessions.

The information function of premarital education also requires the use of a plan. Even though several sessions of random, unstructured conversation amounts to quite a bit of time, that is not enough. Assurance that all the basics will be touched, even if only lightly at times, should be built into the program. Such a plan calls for determining the number of sessions to be held and the actual procedure to be used in each. In Wright's comprehensive book, he recommends five sessions.[10] Following the recommended program of Howard Hendricks, I have used four sessions prior to the marriage, with a fifth session some time after marriage (see Appendix 2). The number of sessions is not as important as their comprehensiveness. You will want to devise your own schedule.

Helping the couple develop the skills needed for a good marriage should be a notable mark of premarital counseling. Aaron Rutledge, in his comprehensive book on premarital counseling, regards the development of skills as being both crucial and possible. He includes skills in two of the counselor's goals listed: "In summary, the counselor's goals with the engaged couple are (1) to test the growth and growth potential of each personality, (2) to develop skills in and to stimulate spontaneous communication, and (3) to expose areas of stress, and develop problem-solving skills."[11]

Note, too, that when "marriageability" traits are mentioned by Wright, skills dominate the list: adaptability and flexibility, empathy, ability to work through problems, ability to give and receive love, emotional stability, similar family backgrounds, similarities between the two individuals, and communication.[12] Though such skills as problem solving, adaptability, and communication are acquired during childhood and adolescence and are, in part, the measure of the person's maturity, you can still seek to foster their development and improvement during the sessions.

For this reason the sessions should be filled with communication, solving of problems, and even conflict resolution. I have often been in some very uncomfortable sessions with couples who were grappling with present problems of adjustment. These issues can be worked through with the couple in order to promote their personal and joint maturity. Testing that exposes problems and areas of disagreement, tension, or needed adjustment is a great help in improving living skills under the counselor's guidance. Even the skills involved in praying together and in reading and studying the Bible and other helpful books can be enhanced.

The final ingredient of premarital counseling is perhaps the most difficult to accomplish—the evaluation feature. Sometimes, when the couple is uncertain, the sessions are necessary to enable the two to come to a decision. At other times, when the decision to marry has been made, it is a matter of their evaluating themselves and their relationship in order to expose strengths as well as expected areas of conflict. All of the activities of the sessions will be called upon for the evaluation: your own observations and insight, the couple's growing self-knowledge, their feelings, their developing skills, and their growing knowledge of biblical truth as it relates to the will of God for them.

Even if you are not a professional counselor, you can utilize tests, questionnaires, and inventories to make the evaluation objective. I have listed several of these in the last part of this chapter. I have found two to be especially precise and revealing.

For a comprehensive look at the marriage, which results in a graph of all the relationships, you can use the *Premarital Inventory,* by Bess Associates. When it is completed, the three of you will hold in your hands a chart showing where the couple agrees with one another in the major areas of marital adjustment: interests and activities, personal adjustment, children, religion and philosophy, interpersonal communication, finances, in-laws, sexuality, and role adjustment. In addition to scores in these areas, a score for general marriage readiness is included, which immediately can alert you to possible problems in the future.

To test for temperament compatibility, *The Taylor-Johnson Temperament Analysis* is a highly recommended and reliable device. Although it is designed to be used by professional counselors, clergy can qualify to use it by attending a one-day seminar. The *TJTA* breaks temperament down into nine traits, which are measured by means of a brief questionnaire of eighty-two questions that is easily scored. The *TJTA* is neither designed to be a thorough analysis nor adequate for diagnosing severe personality disorders. The results, however, can be used to assist you in understanding extremes in behavior patterns of individuals and in foreseeing possible problem areas due to clashes in temperaments.

For example, one area explored is that of attitude toward social life. At one end of the scale the person rates as being socially active; at the other end he or she rates as being quiet and socially inactive. Johnson reported from his experience that there was greater marital stability present when scores in the area of activity were moderate rather than extreme or when the couple scored approximately the same. While these test scores may not call for terminating plans to be married, they may initiate intensive discussion about the decision or may even cause postponement of the marriage. They provide a basis for counseling couples concerning their differences in temperament and the extent to which the divergent temperaments might influence the marriage.

Variations in Premarital-counseling Procedures

Improvements in and modifications of premarital-counseling procedures continue to appear as counselors in growing numbers seize the opportunity to improve or modify these procedures. Some modifications are in the interest of saving the counselor's or pastor's time while the quality of counseling is maintained. Some are aimed at raising the quality of the counseling.

Group premarital counseling is an attempt both to save time and to enrich the experience. Providing a series of sessions for groups of five or six couples at a time adds a valuable dimension: couples can discuss their relationships, problems, and questions with peers facing the same experiences. In addition, outside people with particular skills can more easily be involved in the sessions. A doctor can lecture and answer questions regarding sex, a business person can deal with budgets and finances, and a professor or church staff member can share in the area of biblical interpretation.

The utilization of other people is another current trend. While this procedure sometimes is related only to group sessions, it need not be. You may enlist the cooperation of a trusted physician in order to integrate his session on sexuality with yours. The same can be done for other areas of expertise, such as finances. Having an engaged couple interact with a well-adjusted married couple of the congregation during the sessions can also add a dimension: after the young couple's marriage, when they need support or information, they can consult the other couple, who were in the sessions.

A new and growing trend is the use of audio-visual communication. I know of pastors who are video-taping some of their lectures, requiring the couples to view and listen to them in the church library as part of the assignment package. Though the video cassette offers a lecture only, it does provide a background for ample discussion in the couple's face-to-face sessions with you. It also gives some assurance of information input for those not inclined to read.

Conclusion

In our complex society people are not always properly prepared for marriage. Broken homes and inadequate parent models often leave individuals without any guidelines or skills for making the right decision concerning marriage or for adjusting after marriage. People spend years preparing for a vocation and sometimes hundreds of hours preparing for an athletic contest; four or five sessions along with study seems little to demand as preparation for such an important and valuable relationship as marriage. Premarital education makes sense.

SUGGESTED READING

Books on Premarital Counseling

Ard, Ben, Jr., and Ard, Constance. *Handbook of Marriage Counseling.* Palo Alto, Calif.: Science and Behavior Books, 1969.

Gangsei, Lyle B. *Manual for Group Premarital Counseling.* New York: Association, 1971.

Morris, J. Kenneth. *Premarital Counseling: A Manual for Ministers.* Englewood Cliffs, N.J.: Prentice-Hall, 1960.

Oates, Wayne E. *Premarital Pastoral Care and Counseling.* Nashville: Broadman, 1958.

Peterson, James A. *Education for Marriage.* New York: Scribner, 1956.

Rutledge, Aaron L. *Premarital Counseling.* Cambridge, Mass.: Schenkman, 1966.

Wright, H. Norman. *Premarital Counseling.* Chicago: Moody, 1977.

Family-Life Education

Books to Use in Premarital Counseling

Coble, Betty. *Woman: Aware and Choosing,* new ed. Nashville: Broadman, 1975.
Popenoe, Paul. *Marriage Is What You Make It.* New York: Macmillan, 1950.
Wheat, Ed, and Wheat, Gaye. *Intended for Pleasure.* Old Tappan, N.J.: Revell, 1977.
Williams, Harold Page. *Do Yourself a Favor: Love Your Wife.* Plainfield, N.J.: Logos, 1973.
Wright, H. Norman. *Communication: Key to Your Marriage.* Rev. ed. Glendale, Calif.: Regal, 1979.
Wright, H. Norman, and Roberts, Wes. *Before You Say "I Do."* Irvine, Calif.: Harvest House, 1978.

Cassettes

Wheat, Ed. "Sex Problems and Sex Techniques in Marriage." Christian Marriage Enrichment, 9000 E. Girard, Denver, CO 80231.

Tests, Questionnaires, Inventories

Marriage Expectation Inventory for Engaged Couples

Marital Communications Inventory

Sex Knowledge Inventory

The above three inventories are published by Family Life Publications, Inc., Box 427, Saluda, NC 28773.

California Marriage Readiness Evaluation Profile

Taylor-Johnson Temperament Analysis

These two testing devices are published by Western Psychiatric Services, 12031 Wilshire Blvd., Los Angeles, CA 90025.

Premarital Inventory

Published by Bess Associates, Box 4148, 4700 South Poplar, Caspar, WY 82604.

15

The Family-Life
Conference

Some may react coolly to the suggestion of a family-life conference—and with good reason. For too many years we have taken the annual-conference approach for solving substantial problems or achieving ambitious goals. The heavy investment of time, money, and energy of the planners have made them unaware of the often paltry results. Surely, they have thought, something that cost so much must have accomplished something. But when the people have left the meetings and the speakers left town, what has remained has been embarrassingly little after subtracting the inspiration, which usually has self-destructed after a few weeks. Matthew Miles reported, for example, that the average inspirational speaker is unlikely to bring about permanent attitude change in any intended direction.[1]

As a medium, however, the local-church conference is probably here to stay. Bible-centered proclamation and teaching does seem to make a lasting difference. Miles was reporting on secular conferences, not those where biblical authority prevailed. And, in general, conferences, seminars, symposiums, conventions, and workshops are still a major vehicle for human interaction throughout the world. Actually, there are more conferences of all types than ever before.[2] Abandoning the conference approach seems less sensible than using it wisely. And wisdom dictates two guidelines. First, we must realize that conferences do have limitations and shortcomings. It is unrealistic and unproductive to believe that an annual conference is the only, or even primary, vehicle for arriving at our objectives in any major domain of ministry, whether it be missions, Christian education, or family life. It is the ongoing congregational life, not the annual conference, that will make the biggest difference for families. And second, we should recognize that conference formats are changing. As a result of the turbulent sixties, conferences are no longer obsolete, but they certainly are different, usually calling for more active participation by those who attend.

THE VALUE OF THE CONFERENCE

When deciding on a family conference or seminar, the planners should give primacy to assessing realistically its potential value and purpose. Used in connection with other family-life ministry, the conference contributes a great deal.

Perhaps its greatest benefit is the broadest one. It raises the awareness level of the congregation. Devoting a weekend or a number of weekdays to the subject of family life makes family life more important for individuals as well as for the entire church body. The promotion beforetime, as well as the excitement and involvement during the conference, gives visibility to both the potential and the problems of the Christian home. Once the awareness and value levels of an area of life are raised, people will be much more sensitive to learning and changing in that area. They may purchase and read books, discuss changes with other family members, try new approaches, seek counseling, and generally be more alert to helping, growing, and learning.

The informational aspect of the conference should not be dismissed lightly. John Howell, family-life conference leader, lists three purposes of a local-church family-life conference, all of which relate to information: (1) to provide an opportunity for a systematic presentation of Christian teaching on various aspects of family life, (2) to provide a forum period for discussion of pertinent family problems, and (3) to provide an opportunity to guide the thinking of youth toward a Christian understanding of dating, courtship, and marriage.[3] Since many of the family-living themes are complicated and specialized enough to call for special speakers, the local-church leaders need not be embarrassed by endorsing a ministry that is meant to supplement, not to be a substitute for, the church staff's ministry.

It is not surprising that evangelism can be a major purpose of a conference on family life. So much of life's hurt happens in the family. This prompts many people to seek relief in a church meeting that promises to help them. Many persons find Christ in family-life seminars. Quidnessett Baptist Church in Rhode Island rented facilities outside the church for three evening lectures by the pastor on the home. Scores of outsiders were among the 400-550 people who were there each night, when practical, biblical help on the family was shared along with the gospel message.

The emotional impact of a family-life conference is also worthwhile. It is the emotional impact that is apparent during a conference. Successful conferences are often measured by feeling-oriented statements: "Isn't the speaker wonderful?" "I was so inspired." or "Really terrific!" But the lasting value of that emotional impact is difficult to assess. Conferences, we suspect, generate a momentary enthusiasm that fades away, leaving little practical results. Yet a successful conference without emotional involvement seems impossible, even with today's youth, who are characterized as pragmatic and realistic. Cyril Mill explains that, given the temporariness of subcultures and their beliefs, it is not difficult to understand the sense of play and feeling that permeates the activities of the young. Insisting that the successful conferences of the future will break away, creatively, from old patterns, he identifies this temporariness as the reason for this new direction:

> Even when dealing with the most serious topics they [the young adults] desire immediacy, a short-circuiting of cognition in order to achieve an immersion at the level of feelings. To be "with it," to sense "where it is," or in the sense (it used to be called a peak experience) to "grow" or achieve a full understanding throughout your being, is a highly sought-after goal.[4]

Of course, this feeling orientation marked church conferences of the past. Whether the conferences were evangelistically oriented, Christian-education oriented, or missionary oriented, we often sought for purposes and plans to produce revival, inspiration, and dedication. The difference today lies in a careful explanation of what we mean by these terms. Contemporary conference planners speak more of feeling than of inspiration. And the exclusively speaker-oriented conference has given way to one that also includes various types of involvement. Experiencing is no longer equated with listening, even when people are listening to a proven powerful speaker.

The conference is valuable also as a medium for developing skills. Typical conferences usually include certain workshops in which people can get down to business in solving their problems or learning new techniques. This can be true of a family-life seminar, where individuals according to age groups or as whole families can be involved in practical, small-group-oriented sessions to equip them with new skills in family living.

Obviously, the skills to be mastered as well as the information and attitudes to be gained will depend on the specific purpose of a particular family-life conference.

THE CONFERENCE GOALS

Planners of family-life conferences are susceptible to formulating goals that are too broad and general. Broad goals may seem sensible, particularly when a church has never had such a conference. One speaker or more is summoned to the premises to paint in broad strokes the whole canvas called "The Christian Family," while the attenders look on admiringly and in awe.

It's hard to make a case against this tendency to drop the whole load. But as a starting principle for selecting a purpose, I would suggest you choose a purpose that is narrow in scope. By doing this, you will leave other family topics for future conferences, thus avoiding the continuous repetition of generalities. And in this way you can avoid causing believers to come to the conference and end up feeling bad about all areas of their family life because they were taught to do very little specifically. It would be better to select a goal related to communicating in the home, for example, rather than living in the home. By selecting the narrow topic, you can concentrate better on developing certain skills and on providing specific suggestions than you could if the subject is too broad. The effect on those attending may more likely be a sense of satisfaction in accomplishment and improvement than one of frustration and guilt.

Keeping all age groups in mind when you are choosing conference goals is a good principle to follow. While the larger sessions may be given to broad topics, workshop sessions can be devoted to specific, age-related interests. Reference can be made to the list of objectives of family-life ministry given in chapter 7. S. Autry Brown provides a list of possible goals that can stimulate conference planners.

Among other goals, he includes these:

> Retired adults. To help senior adults (1) face the problem of loneliness, (2) retain or develop a feeling of worth, (3) develop or maintain a sense of purpose in life, (4) face money problems peculiar to retirement, (5) handle physical problems and tasks, (6) face death with dignity. . . .
>
> Adults in their middle years. (1) To help prepare adults for "the empty nest," when children are gone, (2) to help parents effect healthy relation-

ships with sons-in-law and daughters-in-law, (3) to help grandparents understand how to develop healthy relationships with their grandchildren, (4) to help adults keep their marriage exciting. . . .

Parents with teen-agers. To help parents of teen-agers (1) keep the communication lines open, (2) accept their teen-ager's sexual maturity and to help their teen-ager in accepting his own sexuality, (3) understand the physiological changes and personality needs and characteristics of teen-agers, (4) determine how much freedom a teen-ager should be given. . . .

Parents of children in their preteen years. To help parents (1) develop healthy and consistent patterns of discipline, (2) develop skills in communicating with their children, (3) understand the developmental needs of children. . . .

Young married adults. To help young adults (1) effect healthy communication patterns, (2) learn problem-solving techniques, (3) deal with problem areas in marriage . . . (6) understand the physical and emotional needs of the family, and (7) accept their roles in teaching religious and spiritual matters in the family.

Single adults who have been married. To help one-parent families (1) understand discipline problems peculiar to their situation, (2) work through grief caused by separation due to divorce or death, (3) resolve feelings of guilt, anger, and hostility, (4) effect satisfying social adjustments and recreational activities. . . .

Single adults who are looking forward to marriage. To help single adults (1) recognize differences in expectations in marriage, (2) determine healthy bases for mate selection, (3) decide on the qualities they desire in a mate. . . .

Teen-agers. To help teen-agers (1) understand and accept the physiological changes occurring in their bodies, (2) be aware of their feelings toward the opposite sex without having to explore them . . . (4) communicate with their parents . . . (7) develop proper attitudes toward love, sex, courtship, and marriage.

Children (preteens). To help children (1) develop a respect for parental authority, (2) develop positive attitudes toward their parents, (3) develop healthy concepts regarding their bodies, (4) develop a sense of worth and of being loved, (5) feel that they are part of the family. . . .[5]

Although this is not an exhaustive list of goals, these paragraphs offer a look at the potential practical purposes of a family-life conference for any member of the congregation.

A third guiding principle relates to planning the conference: the purpose should arise out of the needs of the congregation. This is a sensible principle but it is not so easily achieved. This is particularly true in the area of family life, in which problems are not so apparent to outsiders. Also, family failure produces embarrassment and guilt, which cause people to be reluctant to admit deficiencies. Even the pastor and other church leaders are not fully aware of the areas in which certain families need help most.

Taking a survey is an appropriate beginning for planning a family-life conference. Questions need to be related and directed to each age group. Provide for ease of response by inserting blocks for checking on the questionnaires and by ensuring that questionnaires will remain anonymous. A respondent can be asked to give a value to his response by circling a number from one to six so that there can be a comparison of the degree of recognized need.

A planning committee can conduct individual interviews as another means of finding relevant goals. Or the committee can ask small groups or Sunday school classes to discuss conference subjects and then to submit reports.

Including representative people on the planning committee can provide further assurance that certain people or possible topics are not ignored in the conference goals. Two authors suggest this approach:

> Select one person who is newly married, one parent who has young children, another whose children are away from home (or who has never had children), someone past sixty, a couple of teen-agers, two children under twelve, and a parent without a partner. Include persons from both sexes.[6]

However it is done, selecting needs that congregational members feel are most important may be the most crucial ingredient of a profitable conference.

Another principle in regard to selecting a purpose is this one: the purpose should determine the type and the program of the conference. Too often in church ministry we begin with a program, not a purpose. Our tendency is a photocopy approach: we copy successful programs or invite dynamic speakers in imitation of things others have done. Instead, we should begin with a carefully selected set of goals, then design a program to achieve those goals. Program format and speaker selections will more easily follow the determination of precise goals. Workshop leaders and platform speakers can be invited on the basis of their strengths in certain areas and not merely because of their general popularity.

THE CONFERENCE CORE

We can gather together under the term *core* a number of features of a family-life conference that are difficult to deal with separately because they are so interrelated. These elements, which grow out of the conference goals, are theme, program format, schedule, methods, and climate. The conference planners usually need to have all of these things out on the table at the same time. An example will explain what I mean.

Suppose a family-life conference is planned for an evangelistic purpose—to present life in Jesus Christ as the basic answer to successful family living. This purpose should dominate all elements. First, the theme will of necessity be one that will attract non-Christians to the meetings; yet it will accurately describe the contents of the meetings. Second, the program format will probably be speaker oriented, with perhaps a more-or-less formal question-and-answer period following. Small-group participation will probably be too threatening for an evangelistic purpose. But small-group participation might be part of the format if such participation is in a nonformal, small-group interaction, with refreshments following the main meeting. This would give people a chance to meet first-time attenders, making personal contact that might become a bridge for sharing Christ eventually. Probably the meeting will include some special music and even testimonies as an added attraction to outsiders. And one can conceive of yet other elements in the format that would serve an evangelistic purpose.

Third, the schedule of the conference will be in keeping with the evangelistic motif. A rigorous schedule requiring a great deal of commitment will be rejected for one that majors on meetings that are convenient and brief. Fourth, the methods used will be aligned with the evangelistic purpose. The workshop approach might be used, with an expert and small-group discussion. But the biblically oriented speaker or teacher in a large-group session might better serve the evangelistic purpose. Fifth, the purpose will determine the climate of the meetings. A cheerful, expectant climate may be most appropriate for an evangelistic purpose. This climate is built through the music, the personality of the speaker, the decoration of the facilities, etc.

The design of a family-life conference is our major concern in the following material.

Determining the Theme

Even though the purpose of the conference may relate to many topics and a variety of persons, one major theme can hold the conference together and provide a basis for promoting it.

A theme can be chosen from an area of family life: the family's spiritual life, family roles, family use of leisure, family responsibilities, family problems and crises, or a Christian view of sex.

Or else the theme can be selected from considering the dynamics of family life. There are certain skills or attitudes involved in relating within a family that can provide the focus of the seminar: communicating love in a practical way, handling conflict, accepting, supporting, maturing together, studying and praying together, handling change, or dealing with crises and problems.

Selecting a theme in regard to the circumstances surrounding family life today can give the theme a contemporary look and a relevant thrust. Some such themes are: living with pressures of family life, handling cultural threats to marriage and family values, struggling with disintegrating factors in family life, understanding changing family patterns, identifying family roles in changing times, dealing with ethical issues related to marriage and family, and biblical teaching about the family in uncertain times.

Once a theme has been selected, it should be expressed in a relevant and brief way that can be used in advertisement. Expressing the theme in pragmatic and personal terms may be more effective than stating it in an academic fashion. "Facing Family Pressures," for example, is more effective than "The Family Under Pressure."

The theme can be the umbrella under which more specific topics fall. For example, if you are using the family pressure theme, you can schedule a workshop on family finances as well as one on sex relationships. Under this theme youth can be invited to participate in a workshop on selecting a mate as easily as the subject of facing loneliness can be assigned to a senior citizens' session.

Designing the Program and the Schedule

No single format dominates the many family-life conferences now being conducted. But educational and practical insight gleaned from the history of conferences in general does offer some practical guidelines for programing and scheduling. First, it is wisest to have the program include both large- and small-group sessions. Whether a speaker, a drama, a film, or a panel discussion is central to the large-group gathering, there are obvious advantages to having a large-group meeting. Visitors are more comfortable in the auditorium, sitting where they can remain anonymous. Besides other benefits, the large session can generate some enthusiasm for the subject and overcome some of the initial inertia that people bring along with them. But the small group provides distinctives that the large group lacks. Offering elective workshops or seminars where there can be interaction and grappling with specific problems provides a dimension for change missing in the large group. Also, if four or five workshops are scheduled for the same period, there is more chance that individual needs can be met. Thus, a Sunday morning conference schedule might look like this:

9:30–10:30: Worship service. Message: The Basis of Christian Family Life

10:45–12:00: Elective sessions for teens through adults: Developing the Family's Spiritual Life—"Homemade Piety."

Handling Anger—"How to Have a Fair Fight."

Building Family Oneness—"Falling Together Instead of Falling Apart."

Expressing Feelings—"How to Avoid Emotional Divorce."

Enjoying the Single Life—"The Unmatched Potential."

Another important principle of scheduling relates to the inclusiveness of the conference. In a zeal to reach parents and husbands and wives in typical nuclear families, it is too easy to exclude large segments of people. People of all ages and in all types of family situations will need the help the family conference offers. A program can use the principle of inclusiveness by making subjects broad enough to include various age groups and peoples. As an example, a session on handling anger could relate to teens as well as adults, singles as well as married couples. Dealing with the dynamics of handling emotions in relationships strengthens individual persons as well as family units. Or else workshops can be offered for special groups. The regular age-group divisions might be followed for the Sunday school hour on Sunday morning. Each class could deal with the same subject, perhaps "Communicating Feelings in Close Relationships." On the other hand, special topics, all family related, could be assigned to the various groups. These topics could be assigned to individual classes or departments or offered as electives for all of the classes. Following the principle this way, the schedule for a Friday-evening-through-Sunday-evening conference might look like this:

Friday: Covered dish for all. Speaker: "Developing Unity in Relationships"

Intergenerational discussion groups follow the speaker.

Saturday evening:

Workshops:

Preschool children: "Loving in the Family"
Primary children: "Biblical Family Roles"
Junior children: "Coping With Parent-child Relationships"
Junior high: "Teen Tensions at Home"
Senior high: "Dating With a View to Marriage"
College age: "The Good Ship Courtship"

Parents with small children: "Family Living Under Pressure"
Parents with teens: "Coping With Conflict"
Parents with empty nest: "Keeping the Match Burning"
Parents without partners: "Handling Pressure"

Sunday morning: Worship hour: Intergenerational worship
Speaker: "Developing Family Unity in the Church."

Sunday school hour: Classes meet by age groups with special topics geared to them.

The principle of including all may also be carried out by having an entire evening or morning relate to one particular group. In this case there is no expectation that everyone in the church attends every scheduled event. A men's Saturday breakfast could be held on the topic "Understanding My Wife." A luncheon for the wives on the same day could deal with "Understanding My Husband." Saturday evening could be called "Couples Night," during which time couples could hear a message and then be guided, as couples, through some exercise to evaluate their relationships. Brown suggests extending the family conference to a whole week so that the conference appeals to persons in various situations:

Sunday

11:00 Morning worship—sermon on the opportunities and hazards of marriage

6:00 Dinner for junior- and senior-high and college youth, followed by discussion on preparing for marriage

7:30 Evening worship—sermon on the Christian basis of the home and family life

Monday

7:30-9:00 Conference for engaged couples and newlyweds on marital adjustment in the early years

Tuesday

7:30-9:00 Conference for couples with children under twelve on "The Couple With Young Children"

Wednesday

7:30-9:00 Conference for the entire family on "A Dialogue Between the Generations"

Thursday

7:30-9:00 Conference for the entire family on "Parent-Teen Relationships"

192

Friday

7:30-9:00 Conference for older married couples on "The Empty-Nest Years."[7]

Certainly, the way the principle of inclusivism is followed will depend on the size of the church, the workshop leaders available, the current needs of the congregation and other variables. Yet it is a sound policy to provide for all of the people, whether the church is large or small. Otherwise, we continue to pass along vague generalities that have little relevance for the many who live in unique and varied conditions. Addressing those persons will force us into a specific application of Scripture that is necessary for the success of the conference.

Choosing Methods

A successful conference will also feature a variety of methods. Not that variety alone is the measure of success. Variety is occasioned by a diversity of goals. Unfortunately, the majority of our evangelical family-life conferences have as their objective the dissemination of information. Therefore, they are usually speaker-centered, large-group settings, where the educational method is limited to the lecture. Sometimes, though, a film or even a panel discussion is included.

Yet, given the needs of contemporary families, a family-life conference should go beyond the mere transmission of knowledge. Methods that lead to evaluation, to learning of skills, and to interaction on an emotional plane should be used. The planners should take into account, however, that any learning models that force family members to face each other in situations that demand openness and honesty raise the threat level of a conference a hundredfold or more. We should use some methods with caution.

Methods can be categorized according to purpose. Methods used to communicate information include lectures, question-and-answer segments, panel discussions, films, dramas, symposiums, etc. Discussion, role playing, small-group working sessions, case studies, couple discussions, family-group discussions, and family-cluster discussions comprise the methods that are used to get people to talk about concepts. These methods are more threatening than lectures or films but still are less threatening than the methods of the third dimension—learning designs for personal evaluation and practice. They include evaluation questionnaires, expressing-feelings exercises, practicing-listening games, and other techniques suggested in the marriage encounter and parent-training chapters of this book. In his guidebook Brown describes in detail a number of fine creative group activities.[8] The right atmosphere and advanced preparation are necessary for the successful use of these designs, which cause people to face themselves and the demands of change. These educational strategies are of such value that effort should be made to include them in the conference. Some of the threat can be overcome by announcing before the conference that persons who attend the session will be asked to be involved in thinking through their own family life. Or an involvement exercise can be scheduled after a lecture session, with the understanding that only those who choose to participate in the exercise will do so.

CONFERENCE ADMINISTRATION

The administration of a family-life conference involves elements essential to any conference administration. One of the major matters to plan for is climate.

Establishing the Climate

The atmosphere of the conference is important to its success, especially in our emotionally sensitive era. But the climate is fostered by more than the musicians and speakers. The form of the promotion and the announcements about the conference determines the attitude that people have when they attend the first session. If the announcement is colorful, eye catching, well written, and couched in creative terminology, those who attend may have a light-hearted, expectant feeling. On the other hand, if the conference advertisement is forthright and serious, having little attractive embellishment, it will attract only those who sense a real need. Even the name you give to the conference will affect its climate. If you call it a workshop, people may come with a desire to participate, and this will result in making it easier to get them involved in discussion and creative activities.

The start of the conference also sets the climate. If there is a registration procedure, it should be handled efficiently and conveniently. Enthusiasm and momentum should characterize the first session. The purpose and nature of the conference itself determine the type of beginning session the planners use. If the intention is to get people involved in small-group activities, it may not be best to begin as if it were a Sunday morning worship service. This could foster a counterproductive tone.

The physical environment is a climate factor, too. Banners and signs and special seating arrangements can generate a feeling of expectation. The places where individual meetings are held contribute to the success of the climate. A question-and-answer session might be hindered in a church sanctuary setting, where the people in the audience customarily do not speak. Small-group discussion is certainly less effective when people are sitting in pews than when they are sitting in a circle in chairs. The physical setting may also contribute to the forming of the attitude toward the subject. The climate produced by a church sanctuary is usually not conducive to a discussion of sex or conflict in marriage.

Providing "white space" for participants is important for the atmosphere. If the scheduling is too tight, where one subject follows another, there is little leisure for the participants to think over the subject matter they have learned and the exercises they have done. Even if the conference continues all day long, there are measures that can be taken to prevent overwhelming people with new information and ideas. Refreshment and discussion breaks can be inserted between major sessions. The methods used can vary to avoid monotony. Exercises and creative methods can follow lecture sessions. And concentrating on the same subject for a large block of time, approaching it from different angles and through various media, can avoid the pitfall of bombarding people with a wide range of unrelated concepts.

Securing Leadership

Obtaining mature and resourceful workshop leaders and speakers is obviously the most important factor in a productive conference. And yet it need not be the most difficult. Major platform speakers are available from seminaries, Bible schools, and other churches. Many pastors are now well known for a family-life emphasis in their ministry. Workshop leaders are often available within the local church congregation or within the community. Brown lists these: doctors, nurses, lawyers, social-service-agency personnel, guidance personnel from local schools, home economics and health teachers, college professors in psychology, child-development and family-life and educational personnel of preschool institutions, state family-life consultants and state age-group workers, institutional chaplains, professional family counselors, and educators.[9] Many of these are Christians who can share their Christian viewpoint along with the technical information from their fields. In fact, unless they have a biblical perspective, it would be unwise to utilize them since no subject is untouched by Christian principles.

When workshops are designed to draw upon the resources of the participants or to interact with what a specialist has already presented, leaders can be enlisted from the congregation. The major requirements in this case are the ability and the training for guiding group activities and discussions.

Handling Finances

Costs for the conference can be met by taking offerings. On the other hand, many conferences can be supported by registration fees. A church will need good publicity and a very large constituency to draw from in order to finance the conference with such fees. Sometimes the costs can be handled by churches banding together to sponsor a conference with widely known speakers. Though financially feasible, this method does reduce the amount of involvement the people can have during the speaker-dominated session, and fewer church members from individual churches will attend than would do so for their own local-church event. Usually, a church will need to underwrite the conference expenses, preferably including them in the annual church budget.

Publicity

Publicity, too, is based on the purpose of the conference. An evangelistic thrust to members of the community will require an extensive promotional effort. Broad media coverage, including radio, television, newspapers, and paid advertisement, not only informs community constituents but also excites church members, who will be motivated to invite others. An attractive brochure and posters contribute to the conference whether the planners propose to reach outsiders or not. Announcements can be made in family-living classes at schools, at community agencies, and at service clubs. The quality of the brochure determines the attitude people will have toward the conference itself. An inexpensive, carelessly produced brochure may even give a negative image. All in-church promotion should portray the importance and the possibilities of such a conference. Public announcements, posters, mailings, and bulletin inserts should convey the importance of the conference by both message and appearance.

Evaluating the Conference

Designing future conferences depends on deliberate assessment of a conference by those who attended it. Evaluation is crucially important. Improvements in a specific conference need to be made on the basis of previous conferences. As in assessing needs prior to a conference, an evaluation after the conference may be taken in three ways. Committee members can meet to discuss how well goals were met. Or committee members can conduct brief personal interviews during the conference. The most thorough means is a written evaluation form. But if it is to be effective, this method needs to include certain features. The form should be distributed to a representative sample of the attendants. Not everyone who attends the conference needs to fill out a form if the committee is careful to get a select number of the attendants from each age group and from each type of person attending. Second, the form needs to provide printed answers for checking or circling. This takes extra time to prepare, but it standardizes the answers so that they can be easily counted. Otherwise, individual answers must be read, listed, and compared in a way that is very time-consuming and ineffective. For example, instead of asking, "Were the methods effective?" the form should include the various parts of the conference:

Evaluate the effectiveness of the methods employed by encircling one number after each item:

	Very effective					Not effective
Lectures by main speaker	6	5	4	3	2	1
Panel discussion	6	5	4	3	2	1
Feeling exercise	6	5	4	3	2	1
Evaluation exercise	6	5	4	3	2	1
Simulation game	6	5	4	3	2	1
Workshop discussion	6	5	4	3	2	1
Relational games	6	5	4	3	2	1

The results obtained from such a form can be easily tabulated and evaluated.

Third, an evaluation form needs to be reviewed wisely. Avoid taking the remarks of one outspoken individual as the sentiment of the whole group. Forms should be tabulated and compared to determine what the majority thinking or feeling was for any item. And finally, the evaluation should be as thorough as possible. Participants should be asked to review biblical conformity of content, practical usefulness of content, effectiveness of communication of speakers and leaders, effectiveness of discussion leaders, suitability and adequacy of methods, adequacy of facilities, effectiveness of scheduling, and relevance of subjects covered. Each of these areas can be covered by a list of questions calling for a yes or no response or by rating various aspects by encircling a number. Space can be made available for respondents to make suggestions for improving future conferences.

The accumulated impact of this information from the congregation along with the committee's and church board's honest appraisal year by year will probably, more than anything else, assure a productive family-life ministry through a local-church conference.

197

SUGGESTED READING

Brown, S. Autry. *Church Family Life Conference Guidebook.* Nashville: Sunday School Board of the Southern Baptist Church, 1973.

Burke, W. Warner. ed. *Conference Planning.* Washington, D.C.: National Training Laboratory, Institute for Applied Behavioral Sciences, 1970.

Nelson, Virgil, and Nelson, Lynn. *Retreat Handbook.* Valley Forge, Pa.: Judson, 1976.

PART SIX

FAMILY
NURTURE

16

Theory of
Family Nurture

Family Ministry is about two major processes: Christian education *of* the home and Christian education *in* the home. The importance of family-life education, the first of these processes, seems uncontested. Although surveys show that many evangelical churches have done little to help the family, there is an abiding conviction that the church ought to do something. Family-life education is stalled by lack of knowledge, lack of resources, and lack of right priorities.

But Christian education in the home—family nurture—is bogged down by controversy. Arguments are a mixture of pragmatic and theoretical themes. Religious educators have generally honored the home for its power to form the child, but in the past quarter century two tendencies have emerged.[1] One tendency is to idealize the family because of its overwhelming power to shape personality. Thus, those who hold this belief build an educational strategy on the basis of what the church can get the family to teach in the home. The other tendency is to depreciate the home. Those who tend to depreciate the home maintain that if Christian education is to be done, the church must do it. A brief historical survey will confirm that there has been vacillation between these two tendencies.

Family-Life Education Is Not New

While the cry "God save the family" may have a recent ring to it, it is genuinely antique. The cry began to be heard in the 1920s. Little had been done for the home before that time. Fairchild maintains that the Protestant Reformers did not guide the church toward this emphasis. "Sixteenth century reformers had little interest in the family as such. Rather than making deep excursions into theological understanding of marriage and the family, they were more concerned with correcting religious abuses of their day."[2]

The intense interest in the family in modern times was not yet evident in the first two decades of the twentieth century. John Charles Wynn offers some compelling evidence for this assertion, referring to a publication of 1931.

> Only thirty-five years ago a survey that was a progenitor of this volume was Lotze and Crawford's *Studies in Religious Education;* yet for all its variegated chapters written by the church educators of that day, not one of them refers to the family, and the index reveals no references to "family," "home," "marriage" or "sex."[3]

Speaking of parent education, Blanche Carrier observed the paucity of early effort: "Before the current movement, we can scarcely say that a program for parents existed in the churches despite the fact that a continuous interest in home life is evident in considerable publications of books and monographs."[4]

The current swing toward family-life education had its major push at the time of the Great Depression and immediately following. The leaders of the International Council of Religious Education announced in 1931 that 1934-35 would be the year given to a special emphasis on the Christian home.[5] Then in 1937 the church was served three meaty books on the family, all calling for strong family-life education programs. Although each book had its distinct approach and vantage point, all three were on the same theme, as is evident from the titles.[6]

Though the style and data of these books are far removed from us, their emphases and slogans have an astonishingly modern sound, and the books even identify the same dilemmas we have. It was almost fifty years ago that Jacob Sheatsley wrote,

> We can only look to Christian homes for religious training; and since many homes are only nominally Christian where likewise no Christian nurture can be expected . . . it becomes apparent how tremendously great the problem of Christian education is—at its roots.[7]

201

Family Nurture

The culmination of this thrust on the Christian home was the publication of the revolutionary statement of the International Council of Religious Education in 1940. This group called for a strategy of religious education that centered in the home. Those interested in church-home relations must realize there is more than fifty years of recent history from which to learn.

Family-Life Education Has Various Causes, but a New Direction

The assorted causes for this new direction in church ministry are clear to see. First, there was the response to the threat to families. The new secular age was challenging family solidarity and success. Quoting a denominational bulletin written earlier, Blanche Carrier in 1937 recalled, "The leaders say that any program which puts the church first would fail to help the home as it struggles realistically to find itself in modern life."[8] Isolated from kin and past tradition, families were undergoing severe stress, which prompted the church's action.

Second, there was the attempt to help the church. Earlier concern for the family was really concern for the church. "Family religion cures sick churches" was a slogan prior to the thirties.[9] Carrier admits that many churches were turning to parent-education classes to help ailing Sunday schools that were experiencing a decline in attendance, particularly among young adults.

And there was a new underlying revolutionary philosophy that was forming, and it would not lie down and be quiet. It was the foundation-shaking idea that Christian education should center in the home. Horace Bushnell had called for it in 1861, but church leaders now began to take it seriously in the formation of church programs. Leaders reversed the drift of past decades with this idea, which is preserved in a statement in Carrier's book:

> The program of Christian education ought to be interpreted as one in which the initial or primary responsibility rests on the parents and the function of the church school leader is to cooperate with them in carrying out their responsibility rather than to seek their cooperation in a responsibility resting primarily on the church.[10]

This dominant thread shows up in different designs and patterns through the garment of twentieth-century history of religious education, as it does in Lewis Sherrill's summons in 1944: "The church has begun to believe again that the family is the chief religious teacher."[11]

Prior to the twenties the church was saying, "We will teach your children; parents should help us." Lewis Sherrill observed this perspective in the *Book of Church Order of the Presbyterian Church in the United States:*

In the supreme task of religious education, parents should cooperate with the church by setting their children an example in regular and punctual attendance upon the sessions of the Church School and the services of the sanctuary and by assisting them in consistent application of the Gospel in their daily activities.[12]

Now a new direction was set: Christian education was to be based not on parents' cooperating with the church but on the church's cooperating with them.

Family Nurture Gained New Sociological and Theological Bases

The family-life emphasis was based on liberal theology and new sociological understanding. The growing understanding of the child in psychology and in sociology was a major influence. Earlier there had been a strong dependence on the public school for values and even for religious training. Along with this there had been a trust in the possibilities of teacher training for Sunday school teachers. In the thirties the emerging sociological understanding was noted by one of the prophets of the family movement: "No matter what the child's formal instruction in religion, his home life has determinative influence on his attitudes, concepts and practices."[13]

Though a theological base for this belief had been laid down earlier, new sociological findings were pressing home the point. The theological drift of the times also was imploring along the same line. Liberal religious educators were decisive about their goal of social change. Earlier they had been dependent mostly on the changes wrought by education, but this began to change. Historian Robert Lynn maintains that "both generations [liberal church leaders before and after the thirties] looked upon the family as the most powerful matrix of social change. Some, in fact, ventured further and claimed that the family was the primary source of social change in America."[14] The impetus for family-life nurture was a liberal viewpoint, in which it was proposed that social change comes through the family. Later, Robert Lynn chastised these religious leaders for holding an inadequate sociological viewpoint that led them in the wrong direction. He affirmed that society changes the family. "It is not the other way around," he wrote.[15]

Evangelicals Tended to Ignore Family Nurture

Fundamentalists and evangelicals largely ignored the family-life emphasis of the thirties and forties for the same reasons that many ignore it today. It was not merely that the movement was on a liberal base nor that they disregarded the sociological understanding of the day. It was because conservatism had an approach to Christian education that was in large part taken from the nineteenth century, and this approach did not include home-centered nurtures. Robert Lynn's careful research has uncovered evidence that there was a powerful system of Christian ministry that was formulated prior to the Civil War and which experienced a forceful development afterward. The features of this system were primarily institutional. While there was some reliance on family and congregational life, the strategy's strength was elsewhere. The elements of the *Paidea* of Protestant Zion (in his terminology) were revivals, the Sunday school, publications, denominational colleges, the confessional seminary, agencies and Sunday school societies, and finally the congregation and the family.

Of this "potent educational ecology" he writes as follows:

> No self-conscious strategist mapped it out as a whole; no committee said, "Now this is what we must do." It came into existence in a haphazard, unplanned manner. Each of its expressions represented an *ad hoc* response to a particular need or opportunity. But what held it together, once it was established in the routines of Protestant church life, was the evangelical spirit.[16]

Evangelicals may have resisted the strong family-life movement because they felt it was not conducive to their aims of reaching the lost and teaching the Bible. Carrier noted, for example, that early attempts to introduce parent training during the Sunday school hour were looked down on because of the traditional Bible curriculum.[17] Lynn observes that in evangelical circles these nineteenth-century institutions continue to thrive. Part of the resistance to a family-centered strategy is the predominance of the institutional approach, which often competes with the home.

The Emphasis on Family Nurture Rose and Then Declined in Mainline Churches

That the new direction of the twentieth century's fourth decade had taken hold seemed evident by what happened in the fifth. The revolutionary statements about the home becoming the center of the church's Christian education efforts produced various programs designed to strengthen family life. So many of the programs familiar to us now began then: parent-education classes in Sunday school, guidance for reading in the home, national family week, encouragement of religious activities in the home, and pastoral counseling.[18] The new direction fostered a changed attitude toward the church school—now seen as a sort of "parent cooperative." The church school was to be maintained by the parents as the responsible parties, who were to pool their resources to train their children.

The family emphasis continued until it culminated in the most far-reaching and most logical program—a church education curriculum that centered in the home. The printing presses turned out this revolutionary curriculum when religious educators were making their most forceful presentations in favor of family-centered Christian nurture.

Wesner Fallaw laid down a solid intellectual and liberal theological case for a family-nurture strategy, assuring the church that "the family is still a cultural moral force." He declared, "Until the home becomes as purposefully a teaching arm of the church as the church school tries to be, we are not likely to find much satisfaction in our programs for religious education."[19] Sounding much like many contemporary evangelicals, Harry Munro warned religious educators that they must "give more attention to helping parents do their job and less attention to acting as substitutes for parents."[20] Studies confirmed the validity of the new direction. Research into the Sunday school's long-range effectiveness showed it was virtually useless when compared to the home's influence on children.[21]

Leaders refuted certain objections, particularly the most obvious one—that parents would not cooperate and that the church would be forced to teach the children anyway. Many, like Martin P. Simon, recognized the existence of this pragmatic argument: "The common fallacy runs like this: 'God made the home responsible for the training of children. But since the home is not doing its duty, we must have schools and Sunday schools.'"[22] The forceful theological and sociological arguments prevailed. There was no other way, the leaders insisted.

Church curricular materials were criticized for omitting the parents. A study of the curricular materials of the denominational publishing houses in 1944 revealed that only in the lower grades were any materials whatever provided for use by parents or in the home.[23] The family-nurture theme was at a crescendo when the Faith and Life Curriculum of the United Presbyterian Church of the U.S.A. appeared in 1948. Seven years in planning, it was hailed as the first serious attempt to implement the reserves of home and church through a common curricula. It was based on the premise that the family is the center of religious education, which takes place not only on Sunday morning, but every morning and every evening in the home.[24] Other denominational publishers followed the same pattern.

But the curriculum designed to launch this Protestant strategy did not have the hoped-for results. Though there were materials for the parent as well as the teacher, parents did not cooperate. By 1961 Fairchild and Wynn were forced to ask, "Has Protestantism overemphasized the family?"[25]

205

Family Nurture

Looking back sixteen years later, Robert Lynn pronounced that the attempt to found religious education in the home had two major faults. It was founded on the unsound premise that the family was the primary source of social change in America. And further, it did not recognize fully the mission of the church.[26]

Wesner Fallaw, who earlier had formed one of the strongest cases for family nurture, did a dramatic turnabout with a new thesis in *Church Education for Tomorrow.*[27] He turned from the parents to the paid staff of the church as the agents of Christian education.

Family-Nurture Approach Abandoned by Mainline Churches

Today, it seems fair to judge that mainline religious educators have turned from a home-centered philosophy. While that philosophy still continues in some way everywhere and in some quarters in particular, the major future drift does not seem to be in that direction.

After the Faith and Life curriculum failure, there were certain signs of renewed attempts in family-life education. Fairchild and Wynn made a very strong appeal for it in an influential volume entitled *Families in the Church: A Protestant Survey.* Observing that "churches as a matter of fact, are confessing that they are in a quandary about the family and its place in their parish life," these two men did extensive field research to uncover the situation. They left no room for doubt that the family-life emphasis was still needed.[28] The Missouri Synod Lutherans made a strong family-life statement in their symposium, *Helping Families Through the Church.* Oscar Feucht, editor of this work, maintained that while it is evident to all that the effectiveness of the church is determined largely by what happens in the family, the "amazing fact is that the typical church gives little attention to marriage and family life education."[29] Feucht's case is built largely on statements made in the early forties, and he fails to mention the inefficiency of the Presbyterian venture. His strong bias causes him to lack objectivity at times. The existence of indifferent parents, he protests, should not make us scuttle a family-centered strategy, but rather should accentuate the need for it. He contends, "The more parents are excused, the less they will do. The more the church gives in to such a situation, the farther it recedes from the heart of the educative task."[30]

But the parental indifference has modified and in some cases altogether nullified the family-nurture push. There is evidence to support the contention that many modern religious educators have little place for the home in their conception of the religious-education task. Writing of the possibilities of family-centered religious-education programs, J. Thomas Leamon exposes his pessimism in a volume on

206

Christian education. After describing a couple's attempt to teach their children, he writes, "I really don't believe there are many Protestants interested enough in the Bible or in religious tradition to go through such a routine as I've described."[31] The most striking barometer reading is the recent survey volume that represents the mainline Protestant religious education movement. *Foundations for Christian Education in an Era of Change* not only omits a chapter on the home, but neither the word *family* nor the word *home* appears in the index.[32] The one reference to family-life education is a historical one. However, twelve years earlier the publication *An Introduction to Christian Education* devoted a chapter to the home in Christian education and contained numerous references to the family, particularly in the curriculum section.

This is not to say that all leaders have surrendered their interest in family-life ministry. But it does seem clear that the home will not soon be given the high profile in religious-education strategy that it had earlier. Even writers of curriculum who continue to seek parental cooperation are not dependent on it in the same way they used to be. The United Church curriculum is built on the family as a partner in the task, but Nelson is careful to point out that "the curriculum is not written so that parental responsibility is necessary, because some parents will not assume responsibility for their children's religious education."[33] Celebrated for its home emphasis, even the Covenant Life curriculum is tempered by its stress on the whole life of the church as well as on the home.

Family Nurture Is an Issue in Evangelical Churches

As discussed in chapter 1, the issue of family nurture is very much alive in evangelical circles. Some argue for a strong family-nurture approach, while others maintain that the church, not the home, should be the center of Christian education.

Arguments for Church-Centered Christian Education

Though the advocates of church-centered Christian education recognize the influence of the home, they argue that it cannot, and should not, occupy center stage in the teaching ministry. They point to the high divorce rate, the large number of working mothers, the early independence of adolescents, and the materialistic attitude of parents and they say that we can make little headway if we try to do most of the Christian education in the home.[34] In certain families and in certain communities the situation just described may largely be the case, and this precludes the use of the home as an agent for Christian education.

The argument most heard from those advocating a church-centered approach is a pragmatic one: "Parents won't do the job, so the church must." The history of the Faith and Life curriculum with its family-nurture emphasis may lend support to this argument, but there is some evidence among evangelicals that the situation is different. Many evangelical leaders believe there are a great many young evangelical parents who want to disciple their own children.

Certainly we can point to some biblical arguments for those who take the side of the church-centered approach. The body concept of the church suggests we can help one another with our responsibilities, and included in those is helping in nurturing one another's children. Too often, however, the church's Sunday school and other church-sponsored programs are not looked at in this way. If they were, they would be seen as a sort of parent cooperative, by which parents conscientiously and responsibly shared the task. Instead, parents look at those educational programs as services offered by the institutional church and bear little of the load for maintaining their quality. Yet Christian education within the church community has a biblical ring to it even though there is no definite children's educational program mentioned in the New Testament. There is scriptural support for our assumption that children were part of the total Christian ministry and that they participated in the house and family churches.

The concept of gifts is offered as another basis for church ministry to children. God may provide members of the body who can minister to other people's children, even though there are no children- and youth-directed gifts mentioned in the New Testament. The general teaching gift may be given for all age groups.

Finally, advocates of church-oriented education point to the success of the Christian-education ecology of the evangelical church with its agency-centered approach. The history of the Sunday school, camping, youth groups, weekday clubs, children's church, and vacation Bible school attests to an impressive accumulative effect in terms of evangelism and Christian growth. Were the church to dismantle all of this effective paraphernalia to center its program in the ailing families, it would be a costly mistake. Besides, they contend, these church-sponsored agencies have consistently won and taught youth from broken and non-Christian homes—those whom the home-centered programs would neglect. "Who would care for these children?" is a question that has been raised over and over again.

These arguments for maintaining the present church-based strategy of Christian education are impressive. With the dark, decaying portrait of the family looming in the background, church leaders are reluctant to adopt an approach that depends so much on the North American home.

ARGUMENTS FOR FAMILY-CENTERED CHRISTIAN EDUCATION

But reasons for a family-nurture approach are also compelling. And the first of these reasons has to do with the contemporary family. The picture is not as bad as it is often portrayed. As shown in an earlier chapter of this book, the family still ranks high in people's value systems. Though the family has problems, it has some unusual functions, among which is the supply of intimate contact so necessary to emotional stability and to personal well-being. Large churches, with their superficial relationships and impersonal, cognitive-dominated agencies are hard-pressed to restructure in order to replace the family.

And the plight of the family is not the bane, but the basis, of family nurture. If the church puts its energies into replacing the family's religious influence, the church will continue to neglect the home, only contributing to its deterioration. Authority Urie Bronfenbrenner contends that a survey of child-rearing practices in the United States over a twenty-five-year period shows a decrease in all spheres of interaction between parent and child.[35] Surely the church program should address this problem. Using this information as a basis for a retreat into its age-segregated classes and agencies is detrimental to the home.

There is a second major line of reasoning among the advocates of home-centered education. They maintain that the impact of the family on lives is so important that it is impossible to ignore it. Research continually tends to confirm the fact that the home is still the best socialization agency despite its problems and the increasing influence of media and peers. This conclusion is based on both the *type* and the *time* of experience in the home. Studies in early childhood continue to confirm the important role of this period in shaping a child's attitudes and values.

One contemporary researcher confirms past results: "The experience of those first years are more important than we had previously thought. In their simple everyday activities, infants and toddlers form the foundations of all later development."[36]

Two prominent religious educators offer similar expressions of the same viewpoint. Catholic educator James Michael Lee writes that "early family life and background constitute the most powerful, the most persuasive, and the most enduring variable affecting virtually all phases of an individual's learning."[37]

Protestant John Westerhoff is equally definite: "Obviously a person's most significant experiences are those in her or his family, particularly in the earliest years. . . . A person's faith, work views, beliefs, attitudes and values cannot be understood without reference to the family and to the early years of child-rearing."[38] And despite the broken homes and the growing use of day-care centers, one or both parents still have a major role in the child's early childhood training. This role may be either good or bad, but it is always significant.

The type of experience is as powerful in its effect as is its time of occurrence. Much research has shown that values, character, beliefs, and personality core are shaped through relationships.[39] Factors that facilitate the communication that takes place in these relationships are frequent, long-term contacts with the model; a warm, loving relationship; and exposure to the inner states of the model while observing him or her in a variety of life settings. The natural place for these experiences to occur is in the family. And when they do occur, their influence is markedly greater than that of other experiences.

In fact, though there is not much evidence to show that the church is hard-pressed to counteract this home influence through its church-centered agencies, the evidence we have tends to show that such is the case. All of us are familiar enough with children who have "grown up" in our church programs and have become Christian leaders though they did not have Christian parents; but research proves that these are by far the exception. The lasting influence on a child reared within the church program usually is accompanied by the nurturing of one or more Christian parents in the child's home. Data accumulated in recent decades uncovers the handicap of an approach that is not linked to home training. For instance, there is this revealing study of dropouts:

> Sixty-nine members of a church school were traced throughout their Sunday school life, from the Beginner's Department to their time of withdrawal. The reasons for their withdrawal were listed. It was found that more than 80 percent of the other-than-good reasons for leaving stemmed directly from parental influence or example, intentionally or unintentionally.[40]

The high percentage of youth (some studies show as much as 90 percent) who stay with the local church come from homes where parents are also actively involved in the church. A study of 239 children done by Donald Joy led him to dogmatize thus: "It was perfectly clear that with middle elementary boys we are only kidding ourselves unless we get the family involved in their Christian nurture."[41]

But neither social nor practical matters constitute the strongest support for the home-centered strategy; the theological base does. This base includes more than Deuteronomy 6:7. In itself this is an important reference, but it is not conclusive. The entire chapter clearly lays the task of religious education on the threshold of the home. Following the *Shema,* which reads, "Hear, O Israel: The LORD our God, the LORD is one. Love the LORD your God with all your heart and with all your soul and with all your strength. These command-ments that I give you today are to be upon your hearts. *Impress them on your children*" (vv. 4–7a) (italics mine). That Moses was pointing to the home experience is made clear by the following words: "Talk about them when you sit at home and when you walk along the road, when you lie down and when you get up. Tie them as symbols on your hands and bind them on your foreheads. Write them on the doorframes of your houses and on your gates" (vv. 7b–9).

At this time in Israel's history there was no synagogue. And the tabernacle services offered no formalized training of youth. That Is-rael's religious education was centered in the home life is clear from the whole Old Testament context. Many of the Jewish festivals were for educational purposes, always including the family. Often the festi-vals were family-centered celebrations. The most prominent festival, the Passover, took place in the home, where answers concerning faith were to be given by the parents. The Book of Proverbs encourages the youth to follow the instruction of their parents (1:8; 13:1; 29:3).

While direct application of this Old Testament practice of home-centered training may not be binding on the church, the principle is relevant. It demands careful consideration most of all because it is confirmed by New Testament practice and instruction. Paul's state-ment makes Christian education a parental matter: "Fathers, do not exasperate your children; instead, bring them up in the training and instruction of the Lord" (Eph. 6:4). This instruction, plus the fact that the church in New Testament times did not provide special church teaching for children, puts the church-centered strategists, not the home-centered strategists, in the defensive position.

All of these arguments on both sides, however, seem to converge and to press upon us one sensible conclusion: both the church and the home are important agents of nurture. The situation being what it is today, we can neither ignore nor idealize the family as a nurturing body. That the church, particularly as a community, can also play a part as an agent of nurture is obvious from the history and experience of religious education.

Our major task is not to choose between the church and the home as agents of nurture but to integrate their efforts. How to do that is really the subject of this book. Everything we do to help the family be more Christlike helps the family be more effective in Christ-communicating. The form of integration in regard to Christian educa-tion *in* the family (or home) can be looked upon separately; it is the major goal of this chapter. That integration will best be accomplished on certain principles.

PRINCIPLES OF FAMILY NURTURE

It Is to Be Based on a Total-Life Concept of Christian Education

Dealt with in an earlier chapter, this view of Christian education is one of the major reasons we look to family nurture in the first place. This view requires (1) a life-related adult ministry that deepens relationships and provides true-to-life experiences, so that adults are truly transformed into Christ's change agents in the home, (2) familylike church experiences along with nonformal and personalized interaction in the church that prepares parents for home-style communication, (3) family training that increases the quality and quantity of interaction among family members, and (4) a curriculum that involves parents and children in a serious attempt to relate scriptural truth to life.

It Requires the Involvement of the Whole Family

In the past, those in Christian education have vacillated between ministering to the individual and ministering to the parents, oddly neglecting the family as a whole. Nurture programs aimed at the whole family are as novel as they are promising. Family clusters, family enrichment, and intergenerational programs are among these original ventures that deserve full treatment, which is given later.

It Is to Be Based on a Realistic View of Today's Family

Literature for the home should shun the traditional picture of the home. Not all of today's children emerge from the womb into a complete Christian home, replete with an ever-present, loving mother and a cheerful, Christian father. Such a picture hastily paints over the vast number of children who are born to unwed mothers, who are living with a divorced parent, or who have a father who works nights or is gone weekdays or suffers from illness. Reality can be lost in the framing of the demands of the curriculum of nurture as well as in the family portrait it presents. Programs can become so ambitious and out of reach for untrained parents in a normal, busy family life that those programs do little more than generate a feeling of guilt.

For example, the leaders in a certain church distributed to all parents a booklet that, if used in conjunction with other sessions held during the year, was to assure preinstruction for the parents' small children.[42] At the year's end the leaders called for the borrowed booklets. All of them were like new. One could tell at a glance that they had hardly been used during the year. The following year it was announced that only those families that actually made a request would receive a booklet. Three weeks passed, and only one family in eight had asked for a booklet. Piveteau and Dillon maintain that "the absurdity of some ambitioning leads to a situation where only the more leisured of Christians can afford the parish program." Often, it is only the affluent and educated who are able to participate.[43]

The need for realism should drive us in two directions. We should be certain to offer opportunities for the family, partial families and singles as well, to be involved together within the time allotment the church activities themselves demand. This refers back to the previous principle.

But a realistic view also requires our offering of the family-nurture process to those who respond to it. Some families and individuals need the support of the church for the nurture of their children more than others do. While we are strengthening these families, we can offer the nurture approach to those who are ready for it, and even want it. I sense that there are great numbers of young evangelical parents who are eager to win and train their children for Christ. My great hope for a growing and potent home-nurture movement rests on such parents. And a church that fails to offer them support and the means of doing the job themselves is failing them and their children.

Scripture Should Be Taught Both Formally and Informally

Nobody argues against the informal communication of Christian truth and values in the home. The interjection of biblical truth into routine family life and talk is a biblical as well as a common-sense approach. However, the development of a more formal home process of teaching Scripture is debated.

Because of their view of nurturing, some give little place to teaching the Bible to little children. The religious-education studies of Ronald Goldman show that children misunderstand the essence of biblical stories.[44] Goldman completed his studies in Great Britain, following the views of developmental psychologist Jean Piaget. But Goldman based his views on a nonevangelical theology. He maintained that children are harmed by misunderstanding the stories, thinking that they are to be taken literally. Therefore, teachers should withhold stories like the crossing of the Red Sea until youth are old enough to understand that such stories are myths. Evangelicals, therefore, have little to learn from Goldman's studies and from his conclusions.

However, following Piaget, we should be aware that many of the abstract truths and much of the reasoning of Scripture are beyond the reach of children until the junior-high age. Then, when they reach the level he calls "formal operations," they can handle concepts such as "light of the world" and "fishers of men." But Piaget's studies need not force us to conclude that all Bible stories and all Bible truth should be withheld from children. They still grasp much that is concrete and within their range of experience and thinking. It is most important to keep them from getting wrong concepts, of course. The parents can help a great deal in this, since they are in the best position for knowing what the child is thinking and, if it is wrong, to correct it.

Some contend that formal home instruction produces an intellectual faith that is unrelated to life. They say that the child is saturated with words about Christianity before she or he has had an opportunity to understand those words experientially.[45] Any formal approach to Christian education will run this risk. A nonformal situation is less likely the occasion for intellectualizing. When parents, engaging in ordinary conversation, respond to a child's question, the possibility that the answer will be too bookish or abstract is less than those times when parents and children sit down together for biblical instruction. Children may better handle abstractions and irrelevant ideas when they come in normal interaction with adults. Children slough off such ideas and forget them just as they forget other adultlike concepts that go over their heads. But those who are opposed to formal home instruction say that forcing them to concentrate on the intellectual content of the Christian faith may give them a distaste for God as well as a distorted view of the Christian life.

The major opposition to formal home instruction, however, is a practical one. Formal instruction intrudes into the otherwise informal home life. Christian education in the church is intentional and prescribed. Sometimes the greatest task of the teacher is to get the pupils to talk about things that do not interest them in the slightest. Teachers do this because they believe it is their duty. Because of the schoollike nature of the church program, it is impossible to do otherwise most of the time. No one has devised a need-oriented, experience-centered curriculum that has been truly satisfying. To transfer this formal way of interjecting truths into family life when no one has asked for them and when no experience demands them is a mistake, according to some. It is better to answer when asked rather than to try to force interest in answers to unexperienced questions. To do the latter takes a great deal of pedagogical skill, especially when the setting for this formal training is in the home, where it is an unexpected and foreign kind of activity.

Taken together, these arguments are impressive. Formal training of children is an intrusion into modern home life, making it difficult for parents to accomplish their goal. And we cannot quarrel with the need for relating biblical truth to experience. Educationally, going from life's events to biblical truths is more rewarding than going from those truths to life's events. Keeping home Christian education within the boundaries of a nonformal atmosphere, therefore, is an attractive option.

But developing some formalized Christian instruction in the home makes sense biblically as well as educationally. Teaching the Scriptures to children at home is well-grounded in Scripture. "Teach them diligently," commanded Moses (Deut. 6:7). Two important considerations make clear God's reason for instructing us to do this. First, the accumulation of vocabulary is important to the child while he is interpreting his experience and framing it into a total world view. While it is true that he is confronted with words beyond his experience, he learns words that explain it. If the child is living with the biblical realities of hope, trust, forgiveness, etc., the teaching he receives confirms and explains the nature of and reasons for those realities. The teaching also provides some basis for discussing these things with others. While this teaching can possibly be done within the regular conversation of the home, it is too important to be left to that alone.

Second, important questions about God and the Christian faith need to be raised. Contemporary life does not always prompt the kinds of questions the Bible addresses. A walk through an airport will prompt all kinds of questions from a fascinated child, but the tour will hardly raise questions about God. Our secular, materialistic, plastic world protects and separates us from some of the major issues of life and death. We cannot be sure that teachings about God will automatically occur in the nonformal processes of the Christian family even if parents are prepared to communicate those teachings. We need to alert and prepare parents for both approaches—the nonformal and the formal—because each contributes to the other. Questions asked during the intentionally planned learning time prompts questions and observations during the informal moments. And informal times provide some of the grist for the formalized instructional moments.

Ideally the system includes an integration of four learning experiences of the child: the formal process in both church and home mixed with church and home nonformal experiences. But a family-nurture program that is truly integrated with the local church has not yet fully emerged. Some programs, such as family devotions, have been encouraged by church leaders but have rarely been related carefully to the church's educational ministry. Some contemporary programs are slowly, painstakingly blossoming. In the next chapter we will appraise the variety of possibilities open to us.

17

Programs of
Family Nurture

In this section we will explore the programs devised for Christian education in the home, both formal and nonformal. Because of the nature of family life, the home is a choice context for the nonformal communication of truth, no doubt more powerful than the formal. Scriptural truth can be injected into the mainstream of life as a response to curiosity and as part of normal conversation; it need not always be dragged in irrelevantly as some awkward flash of parental piety. The emphasis in the Deuteronomy passage is on this insertion of the Word into daily conversation: "Talk about them [God's words] when you sit at home and when you walk along the road, when you lie down and when you get up" (Deut. 6:7). That those words are to shape the values, attitudes, and behavior within the home is clearly part of the process of training: "Tie them as symbols on your hands and bind them on your foreheads. Write them on the doorframes of your houses and on your gates" (Deut. 6:8–9). Though God obviously meant these commands to be figurative expressions of the ways truth was to permeate all of life, the Jews sometimes took these commands literally and attached small leather boxes containing scrolls of Scripture on their arms and foreheads and also attached small cases containing parchment inscribed with Scripture on their doorposts.

Shaping the thought and behavior of the parents in the congregation is the first order of business in an educational enterprise grounded in the home. And we can teach parents about nonformal communication. The concept and practice of nonformal instruction needs to be made clear to the many mothers and fathers who normally associate teaching and learning with books and classrooms.

PREPARING PARENTS FOR INFORMAL TEACHING

We can help parents, first, to watch for the child's questions. The Old Testament pattern capitalized on children's curiosity in order to have truth passed on to the next generation: "In the future, when your son asks you, 'What is the meaning of the stipulations, decrees and laws the LORD our God has commanded you?' tell him . . ." (Deut. 6:20–21). Parents might easily overlook opportunities to teach, since children's questions are most often posed at the wrong time. The wise mother later goes back to the question her impulsive young son asked her just as she was sliding the hot chicken from the pan to the platter. Wise parents make it a pattern to go to the shelf for the Bible as they do for the encyclopedia when children are searching for answers.

And parents can do things to prompt the child to ask questions. Jewish ceremonies were intended to provoke queries. During the home-centered Passover celebration parents were to be ready to explain whenever the children would ask, "What does this rite mean to you?" (Exod. 12:26). Joshua established a monument at Gilgal from twelve stones taken from the Jordan River and then told the Israelites, "In the future when your descendants ask their fathers, 'What do these stones mean?' tell them, 'Israel crossed the Jordan on dry ground'" (Josh. 4:21–22). In the same way Christian holidays, family celebrations, church activities, visits of missionaries, etc., can provide occasions to teach in response to searching questions.

The Christian parent, too, can become skillful at asking questions of the children. This is particularly important because the home is the proper setting for correcting children's misconceptions. At the right moment during conversations the father or mother can ask questions like these: "What is your idea of God?" "What is faith?" "How do you explain the word *forgive*?" During play parents can encourage the child to draw pictures that depict his or her ideas of various spiritual concepts. Discussing the child's picture about forgiveness, for example, can be an occasion of honest exchange of feelings and ideas related to Christian faith and life.

Parents who understand the informal process of instruction can

217

also capitalize on life's momentous occasions, turning them into joyful times of celebration, teaching, and worship. Events surrounding a birth can evoke thoughts about the gift and meaning of life. Parents and children bowing over the newly arrived family member and offering their simple words of thanks to life's Creator constitute a sincere and emotional liturgy unmatched by any church service. To celebrate requires the ability to do three things. First, it demands that we know how to live—to act, to experience, to love. Next, it requires awareness —thinking back over an experience, assessing it, judging it, evaluating it. The third requirement is the foremost one—the ability to share, or to turn private reflections into public awareness of them. And so we ask each family member, "What does having a new baby in the house mean to you?" We give the adult or child time to meditate, to search heart and mind; then we ask him or her to share. And in that sharing of life and awareness and response, we celebrate the gifts and presence of God. In that celebration the Word and the person of God are integrated into our living.

That integration can take place during the negative experiences of life as well, during the crises we endure and the pain we suffer. Our Lord is present in such experiences also, and we speak of Him at such times with dignity and gratitude. We interpret our feelings for ourselves and for each other in the light shed from His truth. Such a perspective offers an occasion for celebration when we suffer; for He always offers hope and light, even when it seems hopelessly dark.

FAMILY DEVOTIONS AND FAMILY WORSHIP

One of the sacred cows of the evangelical subculture is the *family altar.* In our thinking, it has stood as the norm for a healthy Christian family. Some historical evidence seems to point to the fact that regular family devotions were once a part of American Christian family life. During the times before the American Revolution the family altar was the means of giving Christian nurture to the children. Most families had and used the Bible.[1] Many evangelical pastors continue to insist on using the so-called altar. Those who have found it useful speak of it in glowing, dramatic, emotional tones, often making claims unsupported by biblical or practical evidence. "The altar has been a focal point of religious experience since time began," one writer generalizes and then misleadingly confuses family devotions with Israel's bloody altar. "In Old Testament times the Israelites met God at the altar. When the altar lay in ruin, Israel's life was at a low ebb."[2] Central to the problem of the family altar has been the unexamined acceptance of it in theory, while the nonpracticing silent majority "listen with respect, feeling a bit guilty at this hiatus in the family life."[3]

What research we have for its actual practice is not very encouraging. A survey done by the Family Altar League of America revealed that only 5 percent of professing Christian families have any kind of regular, meaningful family worship.[4] And a check of family worship practice in the homes of professional Christian educators was rather disappointing also. A majority of the two hundred youth directors and Christian education directors who responded to a questionnaire reported that they did not have prayer and Bible study with their families more than three times a week. The rest had less than this. And half of these model leaders said that they did not have sufficient time for their families.[5]

Lacking extensive reliable research, we must turn to some theoretical debate on the matter. The editors of *Eternity* magazine once invited some evangelical authors to face the issue squarely, asking them, "Should we have daily family devotions?" The three different replies were "Yes," "Not necessarily," and "No, not if. . . ." Two of the authors mentioned the problem of Christians' guilt feelings over the matter of daily family devotions, which is a subcultural tradition, not a biblical mandate. The author in favor of the family altar never mentioned guilt; he laid it on:

> We need family worship so badly. Parents will then have the opportunity to tell their children about God's saving love revealed in Jesus Christ. If you really believe on the Lord Jesus Christ, how can you fail to make opportunities within your family to tell your children about Him?[6]

To justify such an extreme statement, we must establish whether or not regular family devotions is a biblically sanctioned practice. That is the first issue. Nederhood assures us that the practice is absolutely biblical, citing Psalm 78:3–7, a passage that states there is in Israel a law commanding fathers to communicate God's truth to the next generation. But he fails to produce a specific New or Old Testament text that identifies the so-called family altar as the place for that transfer of truth to take place. Enos Sjogren is thus correct when he asserts that it is not a practice that is expressly commanded in Scripture. In fact, in Scripture the emphasis falls not on some twenty-minute period but on the whole day.[7] And that is the major concern of Harold H. Hess, who is most outspoken in pointing out the weakness of family devotions, maintaining that the practice utterly fails to catch the spirit of the approach mentioned by Moses in Deuteronomy 6. He objects to the formalized, structured, and compartmentalized approach of family devotions, which is a substitute for the rich, nonformal communication available in the home.[8]

The practical results of family devotions are taken for granted as

219

much as the supposed biblical base is. But the results are not all positive. At this point research does not help us much. We have a great deal of individual testimony about their value from parents and their children. Yet, we don't have solid evidence concerning the factors that influence children in Christian homes, particularly because the whole matter of these factors is so complicated and mostly because research is so expensive. However, we do have clear testimony about the negative results of the family altar.

Many young people have been turned off and "case hardened" by this daily routine. In part, this is true because it's tough to keep such a day-by-day ritual from becoming boring. Occasional dinner guests may enliven it from time to time, but it too often is a dull affair from which children are only too glad to escape when they leave home. Certainly, this is not true of all of them; but that it is true of some there can be no doubt. This may be particularly true in homes where the parents have little gift for reading out loud or for creative planning and are primarily prompted by the nagging guilt that if they don't force the family through this daily practice, they surely will fail to communicate Christ to their dearly loved children. A sour and negative attitude soon dominates such a household at the very announcement of the family altar.

As for the suspicion that children who are not exposed to this ritual will not be exposed to Christ, such a suspicion remains just that—a suspicion. It is refreshing to hear a word of testimony from the writer on the other side, Enos Sjogren writes:

> I had the great fortune to be brought up in a Christian home. We never had a family altar, yet the presence of Christ was pervasive. Both children accepted Christ as personal Savior when teen-agers, after passing through the normal period of rebellion. Both have been active in Christian work ever since, at home and overseas. Neither of the two homes have family altars. There are seven grandchildren. All are well adjusted children who have professed Christ and who remain active in evangelical youth movements.[9]

Neither the biblical nor the pragmatic evidence supports the contention that one cannot build a Christian home without a daily family altar. I side with Sjogren in answer to this question: Should we have daily family devotions? Not necessarily.

That we can recommend family devotions in certain church situations and for certain people is fine. But the practice is at best an inferior substitute for a more totally integrated plan for church and home that we will consider later.

Those who do recommend having family devotions will need to do more than preach and teach about it. Few parents seem to be able to take the verbal instructions and then carry them out successfully in their home settings. A pastor who invites families into his home and has sample devotions with them has a workable approach. And parents might profit from some practical guidelines.

Make the devotional period personal. What fits your family is best for your family. Recently a dedicated Christian father told a group of pastors I was with that his family had consistently read the Bible and had sung together early in the morning for over twenty years. In fact, the parents and children had memorized all the hymns in a large hymnal. The temptation to copy such successful parents pressed upon all of us who heard the story. But not all parents are capable of accomplishing such an achievement, particularly a father who sings in a monotone or is not musically inclined. Rather than push individuals to conform to a certain procedure, we would do better to help them personalize their approach to the family altar, offering various options to them.

Make family devotions regular. To be sure, a regular time and place is necessary for this practice. Individual families should be encouraged to give thought to determine what is the best time of day for them. And while the parents need to apply discipline and leadership, they should be instructed to avoid heaping oppressive guilt on themselves if they miss devotions from time to time.

Make family devotions simple. Simplicity is the key; otherwise, the day-by-day demand for creativity will make it impractical to maintain daily devotions. But simplicity does not preclude planning. Someone will need to decide what Bible storybook to read, what cassette to play, or what Bible passage to choose for the weeks to come. Otherwise, too much time will be absorbed in deciding on the spot what to do.

Make family devotions short. This may be the one principle that keeps the experience away from the city limits of "Dullsville." Sharing God's Word and experiencing worship together is the heart of the matter; the length of time spent will not replace the quality of the devotional sharing.

Allow for participation. Though it sounds simple, this principle is not easily applied. It may be great to keep seven-year-old George's interest level up to have him read the passage; but it will do little for his teen-age brother's attention if he has to listen to his young brother stumble along.

Also, a mistake can be made in demanding the wrong kind of participation from an individual. Asking questions of kids, for example, is generally a good practice. But if the answers don't come freely to questions that are too tough, the child ends up being embarassed, and thus sacrificed on the family altar.

221

Permit spontaneity. Granted, it is not easy to be spontaneous during a routine event. Spontaneity means we do something when we feel like it, when we have inner inspiration. And rarely does the inner state seem to cooperate with the outer schedule. Yet, we can provoke some personal thoughts and sharing. After reading about the fruit of the Spirit, we might ask, "Which characteristics do we most see in each other's lives?" We can start with mom: Does she most exemplify love, joy, peace, longsuffering, etc.? Then we can do the same with each member of the family circle, lovingly affirming each one in this way. At times the Bible reading might be replaced by a mere question: "Shall we each share what we've been thinking about that relates to God?"

Following such principles could qualify daily family devotions for a major role in family nurture. But we can't be certain. Beset by difficulties lurking in modern family life and lacking solid biblical sanction, family devotions can hardly constitute the backbone of family nurture. An alternative, or in some cases an addition, has been suggested; it's called "family night."

FAMILY NIGHTS

Developed first by the Church of Jesus Christ of Latter-day Saints, the concept of family night has been adopted, in part, by evangelicals. Local churches have sometimes created printed guides for their congregations' families. One evangelical publisher, Gospel Light Publications, offers a one-night plan for each week in its monthly magazine, *Family Life Today.*

The term *family night* suggests that it is a periodic, not a daily, program. Other features distinguish it from the traditional family altar.

While the teaching of spiritual messages is included in the objectives of a family night, the purposes are much broader than that; they are encompassed by a rather total approach. The family sets aside one night a week to follow lessons outlined in an attractive manual. The manual provides games to enhance family unity. It conducts families through communication exercises and learning activities designed to develop skills and change attitudes. Using the hot seat, for example, is typical. A family member sits in a designated chair while other members communicate how they feel about him or her. Each takes a turn in the chair.

Permeating the whole approach of the family night is the attempt to solidify every family member's commitment to family life. The manual's suggestions are designed to produce worship and appreciation of God, going beyond a simple prayer time. In the lessons, which are geared even to the very young children, a typical activity might call for a list of everything a person "can think of that our Heavenly Father does to show that He loves His children."[10] Sharing the lists prompts an enriched time of prayer.

The Mormon church has called on its psychological, educational, and spiritual experts to put together and circulate a colorful, expensive annual—published since 1965 and called "Family Home Evenings." Gospel Light has offered for sale its useful "Family Night" curriculum since the early seventies. An extensive, scientific study of the effectiveness of each is lacking. A small-scale study of family-night materials by Richards suggests that part of their impact has been the generating of guilt. The manual lies unused on the coffee table for the great majority, who lack the discipline, motivation, or skill to use it. But a recent public account of the Mormon Family Home Evenings called this program the "most important and unique family program in the church,"[11] and the reputation for strong families in the Mormon church tends to support the report of the program's success.

However, like other suggested church-prompted programs, the family-night approach seems doomed to failure unless it is given priority and is integrated into the total life of the church. This the Mormon church does with fierce determination. The Latter-day Saints church supports the program with the full force of its philosophical and theological traditions. The LDS church conceives of marriage as a religious sacrament, and the family is viewed as an indissoluble unit, whose bonds will endure not only for all time, but for eternity. The responsibilities of parenthood are held to be sacred obligations to be given top priority in the life of every parent. Pamphlets tell fathers that "the most important work is within the walls of your home."[12] In actuality they foster a semipatriarchal family in which the authority of the father is not negotiable. The educational philosophy of the LDS church is equally firm: no church organization can supplant the parents in discharging their obligation to nurture their children.[13]

The support system for family night is quite extensive. The Mormon church actually prescribes a certain evening of the week, Monday, at which time denominational leaders do not allow the scheduling of any formal church activities. In addition, Sunday school programs include lessons on effective family living for both parents. Mothers receive additional instruction in the women's auxiliary of the church. And fathers get an additional reminder in the "Priesthood Lessons" presented each Sunday, which feature the family. As if this were not enough, each father is visited monthly by a *home-teaching companion,* who is charged with reporting to the bishop any problems found in the home. The church also focuses on future families by means of a special program for young married couples.

223

Family Nurture

From the preceding material it is clear that the LDS church considers the development and enrichment of family life to be a divine mission. Any evangelical church attempting to adopt a family-night strategy as an answer for family nurture should first consider the level of its commitment and count the cost of a support system to make it truly effective. That some evangelical congregations are doing so is increasingly evident. It seems also clear that some families are using family-night materials without the strong support of the church. But in general, the rule is clear: family nurture must be an integrated program. We will now turn to one church's attempt to integrate a family-nurture program with the church's ministry, examining the pain as well as the possibilities the church experienced.

A Combined Approach

The Peninsula Bible Church of Palo Alto, California, provides a case study of a church groping for a practical way to make the home central to family nurture. The experience of this church is instructive both for the program it has devised as well as the process it has gone through. The beginnings of the program, typical of many such endeavors, had a revolutionary character. Since then the program has gone through a number of phases.

In the first phase the church leaders declared that the decades of Sunday school ministry had been inadequate and then informed parents that it would no longer be responsible for the Christian education of their children. The staff of the church disbanded Sunday school and bused the children to the YMCA for classes on bicycle repairing and crafts during the Sunday morning hours. Parents could not accept this radical approach, and modifications were soon under way.

The next phase was a unique and strenuous effort possible only in a church with the dedication and resources available there. It combined a number of features:

1. A *printed handout* was made available to parents. It explained how the Sunday morning sermon passage could be taught to their children during the week.

2. An *intergenerational Sunday school class* was convened the following Sunday for parents and their elementary-school children. They viewed a puppet show based on the previous Sunday's sermon text.

3. A *family-cluster experience* followed the puppet presentation. Breaking the larger audience into clusters of three or four families, parents and children discussed together their experiences of having learned and having lived the Scripture passage of the past week.

This ambitious program was set aside after it underwent careful evaluation. The staff learned of at least two weaknesses in their approach.

1. Parents were threatened by the family-cluster experience because in it their home lives were being evaluated. The tendency was to focus on failures and weaknesses, resulting in a great deal of guilt feelings the parents had difficulty in handling.

2. Not all parents were capable of entering into the program—because of misunderstanding, disagreement with the approach, or immaturity. The staff now feels that such a program should be entirely voluntary, appealing to those who desire to participate in it.

Phase two did yield some positive results and has led the staff to several convictions. The whole program is worthwhile except for the cluster evaluation and should be launched again after the church is more fully prepared for it, and then the appeal should be made only to those who desire to be in the program. Second, they concluded that intergenerational learning is a unique and outstanding experience. Third, they are convinced that the church's prompting and assisting parents in family nurture has proved to be both possible and practical.

The present phase includes these features:

1. There are handouts to assist parents in communicating the sermon passage. Unique to this is the utilization of an expositional approach to children's Christian education since the sermons are not always topical or narrative, but usually follow an exegetical style.

2. There is a parents' class (on an elective basis) for those who desire to study with a view to teaching in the home. This has been changed to an anticipatory discussion of the coming week instead of an assessment of the past one.

3. Experimental groups in intergenerational learning have been continued, usually meeting on Sunday afternoons.

4. The staff is planning for the time when they will write a children's curriculum that will correspond to the parents' Sunday morning experience; in effect, it will be a totally unified curriculum that includes the sermon, Sunday school, and daily home life.

SUNDAY SCHOOL PLUS

For evangelical churches the most promising system for family nurture is contained in a Sunday school curriculum recently developed, *Sunday School Plus*.[14] It retains much of the traditional Sunday school hour features, with much added to it. It can be readily adopted by any evangelical church because it has two essential features. It is evangelical in its theology and it need not require radical change of the whole church. In fact, a church need not jettison its traditional programs for Sunday School Plus. It can be offered within the standard Sunday school as an alternative for those parents who volunteer to commit themselves to the home-related system.

The producers of this material state their underlying principles as necessary to making the home a nurture center:

1. Shift the primary focus for communication of faith-as-life from church agencies to the home.
2. Equip children's primary natural models, their parents, for effective communication of faith-as-life.
3. Shift the role of in-church staff from the traditional "teacher" role to that of model and friend.
4. Relate faith's belief-content in an organic, meaning-sharing pattern rather than transmit it merely as information to be believed.
5. Free children and adults to express affective as well as cognitive data in the various relationships [parent-child, leader-children, children-children].[15]

Carrying out these theoretical considerations with a heavy emphasis on relational and experience-oriented instructions, the curriculum design focuses on four objectives: (1) helping adults grow in areas they will be exploring with their children, (2) helping adults set realistic expectations for themselves and their children (the tendency is for parents to feel they must turn their children into instant spiritual giants), (3) helping adults see the way to talk meaningfully and informally about truths that are meaningful to children, and (4) gradually opening up communication between parents and children in order to free the data flow of inner states as well as ideas and demands.

To accomplish these objectives, the system has several coordinated elements:

System Elements—In-church. Sunday morning involves adult leaders with children in four kinds of learning. A number of learning activities are suggested in the *Teacher's Guide,* with direction for use in one- or two-hour sessions. The four "times" into which Sunday school is divided are (1) sharing love (activities promote peer relationships and communication), (2) understanding God's truth (children are guided to explore a concept that will be taught, such as *forgiveness*), (3) exploring God's book (when the group goes into the Bible to see the truth taught and/or illustrated), and (4) responding to God's truth (suggested activities guide the children to respond to God and suggest behavioral changes).

System Element—Discovery Packet. Each child takes home his own graded *Discovery Packet.* It features behavioral goals similar to those in secular education's individualized learning packets. The packet also prompts restatement and review of the Bible story and key verses. The learning activities in the packet offer a variety of options,

226

many of which include activities with the child's parents. A series of "How well have you learned?" questions at the end also involve the parents in the child's learning, initiating, and sharing in the home in a natural, easy way.

System Element—Parent's Guide. The *Parent's Sharing Guide* shows parents the way to share the meaning of the week's Bible truth with their children. Parents and children read the key Bible passage together. Questions to stimulate meaningful discussion of the passages are included, along with suggestions for activities that will help reinforce the Bible truth.[16]

Depending on a church's circumstances, it can incorporate Sunday School Plus into its Christian education program in one of three ways.

Whole-school approach. The entire Sunday school, first through sixth grades, adopts Sunday School Plus and provides a *Discovery Packet* for every child and a *Parent's Sharing Guide* for every home. A separate class for parents who have children in these grades can assure parents' understanding of the weekly Bible truth, as well as provide support for the children's home activities. Initial experimental studies show that there is a need for such a parents' class; just giving the *Parent's Guide* to them is not enough to fit them satisfactorily into the system.

Family-elective approach. Not requiring the overhaul of the whole Sunday school, Sunday School Plus in this plan is offered for families who want it. In this case parents meet during the Sunday school hour to study the same lessons as do the children, who constitute a class specially formed for them. The children's class could even be offered during church time.

Partial program. The Sunday school uses the Sunday School Plus approach and curriculum and sends a *Discovery Packet* home with each child. No attempt is made to involve parents or to provide the *Sharing Guide.* This final approach sometimes does involve the parents since the *Discovery Packet* includes parent-child activities. But this approach lacks the essential strength that Sunday School Plus offers—the training of parents. Teaching children in the home requires training of adults in the church.[17]

But it includes even more than this. Making the home a nurture center requires relating activities of church and home. In some churches the only educational system that is active is the church-oriented one. Sometimes both systems are operating, but they run parallel with one another. Parents are involved in a round of church activities that do little to support their home-nurturing attempts. Even though attempts at integration are meager, their results have been satisfying and powerful enough to make every effort worthwhile.

PART SEVEN

FAMILY-UNIT
MINISTRIES

18

Intergenerational
Experiences

For many ecclesiastical leaders, speaking of the church as family conjures up dreams as well as nightmares. Visions of small house churches, where intimacy is enhanced by the very smallness and informality of these house churches, encourage some leaders. Others scoff, claiming these dreamers are hallucinating. Some church leaders are tormented by the nightmarish, impossible task of dismantling their present church structures, which are held in place by huge mortgages to pay and large budgets to meet.

INTERGENERATIONAL GROUPS
Creating a familylike experience in our existing churches need not require a drastic change. All of the existing organization need not come tumbling down in order to give way to a new structure that fosters a familial pattern. A number of actual patterns already exist, and some of these have existed for years in various parts of the world.

Following the guidelines established earlier, a church needs to provide various seasonal, temporary, and occasional intergenerational experiences. But in addition, there should be an ongoing adult and youth small-group experience through which family dynamics can exist, particularly in churches too large for these dynamics to occur.

Outside of the U.S., the setting in which small-group interaction takes place has been called the "base community." For the past eighteen years these "small groups," the term used in the U.S., have existed in places as diversified as France, Italy, Latin America, Africa, and Quebec. The fostering of *koinonia* (community), in which Christians live out their lives of faith in small groups, is a phenomenon among Catholics as well as Protestants, nonevangelicals as well as evangelicals. Small groups have enough history for the informed to paint a realistic picture of their contribution.

A description of the movement must come first. These small groups can consist of seven or eight persons and as many as twenty families. Small groups are distinct from prayer groups, discussion groups, task groups, or committees. Community groups may include the functions of all of these other groups but include more than these functions. They involve most of the elements of the New Testament local church—of both its character and its task. Therefore, they are small groups concerned about service to, and evangelism of, the world; they possess a self-consciousness in regard to being Christ's kind of churches. Elements in them include interpersonal interfacing, closeness and belonging, celebration of life in Christ, encouragement for family units to participate and grow, worship, prayer, intercession, and study of God's Word. They are, therefore, minichurches. Herein is their strength. They are not designed just for one thing like instruction, business, or recreation. Rather, they are groups dedicated to all that is meant by being a church. Yet they do not replace the larger church body. They support the larger group as well as receive its support. Freedom from divisiveness or cliquishness is maintained by semiannual or annual rotation of members; or by the growth, division, or turnover within the groups themselves.

The Small Group's Contribution to the Family

Essentially, we are concerned here about the effect these groups have on family life. Speaking for the third-world groups, one writer describes what has occurred. In some cases, small groups develop such an importance and closeness that a virtual counterculture is created, a way of life that aids the family in the nurturing of its youth. The intimacy fostered in the groups also strengthens the internal interchange of the marriage and the family:

> The experience in many such groups is that when couples participate together they find new things which unite them. Their idealism, tarnished so easily in a skeptical world, is supported in the community (group) relation-

ships. Where intimacy is fostered, people generally emerge the winners. Many couples in base communities speak of having fallen in love once more and those outside the community note it . . . the base community seems to encourage couples to develop more intimacy in their marriage.[1]

Sometimes a group begins without the children, but it is a simple matter to bring the children into the warm circle of relationships after it has been fostered among the adults.

Some small groups are more pointed in their family life purpose than others are. Some groups take time to reflect on the way to train children or prepare them for marriage. In some cases, Bissonnette reports, the small group may take some responsibility for the immediate preparation for marriage of young adults who are in the group.[2]

The small group tends to satisfy some people's need for support as the extended family does. For this reason such communities are growing rapidly among Spanish-speaking people, whose residence in the big city has destroyed their extended-family life.

Some Small-Group Models

A large church in Los Angeles has developed a model small-group program called Chameshemes. The Christian Assembly Foursquare Church sponsors weekly groups of fifties to help the home become more Christlike and influential. After a year of experience with this approach the Minister of Education, Eloise Clarnon, says:

> The results have been most rewarding. Parents have begun to assume spiritual leadership for their children, and age groups are comfortable relating to others than their peers, and a closeness within these groups has brought support and strength to many.[3]

The Neighborhood Groups of the Elmbrook Church in Wisconsin have a similar approach. Elmbrook is a large church known for the expository ministry of its pastor. More than fifty groups were begun at the same time; they were placed strategically within neighborhoods surrounding this large church. The leaders intended the groups to be all that the local church should be, urging on them the development of caring and sharing within a context of the study of God's Word and of prayer. Not all of the groups have been successful in achieving this, choosing rather to be mere study or even lecture groups. But many have succeeded, and some have now become intergenerational, including regularly or periodically the children and youth of the involved adults.

Family Reunion is the name of a regular feature of Our Heritage Church in Scottsdale, Arizona. Leaders there recently realized that children were not part of the warm community life developed over the years among the adults. "Small group experiences, open sharing during Sunday services, and other relationship-building involvement had helped adults feel oneness of the Body," Richards reports. The leaders' solution was not to develop another departmentalized program for children. Family Reunion includes a potluck dinner at the church following a morning service in which children and youth share. In the educational wing, institutional furnishings have been replaced with living-room furniture, and the church family spends Sunday afternoons together. There are games and sports, a TV for the sports addicts, and short-term, elective seminars for those who want them.[4] Most important, there is the daylong experience of belonging to an extended family, a family to which children and young people, not just adults, really belong. As important as small groups are for the church and family, a complete description of their organization and administration does not appear within the bounds of this book, in part because they have been given such full treatment in the current literature on the church.

Our attention now turns to data that might be applied to the small intergenerational group, but which is pointedly educational—intergenerational learning experiences.

INTERGENERATIONAL LEARNING EXPERIENCES

"What did you like the most?" we asked the beaming, ten-year-old boy. "The funny song Bob had us sing," he replied without any hesitation at all. Our next question was to a nine-year-old girl: "What did you like the least?" Her reply also came quickly: "The Bible dramas." We followed with a question about results: "During what did you learn the most?" With a bit of embarrassment and a giggle she said, "The Bible dramas." When I talked with the elderly couple who were there without their own children, now grown and gone, they were mostly impressed by the children's vitality, enthusiasm, good behavior, and ability to interact warmly. "One of them really took to you," the lady reminded her husband. Taking cue, he responded, "Yes, he told me that he wanted to do this again; and if we did, he wanted to be in my group."

These are the varied comments of people after participating in their first intergenerational learning experience. Since the sixties, this type of education has become part of the North American church's life and ministry. Prompted in part by the anxiety and disappointment resulting from the generation gap and in part by the desire to discover unique individuals around us, the intergenerational learning experience satisfies many needs of contemporary individuals, even of the singles. For this reason it may become one of the most promising program elements of Christian-education and family-life ministries.

The Concept

As is true of any novel learning venture, however, the usual hazards and confusions are companion to the introduction of intergenerational education. One basic confusion is over the precise meaning of intergenerational education. It should be singled out of the many possible intergenerational experiences or ministries, which include recreation, worship, field trips, and other special activities. Intergenerational education does include learning, not just experiencing. An early starter in this field, George Koehler, distinguishes intergenerational ministry from intergenerational education, defining the latter as "a planned opportunity for nurture, discovery, or training."[5] Thus, it is planned learning.

To make the experience intergenerational, it must include two or more generations; but the term *generation* is by no means easily defined. The way graduate students fail to understand undergrads, a supreme court justice half-seriously concluded, we have a generation every four years. However, for purposes of definition intergenerational ministry refers to two or more generations out of five different age-groups: children (from birth to twelve), youth (thirteen to twenty-four), young adults (twenty-five to thirty-nine), middle adult (forty to retirement age), and older adult (retirement and upward).

And there is a third distinction: these learning events should include interaction. If several generations view a film, they are not really participating in an intergenerational event; but if intergenerational discussion follows the film, the activity would be an intergenerational one.

The Goals

Intergenerational education has some basic objectives that are similar to those of other learning contexts. Sometimes the learning may be specifically *content* centered, such as learning about biblical concepts of death. If the learning is in the *affective* domain, the goal might be to shape values and attitudes. For example: the goal might be to instill a Christian attitude toward death. Training, too, can be a goal since interpersonal skills, creative Bible study, and serving can be effectively developed in the intergenerational context. At times the goals may be family oriented—when dealing with intimate communication or handling problems or conflict. But learning goals will not always be family related.

The value of intergenerational education is located in the process itself, which becomes both the means of learning and the occasion of gaining certain learning by-products. Of course, the novel aspect of the process is the intermingling of generations.

Since discussion of the value of intergenerational education may prove to be too abstract without a more complete description of the process, let's look at a typical intergenerational event prior to appraising its benefits.

A Typical Intergenerational Event

To assist you in your imagination, I'll invite you to a recent demonstration intergenerational experience I conducted for pastors in our Doctor of Ministry program.

You arrive in the evening at Trinity Evangelical Divinity School with a bit of apprehension, because all you know are the directions to the campus and the fact that you volunteered for an intergenerational learning experience. A friendly man greets you at the door and warmly converses with you as he takes you to a table, at which some children and adults are making something from construction paper. You, too, are asked to make a name tag with your name on it and also to write on it or cut it out to display a favorite animal or interest. While you are printing your name, someone explains he is pinning a picture of an animal on your back as part of a mixer game. You are to ask questions that require merely a yes or no answer in an attempt to discover "your animal." As you wander around, you ask questions and are asked questions. The children's excitement is a bit contagious, you think; but you also notice some apprehension on some of the adults' faces.

You also observe that the room is a bit different than you had expected for a "learning" experience. The walls of the carpeted room are decorated with posters. Only a few chairs and a couple of tables around the edge occupy the room, along with four leaders and the participants. These include eight or so children, a couple of teenagers, one bearded college student, eight or so adults of mixed ages, and a couple of "seasoned citizens." Someone calls you to the center of the "bare room," inviting everyone to sit on the floor and form a large circle while he strums on a ukulele.

After he encourages you to relax and enjoy yourself, he leads you in a ridiculous rendition of "When the Saints Go Marching In." It is obviously for fun, and especially the children know that; everyone enters in.

Another man leads all of you in an old game that you may know as "Zip and Zap." Inside the center of the circle the one who is "it" points to someone, says "right" or "left," and counts rapidly to five while the surprised person attempts to blurt out the newly learned name of the person to his immediate right or left. If "it" says "scramble," everyone moves to another position. You are pleased to find that after ten minutes of this you have talked to a dozen or more of the thirty people and that you remember the names of quite a few. And a number of children now seem to remember your name easily. When the nine-year-old girl suffering from cerebral palsy becomes "it" and struggles to stand in the center of the floor with the assistance of her father, there are numerous sympathetic smiles, and you feel a warmth stealing into your heart.

Another fun song immediately follows the game; this time it is an eleven-year-old boy leading rather effectively in a nonsense-syllable song, "Enimenedesiminy, ohwallawallowmeni." So far it's been a fast-moving, lively evening, and you feel caught up and involved with the group.

The theme of the evening is introduced by the song leader as "Christian Joy," and he leads you in two brief songs about it. "Now it's time to get to know each other a little better," another man announces. After you and the others form two concentric circles, you march in different directions while the ukulele player is singing a Jewish song of joy. When he stops singing, all of you in the circles stop marching; you happen to face off with a six-year-old girl and you tell each other what the leader suggests—one food that each of you most dislikes. Her answer comes quickly: "Spinach." The music starts and you're off again; you stop when it does, this time to share the most joyful time of the past week with a pleasant-looking woman who is the mother of four of the children. Before it is over, you have shared with four other persons, but the exchanges with the children linger most in your mind.

All of you form one circle again—this time for instructions about the evening's main event. You will be divided into three groups, each producing a drama of a biblical event that portrays joy. Your aim is to share with each other what the Bible describes as Christian joy. Each of the three groups is given a passage of Scripture and two tasks: one task is to produce a drama describing joy, and the other is to make a banner that colorfully shows what joy is. Your group is working on the imprisonment of Paul and Silas, who sang hymns at midnight. You don't yet know that the other two groups are working on the discovery of Christ's resurrection at the tomb and the reuniting of Joseph with his brothers and father.

When all groups are ready for the drama, and when the banners have been created with large, white sheets of paper and felt-tip pens, each group in turn presents their drama and tapes their banner to the

236

wall. Your group has created a prison from a clever stacking of folding chairs. One folding chair falls away when the earthquake occurs, leaving an open door. You're a bit surprised by the creative way all of the groups perform, each having had only fifteen minutes to read the passage, decide on the approach, and plan the drama. Some discussion follows each drama, and the groups' energetic actions and words reveal that they are having a lot of fun learning about joy.

Now your smaller group is split into two, as are the other groups, so that there are six small intergenerational groups. A large empty punch bowl is brought into the center of the room while each group receives a large can of juice with a blank label on the can. Each group is asked to write on the label one ingredient of Christian joy, attempting to answer the question "How can Christians rejoice always?" Someone holds up a large sign that says, "Rejoice in the Lord always" (Phil. 4:4). After some discussion one of the children in your group prints "PRAY" on your can of juice. Then the "chef" calls each group in turn to send their can of juice to the center while one of the men writes on the wall under the word *"RECIPE"* what is on each label. When each can of differently colored juice has been poured into the punch bowl, it is full of the "joy drink."

But before you drink any of it, you are part of a large circle again, this time holding hands. You sing with the others, "The Joy of the Lord is Our Strength." Then the leader asks your group (one of three who performed the dramas) to step into the center of the circle. You hold hands while the others sing to your group, "The Joy of the Lord is Your Strength." The song is sung in this manner two more times, one time each for the other two groups.

You form one circle again for closing prayers. The prayers begin with "God, I thank you for . . ."; "God, I praise you for . . ."; or "God, I feel good about . . ." The first to pray is a boy about eleven: "I really feel good about the joy we had tonight and that we all could get together and learn about you, Jesus." You learn later that the adults were surprised how quickly the children prayed in this circle. Adults also prayed.

All are now invited to surround the huge tray of cookies being brought in to be eaten along with the "joy drink" all of you have created. You and the others linger together for twenty to thirty minutes, seemingly reluctant to leave the warm and cheerful atmosphere.

Benefits of Intergenerational Education

What, then, are the benefits of intergenerational education? Learning? Certainly. But not in a traditional classroom manner. Nor is the learning always cognitive, that is, the learning of a new idea or concept. Sometimes there is a new awareness of a doctrine or a new sense of a value, and this is learning in the affective domain. Or the learning is concomitant, that is, the attitudes, ideas, and behavior acquired are sometimes distinct from the actual subject discussed. Adults often say, "I didn't learn anything new." Then they go on to say that they did "learn" something about a particular child, or that they were surprised to see that children would pray so readily or participate so eagerly. While the learning of "content" is also happening in these settings, it is the new awareness, understanding, empathy, and ability to relate to other generations that is most prominent.

Real cognitive learning can also be present, though the method and source of learning are often different than those of normal cognitive learning. Sometimes there are inductive studies or brief lectures; but the teaching-learning is not always directly done from open Bibles. Biblical and practical truth is released from within the individuals, who by their knowledge of the Scriptures and by their Spirit-filled lives are themselves the source of knowledge and wisdom. Learning in the form of nurture is carried on through exposure to adult models.

Affirmation. The acceptance of individuals across the generations is a rewarding outcome. Children are seen as persons to be talked *with* and not merely *to.* The activities themselves provide avenues of support and caring for all present, including the elderly and singles. At the conclusion, the prayer of thanksgiving I have heard most often is "Thank you, God, for each other."

Development of family ties. Whether a particular subject of an intergenerational experience is related to the family or not, the relationships for family participants are strengthened. For one thing, the whole experience is done as a model family. Sensitivity, joy, sharing, and caring all characterize the group in a way that makes us want to practice these qualities in our own families. And individual families within the group have opportunities for meaningful interaction during the sessions that spills over into their home lives.

Understanding. The discovery of one another in the intergenerational setting produces new understanding of the needs, desires, traits, feelings, and anxieties of other generations. Participants usually come away with a new awareness of the extent to which they have been segregated from those outside their own age brackets. Certainly the differences become more apparent, but also less threatening and mysterious.

Joy. Initial enjoyment seems to come from the fact that intergenerational learning is different from cognitive learning; this learning offers a change of pace. But joy also results from the variety of discoveries that occurs as well as from the new dimension of relationships that develops. Spontaneous expressions, kidding, and individual antics mixed with the gleeful responses of the children make it a time of great fun. And the worship and praise that result produce a time of great joy.

We don't have information about these benefits from scientific study of the intergenerational movement since that kind of research has not been done yet. However, the benefits are real, as those of us who have been involved have experienced and have seen. And on this basis we can testify that the enthusiasm level is high. George Koehler has even seen a "new sense of life and unity in the whole congregation" as a by-product of intergenerational education.[6]

But some have concluded that intergenerational experiences require too much effort to initiate or to continue. Difficulties may arise both from the traits of the program and the nature of the participants. It is true that these events take some specialized and extensive planning. Most of the format and methodology has to be developed by those familiar with the discovery educational process. But with the growing reservoir of plans and programs for intergenerational learning, these difficulties will be a less formidable barrier than they have been up to now.

Hazards of Intergenerational Education

Adults may not understand the process. In evangelical churches the understanding of the process of learning in intergenerational education may be the greatest hurdle, since learning is usually viewed as receiving truth or insights in a transmissive manner. Adults may be impatient when the biblical input is not always heavy and direct; but this problem can be overcome by giving them assurances that this is only one form of Christian education. Adults soon discover for themselves that there are different dimensions and methods of learning.

One generation may dominate the discussion. At times the adults may dominate by thoughtlessly speaking over the heads of the children. Or else the adults may feel the children's presence too keenly and thus speak down to them, condescendingly. Often adults have not learned to talk with children. But healthy, meaningful intergenerational communication is a goal of these sessions, not actually a prerequisite. Therefore, the example and guidance of the leaders soon overcome these initial inadequacies. Without a doubt, the most exciting by-product of intergenerational education is contributing to bridging the generation gaps in both church and home.

The wide range of needs may not be met. The strength of the intergenerational experiences, the generation differences, is also its weakness. Formulating a curriculum that appeals to the wide range of

239

interests, knowledge, needs, and behaviors is quite a challenge. In this situation it is easy to slip into planning too narrowly for one age-group and thus miss those in other age-groups. Perhaps the only solution to this weakness is to be found in limiting the use of these experiences in the total church ministry. Intergenerational learning is not intended to replace age-level education, but these experiences can fit into the larger church ministry in a number of ways.

Programing Intergenerational Education

In the most comprehensive and detailed guide to intergenerational learning yet written, George Koehler recommends primarily short-term and voluntary settings. He warns against making this an ongoing educational effort because that is better left to age-level programs. Ninety percent of intergenerational education takes place in elective, short-term situations. For example, an elective, six-week Sunday morning class or a special four weeks of Sunday evening sessions can be offered to those interested. Sometimes only two generations might be involved, as in a parent-teen Sunday school class in which a book of Scripture or a family-related subject such as communication is studied. Imagine, too, the benefits for parents and elementary school children who volunteer for a ten-week intergenerational Sunday school class.

Inserting intergenerational learning into the regular existing programs of the church on a short-term basis is also a feasible option. I know of several churches that have divided the whole Sunday school into intergenerational learning groups for one month. The same could be done for just two generations—youth and parents or children and parents. Making some of the holiday sessions times of intergenerational celebrations is becoming a common practice. Easter, Thanksgiving, and Christmas intergenerational curriculum is becoming readily available.

After gaining some experience in intergenerational education, a church could build a regular option into its total program. Koehler mentions a weekly, Wednesday evening, supper meeting that includes learning and fellowship for all ages as one example and a monthly Sunday evening fellowship as another.

Devising an Intergenerational Event

As in other educational ministries, there are three options open to the planner: select and use a ready-made event from among available printed resources, select a program and adapt it to your situation, or devise your own. The more personalized element of the last two offers more certainty of being relevant to your situation. But they also call for more creativity and experience than the first option does. Drawing on some resources, an inexperienced person can succeed by applying some principles and following the planning steps.

Determine the goals. Because goals give birth to theme and methods, the formulation of objectives must be first. Naturally you begin with the formulation of general goals for the series of sessions. These goals are based on the needs of your congregation in general and the individuals to be involved in the intergenerational experiences and will comply with the potential value of these experiences. For example, an overall goal might be to produce more understanding between adults and teens. Or it might be a family-related goal—to develop communication skills between family members. The goal might be content oriented; for example, it might be to understand the nature of the church as a family.

Individual sessions have two types of goals. The first is the primary goal of the session, which is related to the main event. This goal is primary in the sense that it is the main announced intention of the session. For example, it might be to become more aware of the sovereignty of God in life, or to understand more fully the concept of grace (both cognitive goals), or else to improve our ability to affirm others (affective goal).

Most sessions include more than one objective. Particularly relevant to intergenerational events is a secondary goal, which is related to the anticipated concomitant learning. Along with the primary goal, for example, which is to understand the sovereignty of God in life, the occasion may have this outcome to consider in planning: that the teens and adults understand each other's viewpoints. Another secondary goal could be that the participants get to know each other in more depth, or that the group experience worship.

Incorporating the possible objectives in both of these categories, the list of objectives for the "Joy" session described earlier provides a sample. The goals for the participants in this session are the following:

1. Be able to state elements of Christian joy and to describe ways to maintain it (primary learning aim)
2. Be able to describe some others in the group and state their names
3. Have an enjoyable time so that they will say so when they are asked
4. Feel a closeness to some others from other generations and manifest this in statement or action
5. Realize that the relationships and the closeness to God and others are conditions of joy

241

6. Gain understanding of the thinking and actions of other generations so that they will articulate and use this understanding later

7. Better understand intergenerational experiences so that they can state some of their purposes

Select the methods. Keeping in mind the two types of goals, plan first for the methods related to the primary goals. Certain principles dominate the selection. Methods should (1) provide for intergenerational interaction, (2) allow nonreaders to participate, (3) challenge adult thinking, (4) provide for physical movement between approximately ten-minute segments, (5) offer variety, (6) creatively involve the various senses, (7) make the experience enjoyable, (8) stimulate in-depth relationships, and (9) provoke interaction with God and His truth.

The dramatization we chose for the main event in our "Joy" session was one kind of drama form, one category among many. The drama category also includes role playing, skits, play reading, and pantomime. Discussion methods are another category, which include buzz groups, conversation, pair discussions, panel discussions, etc. Discussion techniques can be attached to some transmissive methods such as films, filmstrips, slides, cassettes, puppets, records, videocassettes, storytelling, or illustrated lecture. For intergenerational learning, discovery forms are best, embracing a whole range of creative activities: paraphrasing, drawing, poster or banner making, producing a puppet show, writing poetry or songs, playing a simulation game, or making collages.

Secondary goals are accomplished, in part, during the main event of the intergenerational experience. Our participants came to know more about each other, for example, when they were formulating their drama about joy. But activities can also be planned with concomitant goals in mind. When a person tried to guess what the picture of the animal pinned on his back was, it facilitated the knowing of others, intergenerational contact, and having fun. The musical circles game was also intended to provoke productive relationships, as was the "Zip and Zap" mixer. These techniques can be planned to take place either before or after the main event and can usually be related to the main theme as well. Some activities are related to developing the Godward relationship: singing, choral reading, praying, poetry writing, and sharing praise verbally or in writing or in art form (posters or banners). Strategies that relate the individuals and the generations to each other consist of such methods as one-to-one sharing, small-group sharing, interviewing, using questionnaires, agree-or-disagree statements, completing sentences, circular response, name-tag making, eating together, wishing and dreaming, making and sharing of gifts, verbally sharing feelings, and personal experiences and concerns.

Keep in mind that normally the intergenerational session should involve people as they arrive so that there is no time for inactive boredom or awkwardness. A schedule for an event might look like this plan for a three-hour-long Thanksgiving celebration devised by Trudy Vander Haar:

Name-tag making (trace hands and turn over for turkey)
Games
Fun songs. Action-oriented such as "I Wiggle My Thumbs Like This"
Bible study dramatizations: Small groups prepare and perform dramatizations of "Ten Lepers" (Luke 17:11–19) and "The Feast of Booths" (Lev. 23:33–44; Neh. 8:13–18; and Deut. 16:13–15)
Brief discussion of gratitude
Midafternoon break
Making of Thanksgiving collages (family groups, singles, and mixed groups)
Sharing of collages
Sandwich supper
Spontaneous sharing (what each is thankful for) listed on newsprint
Singing of "For the Beauty of the Earth" as related to list of items
Carry-over activity: Remove name tags and write on back one thing to do for someone else to express gratitude for God's gifts. (Name tag now becomes a "helping hand" symbol.)[7]

Evaluate the session. The final step, evaluation, is somewhat different for intergenerational events than it is for most other events, since some of the children are not able to write. Other forms of expression than writing may be called for, such as having participants draw a smiling or an unhappy face to express their feelings. Leaders may circulate among the group afterward to get verbal responses to prepared questions. Keep in mind, too, that children may not be able to respond to general questions and may need some specific help. Specific questions are needed to test for achievement of the primary objective, such as these: "What did you learn?" or "Can you finish this statement: 'Joy is' and give three different answers"? or "From what activity did you learn the most?" The concomitant learning can be tested by specific inquiries as well: "What did you enjoy the most?" or "Name one person you came to know," or "How did you feel about the others in the group?" or "What would you change in the program and why?"

CONCLUSION

So far, reaction to the intergenerational learning is mixed. Because of its newness and uniqueness, some have been hurt or disappointed. But the excitement generated by most of those who are experiencing intergenerational learning suggests that it is part of the growing edge of evangelical Christian education.

SUGGESTED READING

Koehler, George E. *Learning Together: A Guide for Intergenerational Education in the Church.* Nashville: Discipleship Resources, 1977. Not a book of programs, it is the most comprehensive guide available for planning intergenerational events. Write to: Discipleship Resources, P.O. Box 840, Nashville, TN 27202.

Nutting, R. Ted. *Family Cluster Programs: Resources for Intergenerational Bible Study.* Valley Forge, Pa.: Judson, 1977. Programs for sessions centered around parables, dealing with interpersonal relationships.

Rogers, Sharee, and Rogers, Jack. *The Family Together: Inter-Generational Education in the Church School.* Los Angeles: Acton House, 1976.

Richards, Lawrence. *Sunday School Plus Curriculum.* Devised for a home-related Sunday school session, these lessons can easily be suited to intergenerational groups. Write to: Sunday School Plus, 1266 Woodingham Drive, East Lansing, MI 48823.

Gospel Light Publications. *Living Word Curriculum.* For all age-groups, this Sunday school literature has possibilities for intergenerational adaptation. Address: P.O. Box 1591, Glendale, CA 91204.

19

Family
Clusters

Margaret Sawin felt hopeless about the task of Christian education after completing her dissertation for her Ph.D. from the University of Maryland. Using an Edwards Preference Scale, she had measured the maturity of Sunday school teachers against that of the average church layman. The laymen came out ahead; Sunday school teachers scored lower in crucial areas of maturity. We were exposing our children to those least prepared to help them, she concluded. She maintains that in order to have an effective ministry we need a model of Christian education that touches the entire family, and thus the children as well.

When she became the Teaching Minister at the First Baptist Church of Rochester, N.Y., in 1969, she initiated plans to develop such a model, called the "family cluster."

The concept makes a lot of sense when it is seen as a sort of artificial extended family. Nuclear families, cut off from relatives, lack what the extended unit could offer. For one thing, the isolated unit misses the support it needs to face its problems. Sawin maintains that the family is a minicommunity that must absorb many of the problems created by our fast-paced, growing society. And the family receives little help from that society in resolving problems and inner tensions unless they grow to crisis proportion. But, she suggests, instead of waiting for crises to develop, churches would do well to begin a preventive family-cluster program.

She rightly holds out "clustering" as a unique approach, defining a cluster as "a group of four or five complete family units who contract to meet together periodically over an extended period of time for shared learning experiences related to the questions, concerns and problems of their lives."[1]

Clustering is distinct from family therapy, though Sawin tends to lean heavily on the writings of family therapist Virginia Satir.[2] Designed to help the entire family communicate, make decisions, and work out internal squabbles, clustering is an educational effort through which the participating families hope to prevent major crises from occurring.

While family clustering is intergenerational, it is also markedly distinct from mere intergenerational learning. One major difference is that family clustering requires whole family units, though the unit may be a whole nuclear family, a one-parent family, a single person, or a couple without children. All who are living together in a home are invited to the sessions as a unit, which would include infants or resident aunts or uncles. Family clustering requires a much more specialized approach than mere intergenerational experiences. Themes and goals arise out of the life of these units rather than from some specified biblical or practical curriculum. The substance of the clustering sessions is the stuff of the family life of those who attend.

GOALS OF FAMILY CLUSTER

Like the intergenerational groups, family clusters also have learning goals; but these goals are more closely related to the family units in family clusters than in intergenerational groups. *Support* and *mutuality* of the individual participants is a major objective, providing individuals with a broader base of people intimately concerned for them than is true in intergenerational groups. Members of the cluster are encouraged to help each other achieve individual goals. Intervention into the family system is also intended. "One family may say, 'Help us help each other feel good about ourselves,'" Sawin explains. "So after a particular exercise the others in the group may say, 'You're not helping so-and-so feel good about himself; you're putting him down.'" In this way the group offers outside feedback and gives support to family members to help them carry out what they say they want to do.[3]

Facilitating intergenerational relationships is another major objective of family clusters. Interaction is such that children can relate easily to adults, and adults to children. A statement often heard is this one: "We've enjoyed seeing relationships build between our children and other adults."

Another objective is to provide models. Families can model for each other aspects of their family systems in decision making, disciplining, interrelating, problem solving, etc. The implications of this goal are quite powerful, considering how such exposure to one another as families is almost completely absent in our society. We see what happens in the contrived family television series while knowing almost nothing about the goings-on in the homes immediately to the right or the left of us. The potential of this revelation is as therapeutic as it is threatening. One participant confessed, "Cluster gives us a chance to compare our style of living with other styles; we have become more confident as parents. I can see who I used to be and where I have grown."

Family clustering also proposes to develop perspective. Parents can gain perspective about their children through contact with other children and also through observing other adults' perception of their children; likewise children can gain perspective about their parents. "Teenagers felt cluster provides an opportunity for them to realize in what ways their parents are unique; thereby allowing for more tolerance in the acceptance of parents' mores," reports Sawin.[4] Singles who are cut off from their nuclear families can gain new insights into their past family lives as well as clearer concepts of reality in regard to family life.

Sharing and discovery are not lacking. Through the joint experiences of clustering, youth and adults can share their concerns regarding the meaning of life amid a time of rapid social change and straying from aberration of traditional values. "Children can deal existentially with their real world experiences, using the group as a place to check out their experiences amid the group's support and value system."[5]

FEATURES OF FAMILY CLUSTER

After a decade of experimenting and ministering with the family-cluster model, those involved insist that any such effort is effective only if it embraces certain features.

Contracting

Contracting marks off family clusters from other intergenerational experiences. In a private session with the leader each family unit agrees to sign a contract, which commits the members of that family to active, regular, and qualitative participation in the cluster. If one member of the family opts not to participate, that is also written into the contract, and the nonparticipating member agrees to have this in

247

the record. Leaders report that one of the frequent misuses of the cluster model is the failure to use the contract mode, since a high degree of commitment is necessary for active involvement and success. Once each family agrees to its contract, the whole cluster of family units then draws up a group contract during the first few meetings that they have.

Lengthy, Regular, Short-Term Meetings

Clustering is a weekly event that requires several hours of an evening; the event includes a potluck supper before the learning activities begin. Clusters meet for about twelve weeks, after which they may decide to continue for another period of time.

Experiential Education

Family clustering draws from the current educational philosophy known as *experiential education.* The core of this concept is sometimes referred to as *phenomenologizing.* It is built on the existential concept that the experiences of human existence are valuable and that life changes result from learning from these experiences. Disciplined reflection applied to experience is thus the means of change.

The family cluster draws upon two types of experience: situational and structural. Situational experiences are those that happen within the bounds of the participating families during the week; these comprise some of the substance for group discussion and reflection. Experiences labeled structural are those contrived by the cluster leader. After living this kind of experience together, the group is led to reflect on it; this provides insight and perspective as well as developing the skills involved in phenomenologizing. Because this is so crucial to family clustering, I am including Margaret Sawin's procedural guidelines for the experiential educator. These guidelines will portray the concept of and procedure for phenomenologizing.

THE ROLE OF THE EXPERIENTIAL EDUCATOR

The Role of the Experiential Educator is to stop the event. (This is never easy since most people are conditioned to go on experiencing—to dismiss the event as unimportant.)

1. *Identifying*—selecting a specific portion of an experience to be recalled. Questions might be: What really happened? To whom? How? The aim is to be concrete and specific, e.g., "When you said. . . ." and "When I did. . . ." and "I felt. . . ."

2. *Analyzing*—moving beyond the first date to deepen the group's understanding of the chosen date; looking at the nature of the event itself. Questions might be: What was helpful? What hindered or blocked the process? How were you affected by this experience?

248

3. *Generalizing*—moving into a possible future situation with questions: What will I do differently another time? What learning can I extract that I can transfer to new behavior? This process is called *E I A G*-ing: *E*xperiencing—*I*dentifying—*A*nalyzing—*G*eneralizing.

In Family Cluster Education:

1. The leader attempts to set an *experience* in which all ages of family members can participate. Therefore, you utilize many techniques and experiences often thought of as child-centered but which really are experience-centered: role-playing, clay modeling, finger painting, simulation games, collage making, form-model building, fantasizing, questionnaire-responding, interviewing, etc. If experiences are real and authentic, most people will respond and have feelings in response that become part of the learning experiences in the group. It is helpful for the leader to move around, observe forms of body behavior, check who is speaking—controlling whom, check lack of response, move in to facilitate people to "do" comfortably, etc.

2. The leader leads the group in *Identifying* quickly, and children will usually "hang in there" when the experience has been real enough and meaningful enough for them. Sometimes the leader needs to help children "zero in" on what they would recall rather than leave it to the adults, as different age level people see the experience in different ways. People also have to be helped to learn how to talk about their feelings . . . to acknowledge their feelings.

3. The leader allows children the freedom to leave the group if it gets too "heavy," too talkative, too discussion-oriented at the *analyzing* point. Many times this is where parents begin to get insights, and they will often want to discuss them at more length. Preadolescents and young adolescents are often ready for this type of discussion in an adult setting when they are ready to understand more abstract ideas.

4. The leader can often help children *generalize* into their future hopes of utilizing this learning—as well as the adults—by sorting out the relevant ideas of children and reinforcing them. This is the point where the leader can sometimes repeat the child's contribution in adult language and use nonverbal language to communicate a child's learning to an adult.

We do not learn by words alone but by the kinds of behavior that are elicited from us and how significant people respond to those behaviors.[6]

At this point an illustration of a structured clustering experience further clarifies the cluster concept. An "affirmation experience" can easily be contrived for one evening. In family groups around tables members make actual gifts for one other person in their family. The person for whom the gift is made is chosen by picking a name from a bowl. The gift is made from construction paper, cloth, poker chips, string, and other materials brought by the leader. While the gift might eventually be a paper airplane or a work of art, it could also likely be a handwritten note that shares loving feelings. After completion, each gift is given with a statement about the reason it is being offered. By this means each individual affirms and is affirmed. That comprises the affirmation experience, but the learning only begins there. Then the family units or the small intergenerational groups or the whole cluster analyze the affirmation experience. What is it like to affirm? Is it hard to do? How does one feel? What is it like to be affirmed? How often should we affirm one another? Why should we affirm each other? At this point the leaders can draw from the Christian knowledge and values of the participants.

Skilled Leadership

The demands of family clustering brings one feature into sharp focus: it requires trained and experienced leadership. The interpersonal and experiential education skills usually are learned in apprenticeship fashion. Because of this, Family Clustering, Inc., operates two types of family clustering training events. The "workshop" is a thirty-hour program that includes actual demonstrations. But, it is not considered to be enough training, unless one already has considerable educational or group-therapy training. For sufficient training, Family Clustering recommends the week-long "Training Laboratory," which is a resident program that includes demonstration and apprenticeships with skilled leaders. While attending, participants' families can join as family clusters with other participants. Yet, there is still no guarantee that all persons-in-training will be ready to lead clusters at the close of the lab.

Need-oriented Planning

Although all educational efforts should ideally be related to persons' real needs, family clustering, with its experience-oriented education, is meticulously so. In fact, the sessions of the clusters are not planned long in advance as might be the case with intergenerational experiences. Each session grows out of the experience of the previous ones. Leaders utilize the data that comes from the accumulating clustering events to plan for each succeeding session. And a particular session is sometimes aimed at particular individuals or families. If the group or the leaders become aware of a certain situation in a family, they might devise an experience for the whole cluster that will meet the one particular need. For example, if one family member appears to be lacking affirmation, the cluster plans may call for an affirmation exercise in order both to meet the need for that one person and to call attention to the family's need to affirm that person. The same is true of the selection of themes for the sessions that will be held in response to questions raised by the group from week to week.

Group Control

Clustering is democratic in that the leaders consult the cluster about decisions to be made and subjects to be discussed. While leaders themselves are in charge of contriving the experiences from week to week, they lead the group in regular contract formulating, contract updating, and planning sessions. All of this is done in such a way that the children also have an influential role in decision making.

FUTURE OF FAMILY CLUSTER

Since it skirts the edge of family therapy and embraces so many unique features, family clustering deserves a close but careful look by evangelical churches. Family Clustering, Inc., has gathered a great deal of testimony and evaluation to confirm the benefits of clustering. The contribution is so great that some clusters have lasted for more than three years.[7]

The potential of the family cluster is closely tied to its objectives. We would be hard-pressed to find fault with the intention of the advocates of family clusters to overcome the isolation of the nuclear family. The family is much endangered by its own temptation to turn in upon itself. "The family may be a minisociety, but it must not be transformed into a minighetto," warns a religious educator who endorses the cluster concept.[8]

Enlarging the perspective of family members by the more-than-normal intimate sharing and exposure can generate insight as well as support. Parents can see their children better through contacts with other children; likewise, children may get a better view of their parents after exposure to other parents.

Providing a support system for nuclear family growth is also badly needed, whether it is provided by the cluster model or by other types of interfamily activity.

Those objectives and features of family cluster that render it so helpful are precisely those that make it difficult to conduct. Nuclear families too often enjoy their exclusive separateness from others. They often guard their privateness carefully because they feel threatened by exposure. The problem of ineffective self-disclosure, which the cluster intends to solve for those who might join, keeps them from joining in the first place. In addition, the careful training required for leadership makes the program too expensive and laborious for many.

The experiential education at the core of the cluster approach discourages some evangelicals who may be suspicious of the origins of experiential education or skeptical about its results. The threat involved in this affective type of involvement no doubt is the most difficult obstacle to overcome. Clustering requires an investment of emotion and total involvement not usually demanded in our usual passive, mentally oriented educational strategies.

Yet, these hindrances need not keep evangelicals from adopting this approach. The suspicion about experiential education can be overcome by clarifying that it is not an exclusive approach. Family clustering need not replace traditional Christian education strategies in other programs. Making it voluntary also somewhat nullifies this objection that clustering replaces traditional Christian education, as well as reduces the threat factor. Family members are not coaxed, but are carefully contracted to participate.

There is reason to believe that the training for leaders will be more readily available as the movement continues to spread to more churches and denominations. Family clustering will no doubt enjoy great success in the years to come.

20

Family
Camping

Some alleged family camps do not really qualify for the designation "family" or "camp." Housed in motellike accommodations, eating meals in a large dining-room setting, and meeting in large speaker-centered sessions, the people are in a conference more than a camp. When, as is sometimes true, parents, youth, and children are separated for recreation and study, the family orientation is nil. Arnold Swanson laments, "To the dismay of some who have gone to family camp, they have found the same fragmentation normally found in the church program."[1]

But genuine, church-sponsored family camping is flourishing, prompted, in part, by society's general craze for camping. There are many different forms of family camps; the form is determined by the camp leaders' philosophy and objectives and by the camp's facilities. In some cases family camping is limited to the provision for tent and camper spaces on the campgrounds. Families rent spaces and use facilities as they might do in commercial campgrounds. A program is not provided or, if it is, it consists of several daily churchlike sessions offered in the camp's chapel. On the other end of the spectrum are those family camps whose leaders engage in carefully planned and supervised living-learning experiences designed for marriage and family enrichment. In these camps relationships plumb depths far beyond what is afforded by the superficial recreational contact in other camps.

Whatever the form, family camping contributes to the contemporary family something not readily available in other settings.

Unique Values of Family Camping

Not everything about family camping is unique, however. Camping activities are similar to church activities; and the benefits can be the same. Individuals and families learn and respond to God's Word at camp as in church. Growth in relating takes place at camp as in intergenerational or cluster times on church grounds. Improvement of family-living skills can happen in camp as in a weekend family-enrichment conference in the church's educational wing.

But two distinct dimensions of camping make their mark in a powerful way, sometimes transforming enthusiasts for the movement into downright, beloved fanatics. The dimensions are wrapped up in this simple, five-word definition: "Camping is simply outdoor living."[2] First, camping offers natural surroundings for people caught up in a fast-paced, complex, concrete, steel-belted existence. In the out-of-doors most people shift gears; they downshift. Attitudes change with the slower pace. Perceptions are sharpened so that one sees and hears novel and welcome sights and sounds.

In that setting the second dimension makes a major spiritual impact. Family camping is a total living together, unlike the partial exposure we have to each other in our churches and homes. The outside environment moves us back to basics, to simple existence. Israel knew this experience during the Feast of Tabernacles. Though the Israelites didn't dwell in a metropolis, God moved them once a year into a simple living style in lean-tos for a week. In that setting the people related to God and to others while being unencumbered by life's routine, day-to-day pressures.

Leisure time in camping affords a kind of relating often lost in home life, contends Ed Branch, Jr.: "Going our separate ways to recreation and when home watching television is not conducive to a dynamic marriage relationship."[3]

Sad to say, not all camps exploit these dimensions. Werner Graendorf argues, "Camping has had to struggle to establish its identity as a total living experience rather than a closely structured conference-type program."[4] Graendorf agrees with Gene Getz in identifying the opposition in this struggle as another form of institutionalism, in this case the unwillingness of church leaders, at times, to encourage the development of camping's own unique potential.[5]

Certainly camping's unique dimensions should not cause us to confuse means and ends. Living together in the out-of-doors is a means, not an end. Growing in relationship to God, to His mission, and to others is the end; Christian education offers many means to this end. And we can capitalize on camping as a unique means.

Values for the Family

Sharing in fun together. Improving family-living skills need not be stressful. One family-living expert challenges the idea that working on family relationships has to be a serious and heavy encounter.[6] Sharing in light-hearted, simple, outdoor recreation can be a binding factor for those who truly enjoy it. The most rewarding discoveries of the morning search for wild flowers, animal tracks, or native birds may, after all, be unity and love.

Learning relational dynamics. The compressed-together living experiences of the family camp give members a better means of seeing the ways they are relating to each other. Relational problems are intensified; thus, they are brought into view and with clearer focus. A camping enthusiast recently told me of the painful times of his two-week, mobile-home trip with his family. Though it was not always easy, they had learned a great deal about their family interrelating that led to some sober reflection and insights.

Changing relational dynamics. It is quite evident that God works in this unique living experience to prompt actual changes in individuals. Responding to the Word of God while interacting with the others in the family in a closely united fashion, a family member may more easily change than in situations when the family is not present. Branch is insightful on this point: "A family camp keeps us with our family group so that one or two of us are not doing some changing that might come as an unpleasant shock to others."[7] In other settings individuals often make behavior changes they are not able to take back into their homes. Studies of growth groups shows this to be true of individual participants.[8] Family camp solves this problem because there the family unit is treated as a whole system.

Sharing with other generations. The intergenerational contacts are among the most valuable commodities of a properly designed family camp. A Christian education director told me that intergenerational contacts had come about naturally during the informal, weekend camping excursion of ten families from his church. In that atmosphere of an extended family, before the weekend was over, children were asking adults other than their parents to tie their shoes and take them boating. In such an atmosphere all of the benefits of intergenerational ministry are added to family camping, including the multiplied modeling of Christian maturity the youth and children are exposed to.

Increasing family identity. Strengthening the individual family-unit identity is important since one's place in the world is helped to be made certain and stable by a secure family identity. Family camping, because it is constructed around the family unit, whether it is a whole nuclear family or not, can make an impact toward reaching this objective.

Developing spiritual dynamics. While any area of family life can be the focus of a family camp, spiritual communication deserves first place. Teaching the family members to talk of God when they are sitting, walking, lying down, and rising up is natural to do in the context of nature (Deut. 6:7). God's gifts in the out-of-doors delight and mystify and provoke discussion both of the meaning of His gifts and of ourselves. Speaker-centered meetings can be replaced or supplemented by designing Bible study, prayer, and worship for the family unit, with the father leading. Joining several family units together also gives momentum to and instruction for family devotional life back home.

Providing interfamily contact. A present-day, powerful, centrifugal force is central to the family-camping surge. This force is the desire of families to relate to other families in more than superficial ways. Family camping fulfills this yearning, and relationships that endure for decades are built. Camp directors tell of families who have returned annually for more than twenty years to fellowship with their friends in the quest to overcome feelings of aloneness. Reunions held in the winter months are not uncommon. When these friends are from the same church group, the unions are strong. In this way family camping has become both a blessing and a threat to churches. Some families camp together regularly, neglecting their church's Sunday services, and are accused of being cliquish. This raises the question about the value of family camping to the church.

Value for the Church

An underlying principle of this book has been that strengthening the family strengthens the church. If you think of the church as the only unit with a divine right to exist, you could challenge that statement. Or you could also do so by embracing an inflated concept of the church as institution, the care and maintenance of which requires the sacrifice of family and other human relationships.

Those who see the church as family, welcome family camping as a means of strengthening the church. Christlike relational patterns learned at camp carry over to the church. The intergenerational and interfamily contacts build the unity of the whole body. This is happening for those churches that regularly sponsor their own family camps. It is also a reality for churches that regularly have eight or ten families attending the area's independent or denominational camp.[9]

In its relational dimension family camping is an expression of the meaning of Christ's church. John Rozeboom describes what happens in a camp setting:

> Just as the needs of every member of the immediate family become the needs of the entire family, so the needs of all the families in a camp setting become the needs of each family and each individual. The members of each family become in reality members one of another, and can experience ministering and being ministered to. They can witness to their belief, and in witnessing, belief and commitment become part of being.[10]

Evangelism in family camps is not uncommon. Some report significant outreach in their family camps, often accomplished through low-key, personal contacts with noncommitted family members brought along by their families. The joyful Christian atmosphere and the sharing of God's Word combine so that the one who witnesses communicates the gospel effectively.[11]

Gustafson maintains that the church denomination has much to gain through its family camps. The Lake Retreat Baptist Camp in Washington has become a center for all types of contact within the Baptist General Conference Northwest District. Families meet other Baptist families, reinforcing ties and broadening awareness. Denominational leaders interact with church families at camp, occasioning nonformal communication about denominational matters and issues. In fact, the objectives of their camp include being a "rallying point for the denomination."[12]

Value for the Camp

Family camping is not always an easy ministry to maintain. Bob Hilts of Hume Lake Christian Camps in California states: "When you try to minister to all age levels at one time you find that you hit one age level here, another one there, and the rest are kind of missed."[13] Some camp leaders also equate family camps with red ink since charges must be minimal in order to make camping affordable for families. But many others are enthusiastic, seeing family camps as a ministry with benefit to the whole camp program.[14] For one thing, family camping offers some firsthand communication between camp leaders and parents of campers who attend the youth weeks. Those contacts increase the bond between camp leaders and youth as well as between parents and youth. Furthermore, the family camp weeks have promotional value; kids attend the youth weeks as a result of exposure to the camp during family camp. And adults who learn firsthand about the camp during family camp sometimes become financial contributors to the camp. They also become supporters in other ways, often joining work crews and offering profitable suggestions. In fact, Gustafson's camp has a family work week, when families attend without cost in exchange for their daily work in the maintenance of buildings and grounds.

PHILOSOPHY OF FAMILY CAMPING

Since family camping is the blending of camping ministry and family ministry, the philosophies underlying these two ministries dictate the type of program that is planned. In a debate on camp philosophy the purists would identify themselves with either centralized or decentralized camping. In centralized camping the scheduled large group is central; the camp is speaker oriented and recreation dominated. Relationships with other campers and with nature are minimal. Those who argue for decentralized camping capitalize on these same ingredients, maintaining that the unique features of camp are the vital living relationships and creation.

Likewise, in family ministry, transmission of knowledge is the key ministry for some, while others stress experiential learning and development of skills. Thus, the terms *centralized* and *decentralized* could be applied to family ministry also. Large audiences hear authoritative lectures in the one approach (centralized), while small groups meet to support each other in experiential growth in the other approach (decentralized).

Applied to family camping, the spectrum of the two approaches in extreme would look like this:

Centralized	Decentralized
Family not in same quarters	Family in same quarters
Sports and supervised fun	Out-of-doors experiences
Planned; tightly scheduled	Informal; loosely scheduled
Planned by program directors	Planned by units
Preparing food and other camp duties done by staff	Preparing food and other duties done by campers
Large-group meetings; speaker	Small-group meetings; leader
Convenient facilities	More rugged facilities (nature)
Programed experiences	Life-related experiences

258

When one is deciding which philosophy to embrace, theology is helpful, but not decisive. Evangelicals have made a strong case for both sides. This is because the issue is not whether the Word of God is included in the program; the question is how. On the surface, the transmissive, centralized approach may appear to be more faithful to biblical proclamation than the decentralized approach. But the endorsement of one or the other approach is a practical matter rather than a theological one, since there are many biblically sanctioned ways of communicating Scripture. It is a question of effectiveness and total results. It is just as easy to make a case for a more effectual communication of God's Word in the small group, where there is a greater change for clarity of meaning and application than in the large group. Nor does a case for special revelation (truth via nature) settle the matter. It is obvious to the evangelical that the more certain sound comes from special revelation. But nature does make an impact that can be integrated with the scriptural word. The heavens declare—along with the prophet. The Christian might do well to be sensitive to both. And the decentralized advocate affirms, "Camp is where it can happen."

But, after all, the experienced Lloyd Mattson has observed, camps rarely exist in pure form. "Camp leaders are reasonable people," he assures us, "and while a person may feel more comfortable with a bias toward one position or the other, most often a blending of the two will be found."[15] What exists more often than not is what he calls the "eclectic approach." In this approach values of traditional (centralized) camping are obtained, while rewarding features from newer approaches (decentralized) are added. As director of educational services of the largest affiliation of camps, Christian Camping International, he writes, "This approach appears to be a basic trend in camping form."[16]

While the eclectic form may exist for camps in general, in family camping the two underlying philosophies give expression to different types of camps. As long as the objectives are scriptural, any one of these designs can contribute to family-life development. A description of the contemporary patterns show us how rich and exciting family camping can be.

Types of Family Camping

Resident-centralized Family Camp

Though this kind of camp is the more traditional type, many of the family camps that fall into this category have vital, ongoing programs. Conference grounds like Camp of the Woods in Speculator, New York, are usually filled to capacity. Lake Retreat Baptist Camp in Washington cannot accommodate all who want to register.

Essentially, the spiritual program revolves around platform speaking sessions. Families live together in tents, campers, or camp facilities. Some recreation is planned: talent nights, sports competition, and special events such as sand-castle building and kite-constructing contests. Families fare for themselves but can use the waterfront, the crafts room, and the sporting and natural facilities of the site. Little or no place is made for contrived learning experiences or skill-development exercises, let alone any cluster or small-group involvement. Meals and program are provided for families, who, the planners assume, don't want to be hassled on their "vacation with a purpose."

Personal care is sometimes given to the family in some camps that try to help the family as a unit. At Timber-Lee in Wisconsin a staff counselor assigned to each family orients them to the program and grounds and relates to them, observing them as a family. The counselor may get a chance to help them with their family relationships. Timber-Lee also gives the family high profile through a family parade that has family floats, through discussion of family-related films, and through family projects like "plant a family tree."

Gustafson of Lake Retreat is careful to gather a great deal of feedback during the family camp, and so the program changes year by year according to expressed family needs. For this reason one of the fathers is appointed the family-camp "dean." He is chosen from among the regular campers and is prepared for his role during the winter months. Everything is done to make the families feel it is their camp.

But generally the goals of these camps and conferences are individualized. Speakers center on evangelistic and Christian-growth themes, usually offering exposition of Scripture. Sometimes family living is a central theme.

Generally, the major obstacle in the pathway toward this kind of camp is facilities. Youth-oriented camps rarely have enough rooms to handle many family units. Separating the families into men's and women's cabins and dorms is unworkable, except for a weekend—when it may be tolerated but not enjoyed. The recent popularity of trailer and recreational-vehicle camping has given many camps a rather easy solution to the problem of lack of facilities and has done much to increase dramatically the number of family camps. The installation of electrical and even sewage hook-ups at camping spots has been a major trend. Special family-camp waterfronts, nature trails, and sporting facilities are also being installed.

Though this type of camp fails to use the more dynamic educational strategies, it is not sterile of dynamic results. Camp leaders and

Family Camping

family members attest to the dramatic changes that occur during family-camp weeks. The growing popularity of these camps indicate that something substantial is happening at them.

Resident-eclectic Family Camp

Drawn by contemporary, family-life, educational approaches, some camps are modifying their centralized camps. California's Mount Hermon attempts to put the family back together at camp. Though the program is carefully scheduled and planned for the campers, the family is generally the central unit for experiences. Dads, trained in special classes, lead the family devotions at breakfast. Families are involved in the projects and contests, such as the annual sand-building competition. In the evening sessions there are experiments with family clusters and intergenerational events. There families participate as families and not as individual spectators. A welcome change to the more traditional family camp, this type could easily be instituted at other camps with the assistance of some family-life educators.

Family-Enrichment Camping

A full-blown, family-enrichment program is now being offered at some camps. A campsite is an ideal setting for some of the marriage and family-enrichment programs discussed earlier in this book. Ed Branch, Jr., writes of the experience of the University of Alberta's Family Studies Department. Their family camp is designed around out-of-doors experiences and experiential education, particularly the Minnesota Couples Communication Program. His chapter in *Marriage and Family Enrichment* contains a complete description of the schedule and particulars.[17] Families are able to participate because the leaders use a long weekend. Beginning on a Friday evening, the sessions continue through the following Wednesday, making it necessary for family members to miss only a few days of work. As with other enrichment programs, we have yet to see evangelicals substantially committed to this kind of camp. But weekend marriage-encounter and family-enrichment programs are increasingly offered at evangelical campsites.

Family-Camporama Camping

"Camporama is for fellowship. Camporama is a rally of families, a weekend outing for families, with fun and enthusiasm." This is John Rozeboom's description of a camporama, a major type of camp, in his booklet, *Family Camping: Five Designs for Your Church.*[18] A camporama can take place at a church resident campsite or a park,

261

anyplace where a large group of families can camp together, usually for a weekend.

I concur with Rozeboom's assessment that "many churches are finding this one of the most exciting activities in their year's schedule."[19] The program is centralized; there is a campfire or a meeting, replete with speaker or film. Usually, families camp at their own sites, cooking meals for themselves. An adaptation can be made for a conference setting, in which families stay in cabins, and meals are served in a central dining hall. I have seen camps where both conditions occurred; cabins and dining room were there for those who wanted them, while some family units set up their own campsites. Rozeboom captures the spirit of the camporama in his description of the activities:

> On the second day, after the individual families have finished their worship, breakfast and tentsite chores, a variety of things begin to happen. A "process" begins to take place. A theme is identified, and the reason for being here emerges. Persons and families begin interacting. Relationships are established and tested. Involvement becomes the order of the day. Since time is short (about fifty hours total time), personal investment is concentrated, and there is sometimes an intensity about the camp not found in some other family camping styles.[20]

Small-group activities for learning, discovery, fellowship, and work are sometimes added to the program along with nature-oriented activities: nature hikes, bird-watching, ecology sessions, etc. These activities usually end up being intergenerational and thus contribute to the relational dimension.

When the camporama is carried over to Sunday, there can be a worship service to which all households are welcome and provided for. This possibility is making the camporama a popular idea in churches today, since it cultivates annually the total relationships the church body is trying to achieve on a daily basis.

Family-Cluster Camping

Cluster camping is distinguished from the camporama by size. A cluster camp includes only about ten family units. But it differs from the camporama in other respects as well. In a cluster camp the group establishes its own objectives, schedule, and program with the help of a *lead family*. Thus, the schedule tends to be much more free and relaxed than in any of the previous designs. Families are free to follow their own wishes at times, but it is generally agreed that the entire cluster of families will be involved together. A common meal, a trip to a nearby point of interest, a nature hike, a game, or a project might bring them all together. These decisions are made in whole-camp meetings early in the week or by delegated representatives of each family.[21]

Naturally, some decisions are made prior to the camp regarding the supply of camping equipment, provision of meals, etc. Sometimes the church can help with the renting or borrowing of equipment. The lead family needs some training ahead of time, and a skeletal schedule of activities needs to be announced.

A church might have four or five family-cluster camps in its annual schedule. Bill Dinkelman, Christian education director in a church of about three hundred in Illinois, started with one such camp one year and ended up with enough demand to hold three the next. The families stayed at the campsite through Sunday afternoon and held their own worship service, thus missing the one at their home church; this was something that was optional according to the local-church convictions and caused no friction.

Family-Colony Camping

If we were to cross the camporama and the cluster camp, the result would be something called the "family colony." Though the clusters are smaller than in a cluster camp, about sixteen people (or three or four families) in each cluster, it acts as a unit and those in the unit plan activities together. But the units, or clusters, attend an occasional experience that is planned for the entire camp. The program is described in *Family Camping: Five Designs* as focusing "on the activities of the three or four families as they study, experience, work, play and explore nature skills, campcraft skills and conservation."[22]

This design calls for more attention to out-of-doors living than the other designs do. It adds a dimension missed by the others, since in the family colony the families are actually forced into a living-together situation in which they share responsibilities for campcraft, cooking, and program planning. This small-group camping offers some true-life experiences of cooperation and even of conflict. Coupling this living arrangement with sessions on interpersonal relations during the entire-camp meetings creates a powerful educational and fellowship setting. The key to the success of this sensitive kind of camping is the lead family of each colony. Rozeboom maintains that the lead families should be selected wisely and trained carefully, preferably in a special lead-family training weekend, which he describes in detail.[23]

Family-Caravan Camping

As the name suggests, caravan camping links camping with travel. Families make excursions together, stopping at designated parks and campgrounds for evenings of study, sharing, and recreation. Caravan camping, like cluster camping, has sometimes been a threat to the local church. The regular weekend departure of a sizeable number of church families to travel and camp together or on their own has caused serious problems in some churches. Not only does this keep them from Sunday worship in their home church, it may also produce cliques in the church. And these, in turn, may cause division.

One leader says the church should face this threat by organizing caravan experiences under church auspices. Though there are problems, the values are worth the risk, he says.[24] Some creative programing can add a spiritual-growth dimension to the trip. Combining the family-caravan idea with a trip to some mission project or site can give the travel an additional purpose. Because caravan camping involves travel, some special precautions and particular long-range plans have to be made; *Family Camping: Five Designs* offers complete guidelines.

CONCLUSION

Some forces are militating against the family-camping movement —the energy crisis for one. But I believe the forces within the Christian family-camping movement will make it thrive. We can use campsites closer to home and use less expensive facilities, if necessary. Camping is not an escape from life; it provides an enrichment of life. Camping is as inexpensive or as uncomplicated as many of our activities. It is a back-to-basics movement—back to God's Word and to creation, to the true body of Christ, and to the family.

CONCLUSION

Conclusion:
Hopeful Reflections

I admit to moments of discouragement when I reflect on what I have written on the preceding pages. So much needs to be done. However, it's not the amount of work but rather the nature of the task that arouses my pessimism. Intergenerational and familylike interaction systems stand in sharp contrast to the institutionalized life of our traditional churches. And I fear that the relational problems that we see within our families are also to be found within our churches.

I have increasing hope for the adoption of the more easily accomplished programs of this text. Specialists will be invited for marriage and family conferences, sermons on the home will multiply, and Sunday-school electives will proliferate.

But I wonder about the more penetrating alterations and additions. Will family-centered nurture become an overwhelming passion instead of a neglected option? Will interaction between the generations become so commonplace that we will remember only with difficulty the time when local-church activities were such segregated affairs? Sometimes I awake early in the morning and wonder about these things.

Again, sometimes in the darkness of early morning I see in my imagination scenes of helplessness that sadden me:

Christian parents, lying awake and consoling one another, waiting in the silent darkness for the sound that will tell them that their alcoholic son has slammed the door and is once again safe at home for the night.

A mother, now single, anxiously trying to explain to her son about girls and sex, and wondering how he will possibly grow up to be the man she hopes he will become without a father to show him the way.

A single girl, staring out the window, praying for a place to belong, a place where she is accepted for who she is without being reminded of her singleness.

An elderly widow tearfully remembering the one she loved and held so intimately yesterday, hoping there will be someone just to talk to tomorrow.

A wife sitting alone in the early evening, wondering why her husband must work late again, and fearing the answer to the question, Why does he so rarely say "I love you" any more?

A Korean, Vietnamese, or Cambodian father in a cold, cramped city apartment instead of a warm village hut, looking out on dirty streets instead of fields, overwhelmed by the confusing problems of trying to raise four children in a place where he himself feels so much like a child.

The frantic seminarian, his voice haltingly making its way through the telephone receiver, reporting that his wife has left and asking, "Can I get her back?" "Can I handle this rejection?" "Can I ever become a minister?"

A dedicated middle-aged Christian woman, bewildered and confused, still hoping after three years of waiting that her husband of three decades will return.

But I dream, too, of churches that will be there to help. Churches that are realistic. Not where every pew is a family pew, where prayer meetings produce only superficial, pious utterings about what ought to be. Not where covered-dish suppers are shared only in family units, each proud of the dish mother has spent much of the day preparing. Not where during worship services we sit looking out the windows, pretending to be kept from all the nasty and perplexing social problems in the world.

Rather, I dream of churches where every pew is anybody's and where everyone feels like a member of a family, the family of God. Where prayer meetings are also praise sessions, celebrating the joys of being single as well as the joys of being married; where we plead tearfully for God to work in the life of the rebellious teen-ager whose parents are sitting next to us, for His love to touch the non-Christian husband of the woman in front of us, and for His power to prevail in the life of the problem drinker who is no longer among us; where we

267

join hands—widows, widowers, single parents, singles, husbands, wives, children, youth—and together thank God for each person, for each calling.

Where covered-dish suppers are intergenerational events for all, and there is gratitude for the Kentucky Fried Chicken brought by the working mother and the Dunkin' Doughnuts brought by the single persons.

Where we look at the world around us with eyes fully open to what is really there and quote God's word to Timothy: "God did not give us a spirit of timidity" (2 Tim. 1:7) and where we sing, "Be strong, we are not here to play, to dream, to drift; we have hard work to do and loads to lift, Fear not the struggle, face it; 'tis God's gift. Be strong, be strong."

This dream is already a reality in many places, and my optimistic side tells me this growth will continue. My hope is bolstered by three already-evident and growing commitments in our evangelical communities.

The first is our commitment to ideals. Of course, idealism, untempered by realism, can be mercilessly harmful. But, in all things, lofty goals are necessary if gains are to be made. Otherwise we settle for less, and mediocrity sets in. In Browning's words, "A man's reach should exceed his grasp."

Lowering our reach will only compound our problem, as in the case of the farmer who wanted to become an archer. Repeated practice with his bow and arrows did not reward him with the coveted bull's-eye. After hours of frustration, he finally shot an arrow into the side of the barn and then promptly drew a target around it.

In much the same way, guilt and frustration in family life often pressure us to settle for unworthy goals. Herbert Otto maintains that a large proportion of marriages and families "are functioning much below optimum despite the couple's love and dedication to each other."[1]

But evangelical faith is wonderfully relevant at this point. It summons us to more than mere existence. Salvation is not equivalent to survival. God's restored person is a new person, to whom God promises even here and now life as God intended it to be.

Therefore family enrichment is based on a theology of hope, not of despair. This hope calls us to an abundant life built on the values of love, justice, and honesty. Though some may fault us for it, it is the evangelical's stubborn commitment to biblical standards and ideals that most qualifies us for leadership in these enrichment ministries. This is the more so because while we hold up God's ideals we also hold out God's grace. Otherwise our ideals will condemn us and drive us to despair instead of guiding us to growth nurtured in the soil of forgiveness. This enables us to minister to people where they are without overlooking where they ought to be. The mechanism for coupling law and grace that Christians possess makes them uniquely suited to minister to stricken and struggling individuals and families.

In the second place, our commitment to the importance of the family also allays my pessimism. Unaffected by cultural changes and fluctuating social mores is the theological affirmation that God has created the family. As contaminated and problematic as this institution sometimes becomes, the evangelical will always resist the impulse to reject the family and will strive instead to heal and improve it.

In the latter days, says the apostle Paul, it will be the non-orthodox who will downplay the home and "forbid to marry" (1 Tim. 4:3). But the Christian will affirm with Paul in 1 Timothy 4:1–4 that marriage is that "which God created to be received with thanksgiving by those who believe and who know the truth. For everything God created is good."

This solid theological affirmation is undergirded by a growing appreciation of the sociological importance of the home. The one experience all humans have in common is that of family membership. Margaret Sawin forcefully states the case:

> Each human being is raised in some type of family, whether that experience is perceived as being positive or negative to the person involved. One's family or origin has the greatest impact on an individual life and provides the "road map" for participating in all other kinds of human experiences.[2]

This impact reverberates to other areas of society. "Each of us developed with a family system which is part of a larger neighborhood system, reflective of the wider cultural system," says Sawin. "It is comparable to a circle within circles which influence each other."[3] Thus, to neglect family life is in reality to neglect church, community, and even national life.

Among evangelical churches, awareness of the family's strategic role is expanding rapidly, if for no other reason than that the family's struggles and problems are spilling like raw sewage into the life of the congregation. Everywhere I see church leaders with a growing realization that the church is located nearest to the scene of the accident and has the responsibility to aid the victims.

Sawin reminds us that "the only organization in our society which has families is the church/synagogue."[4] If any institution needs to be concerned about the family, it is the church and the synagogue. She states: "The religious institution is the one which can take a positive and enriching look at the family and its impact on the society."[5] I am

269

encouraged by the fact that evangelical churches and seminaries are increasingly involved in taking that look.

Finally, I am also encouraged by the evangelical commitment to God's power. I find our churches refreshingly aware of Christ's words "Apart from me you can do nothing" (John 15:5). Bold faith will be required to keep us from becoming discouraged. Those who are already deeply involved in family-life ministry know that progress is always coupled with disappointment. Those who go forth with a hope of harvest in family ministry must be prepared to sow with weeping.

But to keep our ideals, we will have to keep the faith. Not that our faith should become a substitute for the hard work and effort that is needed. Our stance will be like that of Paul who "worked harder than all of them," but who was quick to add, "Yet not I, but the grace of God that was with me" (1 Cor. 15:10).

When another of God's servants, David, faced Goliath, he made clear the source of his confidence: "You come against me with sword and spear and javelin, but I come against you in the name of the LORD Almighty" (1 Sam. 17:45). But David's trust did not exclude wisdom and skill. He had rejected Saul's armor, not to demonstrate faith, but because he had never used this armor before. It would have required more faith to face Goliath with armor and sword than to do so with a sling. David took the best that he had, but his trust remained in his Lord.

Programs and agencies for family-life ministry are not to be trusted to work on their merits alone. They will need to be proposed and carried on with reliance on our redeeming God. The principles and programs of this book are offered in this spirit. And it is in this posture that I find hope.

APPENDIXES

1

Evaluation of Parenting Style

Directions: Circle the statements that seem to sound like things you might say to your children when they disagree, disobey, ask "Why," dawdle, make a mistake, etc. Be honest.

1. You need your sleep. To bed! No arguments!
2. Rules are rules. You're late to dinner. To bed without eating!
3. You're late again to dinner, tiger. How can we work this out?
4. Well, you can stay up this time. I know you like this program.
5. Work it out yourself. I'm busy.
6. I won't stand for your back talk. Apologize (or "Whack!")!
7. You can't get up because the kids wanted to stay out past ten o'clock? That's your problem. I've got to get to work.
8. Good grief! Can't you be more careful?
9. Hey, I wish I could let you stay up, but I don't feel good about you missing your sleep.
10. Late again, huh? Pass the meat, please.
11. When we both cool off, we'd better have a talk about this.
12. You're tired, aren't you? A paper route is a tough job. Sure, I'll take you around.
13. You didn't hear me call for dinner? Well, sit down; I don't want you eating cold food.
14. So you think I'm stupid, huh? That's your problem. Beat it.
15. You're really stuck, aren't you? Well, I'll bail you out this time, and then let's figure a better way for the future.
16. Please don't be angry with me; you're making a scene.
17. I don't have to give you reasons. Just do as I say.
18. No son of mine is going to goof off. You took the job. You get it done.
19. You say all the other girls are going to the party? I'd like to have more information before I say yes or no.
20. Jimmy, please try to hurry. Mommy will be late if we don't start soon.

Scoring Key: Statements 1, 2, 6, 17, 18 are in the authoritarian range. There is a tone of high control but not much support. Statements 5, 7, 8, 10, 14 are in the neglectful range: little or no control, little or no support; revealing an attitude of not caring, of immature lashing out at the child. Statements 4, 12, 13, 16, 20 are in the permissive range. There is low control, generally high support. The child senses he is in the driver's seat and can play the parent accordingly. Statements 3, 9, 11, 15, and 19 are in the authoritative range. There is a tone of control, but this is tempered with a feeling of support. The child knows that he has to work this out (i.e., shape up), but he also knows his parent loves him.

Note: No test of this kind is conclusive. When interpreting remarks like this, the tone of voice, the facial expression, and many other nonverbal communications have to be taken into account. A quiz like this is useful as a checkup or indicator to help you "hear yourself talking" to your children. If you feel comfortable with the idea, it might be interesting to go over the quiz with your children and see what they think!

A Program for Premarital Counseling
(For One Couple and a Counselor)

Prior to the first session administer the *Premarital Counseling Inventory* by Research Press and/or *Premarital Inventory* by Bess Associates.

Session I. Introduction and Discussion of Adjustment

Step 1. Discussion of couple's background to gain rapport
Step 2. Discussion of premarital counseling policies and schedule
  a. Explanation that counseling is no promise to preside at wedding
  b. Explanation of procedures and expectations
  c. Survey of importance of premarital conversations
  d. Presentation of schedule
Step 3. Presentation of assignments
    Give assignments in *Before You Say "I Do"* by Roberts and Wright.
    Give for general reading *Marriage Is What You Make It* by Popenoe and *Communication: Key to Your Marriage* by Wright.
Step 4. Discussion of adjustment areas
    Use results of one of the premarital inventories.
Step 5. Administration of the *Taylor-Johnson Temperament Analysis*

Session II. Discussion of biblical foundations and adjustment

Step 1. Discussion of biblical concepts related to the basis of marriage as commitment (Genesis 2), the nature of marriage as oneness (Genesis 2), and roles in marriage
Step 2. Discussion of adjustment matters
    Utilize further information from *Premarital Inventory.*
Step 3. Discussion of temperament adjustment
    Utilize results of *Taylor-Johnson Temperament Analysis.*
Step 4. Administration of the *Sex Knowledge Inventory*
Step 5. Presentation of assignments
    Assign section 12 in *Before You Say "I Do"* on sex relationship in marriage.
    Give *Intended for Pleasure* for reading (or cassettes) by Wheat.

Session III. Discussion of adjustment areas and sexual relationship

Step 1. Discussion of adjustment with individuals based on results of the *Taylor-Johnson Temperament Analysis*
Step 2. Revelation of results of inventory
    Allow one partner to see the results of *Sex Knowledge Inventory* while the other is in private discussion with you about matters best handled with one person at a time (Step 1).
    Scores are revealed only to the one who has taken the test.
Step 3. Further discussion of adjustment
    Utilize the *Taylor-Johnson Temperament Analysis*, the *Premarital Inventory*, and the substance of past sessions and couple's conversations outside the sessions.

Step 4. Discussion of sexual adjustment

Ask questions about their reading and about areas of weakness un-covered in *Sex Knowledge Inventory.*

Step 5. Presentation of assignment

Administer *Premarital Communication Inventory* by Family Life Publications

Further study in *Before You Say "I Do"*

For reading: *Why Am I Afraid to Tell You Who I Am?* by Powell or *After You've Said "I Do"* by Small

Session IV. Discussion of financial planning and wedding details

Step 1. Discussion about communication and adjustment

Utilizes results of past sessions, questions from reading, and results of *Premarital Communication Inventory.*

Step 2. Presentation and discussion of financial planning

Step 3. Discussion of wedding plans

a. Analyze the meaning of the wedding ceremony.

b. Emphasize the importance of making it a worship service.

c. Plan with the couple details of the rehearsal and wedding.

Step 4. Make tentative plans for session V.

Session V (after the marriage). Discussion about marriage adjustment and spiritual lives together.

Step 1. Discussion with the couple about their marital adjustment to date

Step 2. Discussion about the importance and practice of personal and family devotions

Step 3. With invited guests or with the couple alone, lead them in a dedication service establishing their relationship in their home.

Step 4. Establishment of open-door policy; assure couple you are available for future counseling and help if they wish.

NOTES

Introduction

[1]J. Richard Udry, *The Social Context of Marriage* (New York: Lippincott, 1974), p. 399.

[2]U.S. Department of Health and Human Services, *Healthy People: The Surgeon General's Report on Health Promotion and Disease Prevention* (Washington D.C.: Government Printing Office, 1979), p. 125.

[3]White House Conference on Families, *Families: Challenges and Responsibilities, Delegate Workbook* (Washington D.C.: Government Printing Office, n.d.), p. 64.

[4]In 1978, Census Bureau data revealed that 10 percent of all families include only one parent. The number of single-parent families has doubled since 1960. White House Conference on Families, *Families: Challenges and Responsibilities*, pp. 9, 29.

[5]National Conference of Catholic Bishops, *A Vision and Strategy* (Publications Office, U.S. Catholic Conference, 1978).

[6]Alvin Toffler, *The Third Wave* (New York: Morrow, 1980), p. 198.

[7]"The Changing American Family," *Chicago Tribune*, November 26, 1979, sec. 1, p. 12.

[8]Ibid.

1 / In Defense of Family Ministry

[1]Dwight H. Small, *Design for Christian Marriage* (Old Tappan, N.J.: Revell, 1959).

[2]Regina Wieman, *The Modern Family and the Church* (New York: Harper, 1937), p. 18.

[3]Nathan Ackerman, *Marriage: For and Against* (New York: Hart, 1972), p. 12.

[4]Hazen Werner, *Look at the Family Now* (New York: Abingdon, 1970), p. 19.

[5]Kenneth O. Gangel, *The Family First* (Minneapolis: His International Service, 1972).

[6]Howard Hendricks, *Heaven Help the Home* (Wheaton: Victor, 1973).

[7]Betty Yorburg, *Changing Families* (New York: Columbia University Press, 1973), p. 130.

[8]Edward Shorter, *The Making of the Modern Family* (New York: Basic, 1975), p. 150.

[9]David Cooper, *Death of the Family* (New York: Random, 1971).

[10]Michael Gordon, *The Nuclear Family in Crisis: The Search for an Alternative* (New York: Harper, 1972).

[11]"American Family Life," *Family Life Enrichment: Marriage and Family Resource Newsletter*, vol. 1, no. 2 (February 1975).

[12]Shorter, *Making of the Modern Family*, p. 277.

[13]Arthur J. Norton and Paul C. Glick, "Marital Instability: Past, Present and Future," *Journal of Social Issues* 32 (1976): 5–20.

[14]Paul C. Glick and Arthur J. Norton, "Perspectives on the Recent Upturn in Divorce and Remarriage," *Demography* 10 (1973): 301–14.

[15]Lyle Schaller, *The Impact of the Future* (Nashville: Abingdon, 1969), p. 44.

[16]Arlene and Jerome Skolnick, *Family in Transition* (Boston: Little, Brown, 1971), p. 3.

[17]Continental Congress on the Family, *Affirmation of the Family* (St. Louis, 1975).

[18]Vincent P. Barabla, "Hearing on American Families: Trends and Pressures," *Congressional Record* 199, no. 142 (Washington, D.C., September 26, 1973): 6–10.

[19]Urie Bronfenbrenner, Testimony Before the Senate Subcommittee on Children and Youth, Hearing on American Families, *Congressional Record* (September 26, 1973).

[20]J. Richard Udry, *The Social Context of Marriage* (Philadelphia: Lippincott, 1974), pp. 1–22.

[21]Shorter, *Making of the Modern Family,* p. 280.

[22]Letha and John Scanzoni, *Men, Women and Change: A Sociology of Marriage and the Family* (New York: McGraw-Hill, 1975), preface.

[23]Shorter, *Making of the Modern Family,* p. 79.

[24]David Yankelovich, *The New Morality: A Profile of the American Youth of the Seventies* (New York: McGraw-Hill, 1974), p. 59.

[25]Shorter, *Making of the Modern Family,* p. 119.

[26]Yorburg, *Changing Families,* p. 199.

[27]Ibid.

[28]Tim and Beverly LaHaye, *The Act of Marriage* (Grand Rapids: Zondervan, 1976).

[29]Jim Reapsome, *Youth Letter* (July 15, 1972).

[30]Continental Congress on the Family, *Affirmation.*

[31]Gordon, *Nuclear Family,* p. 11.

[32]Shorter, *Making of the Modern Family,* p. 280.

[33]Gordon, *Nuclear Family,* p. 13.

[34]Helen DeRosis, *Parent Power/Child Power* (New York: McGraw-Hill, 1974).

[35]Henry Biller and Dennis Meredith, *Father Power* (Garden City, N.Y.: Doubleday, 1975).

[36]Bert N. Adams, *The American Family* (Chicago: Markham, 1971), p. 134.

[37]Urie Bronfenbrenner, Hearing on American Families.

[38]Ibid., p. 9.

[39]Roy Fairchild and John Charles Wynn, *Families in the Church: A Protestant Survey* (New York: Association, 1961), p. 37.

[40]Bronfenbrenner, Hearing, p. 8.

[41]Shorter, *Making of the Modern Family,* p. 7.

[42]Ibid.

[43]Ibid., p. 148.

[44]Bronfenbrenner, Hearing, p. 9.

[45]White House Conference on Youth, *Profiles on Children,* pp. 78–79, 108, 179–80.

[46]Bronfenbrenner, Hearing, p. 9.

[47]Daniel Offer, *The Psychological World of the Teenager* (New York: Basic, 1969).

[48]John Charles Wynn, "The Home and Christian Education," in *Introduction to Christian Education,* ed. Marvin Taylor (Nashville: Abingdon, 1966), p. 293.

[49]Yorburg, *Changing Families,* p. 204.

[50]Larry Richards, "How the Church Can Help the Family Face the Future" (Plenary Session, St. Louis Continental Congress on the Family, 1975), p. 15.

[51]"Family Life Ministry," Paper of the Peninsula Bible Church, Palo Alto, California.

[52]Robert Lynn, *Protestant Strategies in Education* (New York: Association, 1964), p. 25.

[53]C. B. Eavey, *History of Christian Education* (Chicago: Moody, 1964), pp. 418–19.

[54]Wesner Fallaw, *The Modern Parent and the Teaching Church* (New York: Macmillan, 1947), pp. 44–45.

[55]Imogene McPherson, "Trends in Parent Education," *Religious Education,* 28 (1933): 67.

Notes

[56]"Christian Family Today" (Declaration of the International Council of Religious Education), 1940.

[57]Edward and Frances Simpson, "The Sunday School," in *Introduction to Evangelical Religious Education,* ed. J. Edward Hakes (Chicago: Moody, 1964), p. 299.

[58]Ted Ward, "The Influence of Secular Institutions on the Family" (Plenary Session, St. Louis Continental Congress on the Family, 1975), p. 4.

[59]Dean Kelley, *Why Conservative Churches are Growing* (New York: Harper, 1972).

[60]Lynn, *Protestant Strategies in Education,* p. 25.

[61]Ron Rose, "The Family Unit: Turn the Key—Open the Door," *Christian Bible Teacher* (May 1972): 188–89.

[62]Samuel Hamilton, International Conference on the Family, 1948, *Helping Families Through the Church,* ed. Oscar Feucht (1957), p. 100.

[63]Ward, "Influence of Secular Institutions," p. 6.

[64]Wynn, "Home and Christian Education," p. 292.

[65]Norman Wright, "The Church Building Families: Myth or Possibility" (Report, Talbot Theological Seminary, 1972).

[66]"American Family Life," in *Christian Marriage Enrichment,* Marriage and Family Resource Newsletter, newsletter 1, 2 (February 1975): 1.

[67]Larry Richards, "Greatest Need," in *Interchange* vol. 1, no. 5, p. 1.

[68]Julie Gorman, "Family Enrichment Through the Church" (Paper, Lake Ave. Congregational Church, Pasadena, Calif.), p. 1.

[69]Fairchild and Wynn, *Families in the Church,* p. 16.

[70]Wynn, "Home and Christian Education," p. 292.

[71]Richards, "How the Church Can Help," p. 14.

[72]*Wheat Ridge Newsletter* (Chicago: Wheat Ridge Foundation, Spring, 1979), p. 1; and telephone conversation with Richard Bennett, former Executive Director, Lutheran Social Services of Northwest Indiana.

[73]Donna Joy Newman, "Can Families Survive Our Fractured Life?" *Chicago Tribune* (November 2, 1975), sec. 5, p. 1.

[74]Frances E. Kobrin, "The Primary Individual and the Family: Changes in Living Arrangements in the United States Since 1940," *Journal of Marriage and the Family* 38, no. 2 (May 1976).

2 / Today's Family

[1]Larry Richards, "Developing Family Life Ministries," in *Family Life Education,* ed. Gil Peterson (Glen Ellyn, Ill.: Scripture Press Ministries, 1978), p. 39.

[2]Daniel Yankelovich, *The New Morality, A Profile of American Youth in the Seventies* (New York: McGraw-Hill, 1972), p. 88.

[3]J. Richard Udry, *The Social Context of Marriage* (New York: Lippincott, 1974), p. 16.

[4]R. W. Fairchild and John Charles Wynn, *Families in the Church: A Protestant Survey* (New York: Association, 1961), p. 15.

[5]William J. Goode, *World Revolution and Family Patterns* (New York: Free Press, 1963), pp. 6–7.

[6]Yankelovich, *New Morality,* p. 59.

[7]Letha and John Scanzoni, *Men, Women and Change: A Sociology of Marriage and Family* (New York: McGraw-Hill, 1975), pp. 135–97.

[8]Ibid., p. 154.

[9]Leslie Y. Rabkin, "The Institution of the Family Is Alive and Well," *Psychology Today* (February 1976), pp. 66–73.

[10]"The Changing Soviet Family," in *The Nuclear Family in Crisis: The Search for an Alternative,* ed. Michael Gordon (New York: Harper, 1972), pp. 119–42.

[11]Betty Yorburg, *The Changing Family* (New York: Columbia University Press, 1973), p. 191.

[12]Philippe Aries, "The Family, Prison of Love," *Psychology Today* 9, no. 3 (August 1975): 53–58.

[13]Michael Gordon, *The Nuclear Family in Crisis: The Search for an Alternative* (New York: Harper, 1972), p. 2.

[14]John Demons, *A Little Commonwealth* (New York: Oxford University Press, 1970), p. 124.

[15]Yorburg, *Changing Family,* p. 13.

[16]Marvin B. Sussman, "The Isolated Nuclear Family: Fact or Fiction?" *Social Problems* (Spring 1959), pp. 330–40.

[17]Yorburg, *Changing Family,* p. 110.

[18]Ibid., p. 16.

[19]Robert F. Winch, "Some Observations on Extended Families in the United States," in *Selected Studies in Marriage and the Family,* ed. Robert F. Winch and Graham B. Spanier, 4th ed. (New York: Holt, Rinehart and Winston, 1974), pp. 155–59.

[20]Frederick H. Stoller, "The Intimate Network of Families as a New Structure," in *The Family in Search of a Future,* ed. Herbert Otto (New York: Appleton Century Crofts, 1970), p. 147.

[21]J. Seeley, R. A. Sim, and E. W. Loosley, "Differentiation of Values in a Modern Community," in *Crestwood Heights* (New York: Basic, 1956) as quoted in J. Richard Udry, *The Social Context of Marriage,* 3rd ed. (New York: Harper, 1974), p. 28.

[22]Aries, "The Family," p. 55.

[23]Edward Shorter, *The Making of the Modern Family* (New York: Basic, 1975), p. 7.

[24]Ibid., p. 3.

[25]Ibid., p. 4.

[26]Udry, *Social Context,* p. 17.

[27]Philippe Aries, *Centuries of Childhood* (New York: Vantage, 1962).

[28]Shorter, *Making of the Modern Family,* pp. 22–78; 205–54.

[29]Ibid., p. 58.

[30]Ibid., p. 27.

[31]Ibid., p. 175.

[32]Ibid., p. 181.

[33]Ibid., p. 28.

[34]Ibid., p. 6.

[35]Udry, *Social Context,* p. 1.

[36]Ibid., p. 16.

[37]John A. Hostetler, "The Amish Family," in *Marriage and Family in the Modern World,* ed. Ruth Cavan (New York: Thomas Crowell, 1969), p. 56.

[38]John Scanzoni, "Can Marriages Last Forever?" *U.S. Catholic* (February 1977), p. 7.

[39]Richard Sennett, "The Brutality of Modern Families," *Transaction* (Sept. 7, 1970), p. 31.

[40]Shorter, *Making of the Modern Family,* p. 254.

[41]Sennett, "Brutality," p. 32.

[42]Ralph Keyes, *We, The Lonely People* (New York: Harper, 1973), p. 26.

[43]Shorter, *Making of the Modern Family,* p. 22.

[44]Letha and John Scanzoni, *Men, Women and Change,* p. 269.

[45]Ibid., p. 269.

[46]Ibid.

[47]Frances E. Kobrin, "The Primary Individual and the Family: Changes in Living Arrangements in the U.S. Since 1940," *Journal of Marriage and the Family* vol. 38, no. 2 (May 1976): 233–39.

[48]Shorter, *Making of the Modern Family,* p. 255.

[49]Richards, "Family Life Ministries," pp. 14–15.

3 / The Nature and Basis of Marriage

[1]Edward H. Schroeder, "Family Ethos in the Light of the Reformation," in *Family Relationships and the Church,* ed. Oscar Feucht (St. Louis: Concordia, 1970), p. 99.

[2]Pierre Grelot, *Man and Wife in Scripture* (New York: Herder and Herder, 1964), p. 27.

[3]There is solid exegetical basis for interpreting both marriage and foods as antecedents of the pronoun *which.*

[4]Gerhard von Rad, *Genesis: A Commentary,* rev. ed. (Philadelphia: Westminster, 1973), p. 85.

[5]Adrian Hastings, "Christian Marriage in Africa: Being a Report Commissioned by the Archbishops of Cape Town, Central Africa, Kenya, Tanzania and Uganda" (London: SPCK, 1974), p. 74.

[6]Walter Wegner, "God's Pattern for the Family in the Old Testament," *Family Relationships and the Church,* ed. Oscar Feucht (St. Louis: Concordia, 1970), p. 29. See also *New Bible Dictionary,* s.v. "Marriage."

[7]Ibid.

[8]L. Koehler, *Hebrew Man* (New York: Abingdon, 1956), p. 78.

[9]Charlotte and Howard J. Clinebell, *The Intimate Marriage* (New York: Harper, 1970); Gordon MacDonald, *Magnificent Marriage* (Carol Stream, Ill.: Tyndale, 1976).

[10]Cornelius J. van der Poel, "Marriage and Family as Expressions of Communion in the Church," *The Jurist,* 26, no. 1 (Winter and Spring 1976): 64.

[11]Charlotte and Howard J. Clinebell, *Intimate Marriage,* pp. 30–31.

[12]Von Rad, *Genesis,* p. 83.

[13]*Encyclopaedia Britannica,* 1969 ed. s.v. "Marriage, Law of."

[14]Peter Berger, *The Sacred Canopy* (New York: Doubleday, 1961), pp. 106–9.

4 / Permanence of Marriage and Nature of Family

[1]John Warwick Montgomery, "Commentary and Response," *The Jurist* (Winter 1975), p. 84.

[2]"Divorce and Remarriage," *Christianity Today* 23, no. 16 (May 25, 1979): 9.

[3]Charles Mount, "Divorce Cases Here Take Record Leap," *Chicago Tribune* (January 8, 1979), sec. 1, p. 1.

[4]Montgomery, "Commentary and Response," p. 84.

[5]John Scanzoni, "Can Marriages Last Forever?" *U. S. Catholic* 42, no. 2 (February 1977): 6.

[6]Ibid., p. 8.

[7]Bernard Ramm, "To Love and Cherish Till," *Eternity* (June 1976), p. 51.

[8]Dwight Small, *Right to Remarry* (Old Tappan, N.J.: Revell, 1975), p. 12.

[9]Guy Duty, *Divorce and Remarriage* (Minneapolis: Bethany Fellowship, 1967).

[10]James Montgomery Boice, "The Biblical View of Divorce," *Eternity* (December 1970), p. 21.

[11]Ramm, "To Love and Cherish," p. 51.

[12]Ibid.

[13]Ibid.

[14]Scanzoni, "Can Marriages Last?" p. 7.

[15]Ibid.

[16]Fritzie Pantoga, "Broken Marriages: Picking Up the Pieces," *U. S. Catholic* 42, no. 7 (July 1977): 8.

[17]Ibid.

[18]Ibid.

[19]Helen Kooiman Hosier, *The Other Side of Divorce* (New York: Hawthorne, 1975), p. vii.

[20]Ibid.

[21]Dwight Small, *The Right to Remarry* (Old Tappan, N.J.: Revell, 1975).

[22]James G. Emerson, Jr., *Divorce, The Church and Remarriage* (Philadelphia: Westminster, 1961).

[23]Ibid.

[24]"Divorce and Remarriage," p. 8.

[25]Boice, "Biblical View," p. 19.

[26]Ibid.

[27]Small, *Right to Remarry*, p. 184.

[28]Norman Geisler, *The Christian Ethic of Love* (Grand Rapids: Zondervan, 1973).

[29]Helmut Begemann, *Strukturwandel der Familie* (Hamburg: Furche-Verlag, 1960), pp. 102–3, quoted in Walter Wegner, "God's Pattern for the Family in the Old Testament," *Family Relationships and the Church* (St. Louis: Concordia, 1970), p. 28.

[30]Wegner, "God's Pattern," p. 28.

[31]James J. Lynch, *The Broken Heart: The Medical Consequences of Loneliness* (New York: Basic, 1977), quoted in Lawrence Crabb, "The Family: Manipulation or Ministry," in *Family Life Education* (Glen Ellyn, Ill.: Scripture Press Ministries, 1978), p. 9.

[32]Edward H. Schroeder, "Family Ethos in the Light of the Reformation," in *Family Relationships and the Church* (St. Louis: Concordia, 1970), p. 111.

[33]Ted Ward, "The Influence of Secular Institutions on Today's Family" (Published Address to the Plenary Session of the Continental Congress on the Family, St. Louis, 1975), p. 6.

[34]Ibid., p. 3.

5 / Family Ministry in the Church's Life

[1]George Webber, *The Congregation in Mission* (Nashville: Abingdon, 1946), p. 122.

[2]Elizabeth O'Connor, *Journey Inward, Journey Outward* (New York: Harper, 1968), p. 182.

[3]Webber, *Congregation in Mission*, p. 123.

[4]Michael Otto, s.v. *oikos*, *Theological Dictionary of the New Testament*, ed. Gerhard Kittel and Gerhard Friedrich (Grand Rapids: Eerdmans, 1967).

[5]Hans Freiheer Von Soden, s.v. *adelphos*, *Theological Dictionary*.

6 / Family Ministry in the Educational Program

[1]Lawrence Richards, "Developing Family Life Ministries," in *Family Life Education* (Glen Ellyn, Ill.: Scripture Press Ministries, 1978), p. 40.

[2]Ibid., p. 43.

[3]Ibid., pp. 41–42.

[4]Didier-Jacques Piveteau and J. T. Dillon, *Resurgence of Religious Instruction* (Notre Dame, Ind.: Religious Education, 1977), p. 167.

[5]Ibid.

[6]Wayne R. Rood, *On Nurturing Christians: Perhaps a Manifesto for Education* (New York: Abingdon, 1972); John H. Westerhoff III, ed., *A Colloquy on Christian Education* (Philadelphia: Pilgrim, 1972), and C. Ellis Nelson, *Where Faith Begins* (Atlanta: John Knox, 1967).

[7]Lawrence Richards, *A Theology of Christian Education* (Grand Rapids: Zondervan, 1975).

[8]Edward Zigler and Irvin L. Child, *Socialization and Personality Development* (Reading, Mass.: Addison-Wesley, 1973).

[9]John H. Westerhoff III, and Gwen Kennedy Neville, *Generation to Generation* (Philadelphia: Pilgrim, 1974), p. 159.

[10]Ibid., p. 129.

[11]Piveteau and Dillon, *Resurgence of Religious Instruction,* p. 168.

7 / Home/Church Symbiosis: A Proposal

[1]Robert Worley, *Change in the Church: A Source of Hope* (Philadelphia: Westminster, 1971), p. 38.

[2]Lawrence Richards, "Developing Family Life Ministries," *Family Life Education,* ed. Gil Peterson (Glen Ellyn, Ill.: Scripture Press Ministries, 1978), p. 41.

[3]Britton Wood, *Single Adults Want to Be the Church, Too* (Nashville: Broadman, 1977).

[4]Gene Getz, *Sharpening the Focus of the Church* (Chicago: Moody, 1974); Donald L. Bubna, *Building People* (Wheaton, Ill.: Tyndale, 1978); Gene Getz, *Building Up One Another* (Wheaton, Ill.: Victor, 1977).

[5]Richard Schunck and Phillip Runkel, *The Second Handbook of Organizational Development* (Washington, D.C.: Capital, 1977); Lyle Schaller, *The Change Agent* (New York: Abingdon, 1972).

[6]Gary Collins, *How to Be a People Helper* (Santa Ana, Calif.: Vision, 1976).

8 / Marital Dynamics and Roles

[1]Herbert Otto, ed., *Marriage and Family Enrichment* (New York: Abingdon, 1976), p. 11.

[2]Stanley Rosner and Laura Hobe, *The Marriage Gap* (New York: McKay, 1974), p. 11.

[3]Carl Rogers, *On Becoming a Person* (Boston: Houghton, Mifflin, 1961); Paul Tournier, *The Meaning of Persons* (New York: Harper, 1957).

[4]Hazen Werner, *Look at the Family Now* (Nashville: Abingdon, 1970), pp. 121–22.

[5]Lawrence Crabb, "Manipulation or Ministry," *Family Life Education,* ed. Gil Peterson, (Glen Ellyn, Ill.: Scripture Press Ministries, 1978), p. 14.

[6]A. T. Robertson, s.v. "Paul, the Apostle," in *The International Standard Bible Encyclopedia,* ed. James Orr (Chicago: Severance, 1915).

[7]S. Craig Glickman, *A Song For Lovers* (Downers Grove, Ill.: InterVarsity Press, 1976), p. 38.

[8]John Powell, *The Secret of Staying in Love* (Niles, Ill.: Argus, 1974).

[9]Gibson Winter, *Love and Conflict,* quoted in Helen Kooiman Hosier, *The Other Side of Divorce* (New York: Hawthorne, 1975), p. 141.

[10]"How Men Are Changing," *Newsweek* 91, no. 3 (January 16, 1978): 53–61.

[11]Letha and John Scanzoni, *Men, Women and Change: A Sociology of Marriage and Family* (New York: McGraw-Hill, 1975), pp. 201–52.

[12]Herb T. Mayer, "Family Relations in North America," in *Family Relationships in the Church* (St. Louis: Concordia, 1970), p. 126.

[13]Arthur W. Calhoun, "Democracy in the American Family," in *A Social History of the American Family* (New York: Barnes and Noble, 1917), quoted by Mayer, ibid., p. 132.

[14]Research Summaries Unpublished Report (1953), quoted by Mayer, ibid., p. 130.

[15]Letha Scanzoni and Nancy Hardesty, *All We're Meant to Be* (Waco: Word, 1974).

[16]Paul Jewett, *Man as Male and Female* (Grand Rapids: Eerdmans, 1975).

[17]Herbert and Fern H. Miles, *Husband-Wife Equality* (Old Tappan, N.J.: Revell, 1979).

[18]Mayer, *Family Relationship in the Church,* p. 30.

[19]John Calvin, *Commentaries on the First Book of Moses Called Genesis,* trans. John King (Grand Rapids: Eerdmans, 1948), p. 172.

9 / Marital Sex, Dating, Engagement

[1]Thomas Oden, *Game Free: The Meaning of Intimacy* (New York: Delta, 1974), p. 32.

[2]Cited by Herbert Otto, *Total Sex* (New York: Wyden, 1972).

[3]Claire Safran, "Why Religious Women Are Good Lovers," *Redbook* 146, no. 6 (April 1976): 103, 155.

[4]Helmut Theilicke, *The Ethics of Sex* (New York: Harper, 1976), pp. 3–6.

[5]James Dobson, *What Wives Wish Their Husbands Knew About Women* (Wheaton: Tyndale 1975), p. 59.

[6]Elton and Pauline Trueblood, *The Recovery of Family Life* (New York: Harper, 1953), p. 54.

[7]Leland Ryken, "Were the Puritans Right About Sex?" *Christianity Today* 22, no. 14 (April 7, 1978): 14.

[8]John Calvin, *Institutes of the Christian Religion,* trans. Ford Lewis Battles, vol. 20 of Library of Christian Classics, (Philadelphia: Westminster, 1960), p. 408, II. 8. 44.

[9]Theilicke, *The Ethics of Sex,* p. 303.

[10]Ibid., p. 302.

[11]Ryken,"Were the Puritans Right?" p. 18.

[12]Ibid.

[13]S. Craig Glickman, *A Song for Lovers* (Downers Grove, Ill.: InterVarsity, 1976).

[14]Norman Wright, *Premarital Counseling* (Chicago: Moody, 1976), p. 38.

10 / Concepts of Christian Parenting

[1]Catherine Brown, "It Changed My Life," *Psychology Today* (November 1976), p. 47.

Notes

[2]Haim Ginott, *Between Parent and Child* (New York: Macmillan, 1965), p. 91.

[3]Brown, "It Changed My Life," p. 48.

[4]Myron R. Chartier, "Parenting: A Theological Model," *Journal of Psychology and Theology* (Winter 1978), pp. 54–61.

[5]William Glasser, *Reality Therapy* (New York: Harper, 1965).

[6]Brown, "It Changed My Life," p. 57.

[7]Ibid., p. 53.

[8]Ibid., p. 109.

[9]James Dobson, *Dare to Discipline* (Wheaton, Ill.: Tyndale, 1970).

[10]Brown, "It Changed My Life," p. 57.

[11]Ibid.

11 / Family Matters

[1]Larry Burkett, *What Husbands Wish Their Wives Knew About Money* (Wheaton, Ill.: Victor, 1977), p. 6.

[2]Anthony Pietropinto and Jacqueline Simenauer, *Husbands and Wives* (New York: Times Books, 1979), p. 23.

[3]Howard and Jeanne Hendricks, "Preparing Young People for Christian Marriage," in *Adult Education in the Church,* ed. Roy Zuck and Gene A. Getz (Chicago: Moody, 1970), p. 279.

[4]Charlie Shedd, "My Number One Job as a Dad," *Family Life Today* 5, no. 7 (June 1979): 3.

12 / Marriage Enrichment

[1]Lawrence Crabb, "The Family: Manipulation or Ministry," in *Family Life Education,* ed. Gil Peterson (Wheaton: Scripture Press Ministries, 1978), p. 5.

[2]Herbert Otto, ed., *Marriage and Family Enrichment* (New York: Abingdon, 1976), p. 15.

[3]Ibid.

[4]Susan Middaugh, "Marriage Encounter, Is It for Everyone?" *Sign* 55, no. 4 (December 1975–January 1976): 10.

[5]Antoinette Bosco, "Marriage Encounter: An Ecumenical Enrichment Program," in *Marriage and Family Enrichment,* p. 100.

[6]Antoinette Bosco, *Marriage Encounter* (St. Meinrad, Ind.: Abbey, 1972), p. 11.

[7]Otto, *Marriage and Family Enrichment,* p. 144.

[8]Bosco, "Marriage Encounter," p. 94.

[9]David Mace, "We Call It ACME," in *Marriage and Family Enrichment,* p. 170.

[10]Bosco, *Marriage Encounter,* p. 170.

[11]Ignace Lepp, *Communication of the Existences,* quoted in Bosco as being one of the psychologists whose thought framed a philosophical basis for marriage encounter in Spain, *Marriage Encounter,* p. 23.

[12]Bosco, "Marriage Encounter," p. 99.

[13]Ibid.

[14]Bernard Kligfeld, "The Jewish Marriage Encounter," in *Marriage and Family Enrichment,* p. 129.

[15]Bosco, "Marriage Encounter," p. 47.

[16]Bosco, *Marriage Encounter,* p. 9.

[17]Middaugh, "Marriage Encounter," pp. 9–11.

[18]Del and Trudy Vander Haar, "The Marriage Enrichment Program—Phase I," in *Marriage and Family Enrichment,* ed. Otto, p. 194.

[19]Mace, "We Call It ACME," p. 171.

[20]James Kilgore, *Try Marriage Before Divorce* (Waco: Word, 1978).

[21]Charlotte and Howard J. Clinebell, *The Intimate Marriage* (New York: Harper, 1970), p. 29.

[22]Bud and Bea Van Eck, "The Phase II Marriage Enrichment Lab," in *Marriage Enrichment,* ed. Otto, p. 223.

[23]Herman Green, Jr., "A Christian Marriage Enrichment Retreat," in *Marriage and Family Enrichment,* ed. Otto, p. 91.

[24]Ibid.

[25]Charlotte and Howard J. Clinebell, *The Intimate Marriage,* pp. 29–32.

[26]David Johnson, *Reaching Out* (New York: Prentice-Hall, 1972).

[27]See a complete worksheet in Del and Trudy Vander Haar, "The Marriage Enrichment Program—Phase I," p. 209.

[28]Robert Taylor, *Taylor Johnson Temperament Analysis* (Los Angeles: Psychological Publications, 1967).

[29]Millard J. Bienvenu, Sr., "Marital Communication Inventory," (Saluda, N.C.: Family Life Publications, 1969).

[30]Herbert Otto, *More Joy in Your Marriage* (New York: Hawthorne, 1969).

[31]Geolo and Thomas McHugh, *Sex Attitudes Survey and Profile* (Saluda, N. C.: Family Life Publications, 1976).

[32]Mace, "We Call It ACME," p. 171.

[33]Ibid.

[34]Middaugh, "Marriage Encounter," p. 10.

[35]Bosco, *Marriage Encounter,* p. 98.

[36]Van Eck, "The Phase II Marriage Enrichment Lab," pp. 217–26.

[37]Bosco, *Marriage Encounter,* p. 102.

[38]Ibid.

13 / Parent Training: A Model

[1]Catherine Caldwell Brown, "It Changed My Life," *Psychology Today* (November 1976), p. 47.

[2]A. Bandura, "Influences of Model's Reinforcement Contingencies on the Acquisition of Imitative Responses," *Journal of Personality and Social Psychology* (1965), pp. 589–95.

[3]Sidney Simon, Leland W. Howe, and Howard Kirschenbaum, *Values Clarification* (New York: Hart, 1972), pp. 17–18.

[4]James Dobson, *Dare to Discipline* (Wheaton: Tyndale, 1970).

[5]Don Dinkmeyer and Gary McKay, *Systematic Training for Effective Parenting* (Circle Pines, Minn.: American Guidance Services, 1976).

[6]Richard R. Abidin, *Parenting Skills* (New York: Human Sciences Press, 1976).

[7]Dinkmeyer and McKay, *Systematic Training*.

[8]Dennis Guernsey, "What Kind of Parent Are You?" *Family Life Today* (January 1978), pp. 29–30.

[9]Ibid. Used by permission.

[10]Kenneth G. Prunty, "The Care-Lab: A Family Enrichment Program," in *Marriage and Family Enrichment,* ed. Herbert Otto (New York: Abingdon, 1976), p. 68.

Notes

[11]Lyman Coleman, *Serendipity Books* (Waco: Word, 1972).

[12]David Johnson, *Reaching Out* (Englewood Cliffs, N. J.: Prentice-Hall, 1972).

[13]Dorothy Law Nolte, "Children Learn What They Live," from the L. A. American Institute of Family Relations, quoted in Barbara Bolton, *Ways to Help Them Learn: Grades 1–6* (Los Angeles, Calif.: Regal, 1971), pp. 29–30.

[14]Herbert Brayer and Zella W. Cleary, *Valuing in the Family: A Workshop Guide for Parents* (San Diego: Pennant, 1972).

14 / Premarital Counseling

[1]Howard Hendricks, "Practical Process of Premarital Counseling" (Transcript of cassette, Dallas, Texas).

[2]Thomas J. Schmidt, "Premarital Counseling: A Preventive Measure in Reducing Marital Conflicts" (Transcript of cassette), p. 2.

[3]Antonio Florio, "The Importance of Premarriage Counseling" (Transcript of cassette), pp. 3–4.

[4]Howard D. Vanderwell, "The Development of an Appropriate Program of Premarital Guidance for Bethel Christian Reformed Church" (unpublished paper, Lansing Michigan), p. 2.

[5]H. Norman Wright, *Premarital Counseling* (Chicago: Moody, 1977), p. 40.

[6]Ibid., p. 35.

[7]Cited by Hendricks, "Practical Process," pp. 3–4.

[8]Wright, *Premarital Counseling,* pp. 39–41.

[9]Ibid., p. 41.

[10]Ibid.

[11]Aaron Rutledge, *Premarital Counseling* (Cambridge, Mass.: Schenkman, 1966), p. 22.

[12]Wright, *Premarital Counseling,* p. 28.

15 / The Family-Life Conference

[1]Matthew Miles, *Designing Training Activities,* cited by Lawrence O. Richards, *A New Face for the Church* (Grand Rapids: Zondervan, 1970), p. 156.

[2]W. Warner Burke, ed., *Conference Planning* (Washington, D. C.: National Training Laboratory Institute for Applied Behavioral Sciences, 1970), p. vii.

[3]Cited by S. Autry Brown, *Church Family Life Conference Guidebook* (Nashville: Sunday School Board of the Southern Baptist Church, 1973), p. 5.

[4]W. Warner Burke, "Conference Planning for the Seventies," in *Conference Planning,* ed. Burke, p. 6.

[5]Brown, *Church Family Life,* p. 9–10.

[6]T. Garvice and Dorothy Murphree, "Implementation Guide for Christian Home Week, May 7–14, 1972," *Church Administration* (April 1972), pp. 25–28.

[7]Brown, *Church Family Life,* p. 15.

[8]Ibid., pp. 23–43.

[9]Ibid., p. 16.

16 / Theory of Family Nurture

[1]C. Ellis Nelson, *Where Faith Begins* (Atlanta: John Knox, 1971), pp. 209–10.

[2]Roy Fairchild and John Charles Wynn, *Families in the Church: A Protestant Survey* (New York: Association, 1961), p. 93.

[3]John Charles Wynn, "The Home and Christian Education," in *An Introduction to Christian Education*, ed. Marvin Taylor (Nashville: Abingdon, 1966), p. 293.

[4]Blanche Carrier, *Church Education for Family Life* (New York: Harper, 1937), p. 16.

[5]Ibid., p. 9.

[6]Regina Westcott Wieman, *The Modern Family and the Church* (New York: Harper, 1937; Carrier, *Church Education;* and Lewis Sherrill, *Family and Church* (New York: Abingdon, n.d.).

[7]Jacob Sheatsley, "The Bible in Religious Education," quoted by Oscar E. Feucht, ed., *Helping Families Through the Church* (St. Louis: Concordia, 1957).

[8]Carrier, *Church Education*, p. 9.

[9]Ibid., p. 10.

[10]Ibid., p. 16.

[11]Lewis Sherrill, *Lift Up Your Eyes* (Richmond: John Knox, 1949), p. 161.

[12]Ibid.

[13]Ibid., p. 6.

[14]Robert Lynn, *Protestant Strategies in Education* (New York: Association, 1964), p. 25.

[15]Ibid., p. 14.

[16]Robert Lynn, "Sometimes on Sunday: Reflections on Images of the Future in American Education," *Andover Newton Quarterly* 12, no. 3 (January 1972): 135.

[17]Carrier, *Church Education*, p. 16.

[18]Ibid.

[19]Wesner Fallaw, *The Modern Parent and the Teaching Church* (New York: Macmillan, 1947), p. 26.

[20]Cited in Feucht, *Helping Families*, p. 93.

[21]Ibid., p. 92.

[22]Ibid., p. 93.

[23]Harry Munro, *Protestant Nurture* (Englewood Cliffs, N. J.: Prentice-Hall, 1956), p. 244.

[24]R. V. Kearnes, at the International Conference on Christian Family Life (1948), in Feucht, ed., *Helping Families*, p. 96.

[25]Fairchild and Wynn, *Families in the Church*, p. 16.

[26]Lynn, *Protestant Strategies*.

[27]Wesner Fallaw, *Church Education for Tomorrow* (Philadelphia: Westminster, 1960).

[28]Fairchild and Wynn, *Families in the Church*.

[29]Feucht, *Helping Families*, p. 92.

[30]Ibid., p. 95.

[31]J. Thomas Leamon, "The Family Alternative," in *A Colloquy on Christian Education*, ed., John H. Westerhoff III (Philadelphia: United Church, 1972), p. 151.

[32]Marvin Taylor, ed., *Foundations for Christian Education in an Era of Change* (New York: Abingdon, 1976).

[33]C. Ellis Nelson, "The Curriculum of Christian Education," in *An Introduction*, ed. Taylor, p. 164.

[34]Nelson, *Where Faith Begins*, p. 210.

[35]Urie Bronfenbrenner, "Testimony Before the Senate Subcommittee on Children and Youth," *Congressional Record* 119, no. 142 (Sept. 26, 1973): 8.

[36]Burton White, *The First Three Years of Life* (Englewood Cliffs, N. J.: Prentice-Hall, 1975), p. xi.

[37]James Michael Lee, *The Flow of Religious Instruction* (Notre Dame, Ind.: Religious Education, 1973), p. 60.

Notes

[38]John Westerhoff, *Generation to Generation: Conversations on Religious Education and Culture* (Philadelphia: Pilgrim, 1975), p. 45.

[39]Larry Richards, "Nurturing the Family," *Action* (Summer 1977), p. 16.

[40]Feucht, *Helping Families,* p. 55.

[41]Ibid.

[42]Didier-Jacques Piveteau and J. T. Dillon, *Resurgence of Religious Instruction* (Notre Dame, Ind.: Religious Education, 1977), p. 186.

[43]Ibid.

[44]Ronald Goldman, *Religious Thinking from Childhood to Adolescence* (London: Routledge and Kegan Paul, 1964).

[45]Piveteau and Dillon, *Resurgence,* p. 196.

17 / Programs of Family Nurture

[1]Herbert T. Mayer, "Family Relations in North America," in *Family Relationships and the Church,* ed. Oscar E. Feucht (St. Louis: Concordia, 1970).

[2]Joel Nederhood, "Should We Have Daily Family Devotions: Yes," *Eternity* (March 1971), p. 14.

[3]Enos Sjogren, "Should We Have Family Devotions: Not Necessarily," *Eternity* (March 1971), p. 15.

[4]T. C. Van Kooten, *Building the Family Altar* (Grand Rapids: Baker, 1969), p. 15.

[5]H. Norman Wright, "The Church Building Christian Families—Myth and Possibilities" (report at Talbot Theological Seminary, Los Angeles, n.d.).

[6]Nederhood, "Should We Have Daily Family Devotions," p. 15.

[7]Sjogren, "Should We Have Daily Family Devotions," p. 15.

[8]Harold H. Hess, "Should We Have Daily Family Devotions: No," *Eternity* (March 1971), p. 15.

[9]Sjogren, "Should We Have Daily Family Devotions," p. 15.

[10]Au-Deane S. Cowley and Ramona S. Adams, "The Family Home Evening: A National Ongoing Family Enrichment Program," in *Marriage and Family Enrichment,* ed. Herbert A. Otto (Nashville: Abingdon, 1978), pp. 73–84.

[11]Ibid.

[12]Harold B. Lee, "Strengthening the Home," Pamphlet 032-B (1973), p. 7.

[13]*Family Home Evening Manual* (Salt Lake City: Corporation of Pres. of the Church of Jesus Christ of Latter-Day Saints, 1965), p. iii.

[14]*Sunday School Plus* (1266 Woodingham Drive, East Lansing, Michigan 48823).

[15]Lawrence Richards, *A Theology of Christian Education* (Grand Rapids: Zondervan, 1975), p. 207.

[16]Ibid., p. 224.

[17]"Introducing Sunday School Plus" (Phoenix, Arizona: Renewal Research Associates, n.d.), pp. 15–16.

18 / Intergenerational Experiences

[1]Thomas G. Bissonnette, "Comunidades Ecclesiales De Base: Some Contemporary Attempts to Build Ecclesial Koinonia," *The Jurist* 26, no. 1 (Winter and Spring 1976): 37.

[2]Ibid.

[3]Lawrence Richards, "Developing Family Life Ministries," in *Family Life Education* (Glen Ellyn, Ill.: Scripture Press Ministries, 1978), p. 45.

[4]Ibid.

[5]George Koehler, *Learning Together, A Guide for Intergenerational Education in the Church* (Nashville: Discipleship Resources, 1977), p. 14.

[6]Ibid., p. 15.

[7]Trudy Vander Haar, *Generations Learning Together in the Congregation* (Orange City, Iowa: Office of Family Life, General Program Council, Reformed Church in America, 1976), pp. 2–4.

19 / Family Clusters

[1]Margaret Sawin, "An Over-All View of the Family Cluster Experience: Historically, Leadership-wise, Family-wise," *Religious Education* (March–April 1974), p. 184.

[2]Virginia Satir, *Conjoint Family Therapy* (Palo Alto, Calif.: Science and Behavior Books, 1964).

[3]Sawin, "An Over-All View," pp. 188–89.

[4]Ibid., p. 188.

[5]Ibid., p. 185.

[6]Margaret Sawin, "The Role of the Experiential Educator," a paper, pp. 1–2. (Distributed by Family Clustering, Inc., P.O. Box 18074, Rochester, N. Y. 14618.)

[7]Didier-Jacques Piveteau and J. T. Dillon, *Resurgence of Religious Instruction* (Notre Dame, Ind.: Religious Education Press, 1977), p. 191.

[8]Ibid.

20 / Family Camping

[1]Arnold Swanson, "Family Camping," *Journal of Christian Camping* 73, no. 2 (March–April 1973): 11.

[2]Werner Graendorf, "Camping Purpose," in *Introduction to Christian Camping,* eds. Werner C. Graendorf and Lloyd D. Mattson (Chicago: Moody, 1979), p. 18.

[3]Ed Branch, Jr., "The Family Camp: An Extended Family Enrichment Experience," in *Marriage and Family Enrichment,* ed. Herbert A. Otto (Nashville: Abingdon, 1976), p. 51.

[4]Graendorf, "Camping Purpose," p. 21.

[5]Gene Getz, *Sharpening the Focus of the Church* (Chicago: Moody, 1974), pp. 202–10.

[6]Branch, "The Family Camp," p. 51.

[7]Ibid.

[8]Ibid.

[9]Clifford Gustafson, "Philosophy and Styles of Family Camping," cassette recording of a workshop at the International Camping Convention, Christian Camping International (Banff National Park, Alberta, Canada, 1977).

[10]John Rozeboom, *Family Camping: Five Designs for Your Church* (Nashville: Board of Discipleship of the United Methodist Church, 1973), p. 4.

[11]Gustafson, "Philosophy and Styles."

[12]Ibid.

[13]Personal correspondence between author and Bob Hilts, March 23, 1977.

[14]Gustafson, "Philosophy and Styles."

[15]Lloyd Mattson, "Forms of Camping," in *Introduction to Christian Camping,* p. 57.

[16]Ibid.

Notes

[17]Branch, "The Family Camp."
[18]Rozeboom, *Family Camping,* p. 39.
[19]Ibid.
[20]Ibid.
[21]Ibid., p. 29.
[22]Ibid., p. 33.
[23]Ibid., pp. 12–15.
[24]Ibid., p. 43.

Conclusion

[1]Quoted by Richard F. Houts, "Learning to Be a Family," *Christianity Today,* vol. 24, no. 11 (June 6, 1980): 686.
[2]Margaret Sawin, "Family Enrichment: The Challenge Which Unites Us," *Religious Education,* vol. 75, no. 3 (May–June, 1980): 343.
[3]Ibid., p. 342.
[4]Ibid.
[5]Ibid.

SELECTED
BIBLIOGRAPHY

Selected Bibliography

THE FAMILY

General

Adams, Jay. *Christian Living in the Home*. Grand Rapids: Baker Book House, 1972.
Denton, Wallace. *Family Problems and What to Do About Them*. Philadelphia: Westminster Press, 1976.
Gaulk, Earle H. *You Can Have a Family Where Everybody Wins*. St. Louis: Concordia Publishing House, 1977.
Getz, Gene A. *The Christian Home in a Changing World*. Chicago: Moody Press, 1972.
Hendricks, Howard G. *Heaven Help the Home*. Wheaton, Ill.: Victor Books, 1973.
Schaeffer, Edith. *What Is a Family?* Old Tappan, N.J.: Fleming H. Revell, 1975.
Zuck, Roy B., and Getz, Gene A., eds. *Ventures in Family Living*. Chicago: Moody Press, 1971.

Sociology of the Family

Bane, Mary Jo. *Here to Stay: American Families in the Twentieth Century*. New York: Basic Books, 1977.
Cox, Frank. *American Marriage: A Changing Scene?* Dubuque, Iowa: Wm. C. Brown, 1972.
Miller, Levi, ed. *The Family in Today's Society*. Scottdale, Pa.: Herald Press, 1976.
Otto, Herbert A., ed. *The Family in Search of a Future: Alternate Models for Moderns*. Englewood Cliffs, N.J.: Prentice-Hall, 1970.
Scanzoni, John, and Scanzoni, Letha. *Men, Women and Change: A Sociology of Marriage and Family*. New York: McGraw-Hill Book Company, 1976.
Skolnick, Arlene S., and Skolnick, Jerome. *Family In Transition: Rethinking Marriage, Sexuality, Child Rearing and Family Organization*. Boston: Little, Brown and Company, 1971.
Tufte, Virginia, and Myerhoff, Barbara. *Changing Images of the Family*. New Haven, Conn.: Yale University Books, 1979.
Udry, J. Richard. *The Social Context of Marriage*. Philadelphia: J. B. Lippincott, 1974.

Single Life

Andrews, Gini. *Your Half of the Apple: God and the Single Girl*. Grand Rapids: Zondervan Publishing House, 1972.
Collins, Gary. *It's OK to Be Single*. Waco, Tex.: Word Books, 1976.
Krebs, Richard. *Alone Again*. Minneapolis: Augsburg Publishing Company, 1978.
Lum, Ada. *Single and Human*. Downers Grove, Ill.: InterVarsity Press, 1977.
Reed, Bobbie. *Developing a Single Adult Ministry*. Glendale, Calif.: International Center For Learning, 1978.
Wood, Britton. *Single Adults Want to Be the Church, Too*. Nashville: Broadman Press, 1978.

Family and Church

Duvall, Evelyn R.; Mace, David; and Popenoe, Paul. *The Church Looks at Family Life*. Nashville: Broadman Press, 1964.
Fairchild, Roy W., and Wynn, John C. *Families in the Church: A Protestant Survey*. New York: Association Press, 1961.
Feucht, Oscar E., ed. *Family Relationships and the Church*. St. Louis: Concordia Publishing House, 1970.

_____. *Helping Families Through the Church: A Symposium on Family Life Education.* St. Louis: Concordia Publishing House, 1957.

_____. *Ministry to Families.* St. Louis: Concordia Publishing House, 1963.

Louthan, Sheldon, and Martin, Grant. *Family Ministries in Your Church.* Glendale, Calif.: Regal Books, 1978.

Otto, Herbert A., ed. *Marriage and Family Enrichment: New Perspectives and Programs.* Nashville: Abingdon Press, 1976.

FAMILY-LIFE EDUCATION

Preparing for Marriage

Fryling, Robert, and Fryling, Alice. *Handbook for Engaged Couples.* Downers Grove, Ill.: InterVarsity Press, 1978.

Miles, Herbert J. *Sexual Understanding Before Marriage.* Grand Rapids: Zondervan Publishing House, 1971.

_____. *The Dating Game.* Grand Rapids; Zondervan Publishing House, 1975.

Popenoe, Paul. *Preparing for Marriage.* Los Angeles: The American Institute of Family Relations, n.d.

Scanzoni, Letha. *Sex and the Single Eye.* Grand Rapids: Zondervan Publishing House, 1968.

Shedd, Charlie. *Letters to Karen: On Keeping Love in Marriage.* Nashville: Abingdon Press, 1965.

_____. *Letters to Philip: On How to Treat a Woman.* Garden City, N.Y.: Doubleday & Company, 1968.

_____. *The Stork Is Dead: A Man Becomes a Man When He Becomes What God Wants Him to Be.* Waco, Tex.: Word Books, 1968.

Smith, Kenneth G. *Learning to Be a Man.* Downers Grove, Ill.: InterVarsity Press, 1970.

_____. *Learning to Be a Woman.* Downers Grove, Ill.: InterVarsity Press, 1970.

Trobisch, Walter. *I Loved a Girl.* New York: Harper & Row Publishers, 1965.

Trobisch, Walter, and Trobisch, Ingrid. *My Beautiful Feeling: Correspondence with Ilona.* Downers Grove, Ill.: InterVarsity Press, 1977.

Wright, Norman. *A Guidebook to Dating and Choosing a Mate.* Irvine, Calif.: Harvest House Publishers, 1978.

Wright, Norman, and Inmon, Marvin. *Preparing Youth For Dating, Courtship and Marriage.* Irvine, Calif.: Harvest House Publishers, 1978.

Wright, Norman, and Roberts, Wes. *Before You Say "I Do."* Irvine, Calif.: Harvest House Publishers, 1978.

Premarital Counseling

Ard, Ben, Jr., and Ard, Constance. *Handbook of Marriage Counseling.* Palo Alto, Calif.: Science and Behavior Books, 1969.

Coble, Betty J. *Woman: Aware and Choosing.* New ed. Nashville: Broadman Press, 1975.

Gangsei, Lyle B. *Manual for Group Premarital Counseling.* New York: Association Press, 1971.

McDonald, Patrick J., and Nett, Sandra F. *Pre-Marriage Handbook.* St. Meinrad, Ind.: Abbey Press, 1976.

Morris, J. Kenneth. *Premarital Counseling: A Manual for Ministers.* Englewood Cliffs, N.J.: Prentice-Hall, 1960.

Oates, Wayne E. *Premarital Pastoral Care and Counseling.* Nashville: Broadman Press, 1958.

Selected Bibliography

Peterson, James A. *Education for Marriage.* New York: Scribner's, 1956.

Rutledge, Aaron L. *Premarital Counseling.* Cambridge, Mass.: Schenkman Publishing Company, 1966.

Wright, H. Norman. *Premarital Counseling.* Chicago: Moody Press, 1977.

Marriage: General

Augsburger, David. *Caring Enough to Confront.* Glendale, Calif.: Regal Books, 1973.

Bach, George. *The Intimate Enemy.* New York: William Morrow and Company, 1969.

Barbeau, Clayton. *Creative Marriage: The Middle Years.* New York: Seabury Press, 1976.

Boldrey, Richard, and Boldrey, Joyce. *Chauvinist or Feminist?: Paul's View of Women.* Grand Rapids: Baker Book House, 1976.

Brandt, Henry, and Landrum, Phil. *I Want My Marriage to Be Better.* Grand Rapids: Zondervan Publishing House, 1976.

Burkett, Larry. *What Husbands Wish Their Wives Knew About Money.* Wheaton, Ill.: Victor Books, 1977.

Clinebell, Charlotte H., and Clinebell, Howard J. *The Intimate Marriage.* New York: Harper & Row, 1970.

Dobson, James. *What Wives Wish Their Husbands Knew About Women.* Wheaton, Ill.: Tyndale House, 1975.

Edwards, Cliff. *Biblical Christian Marriage.* Atlanta: John Knox Press, 1977.

Elliot, Elisabeth. *Let Me Be a Woman.* Wheaton, Ill.: Tyndale House, 1976.

Fields, Wilbert J. *Unity in Marriage.* St. Louis: Concordia Publishing House, 1962.

Fooshee, George, Jr. *You Can Be Financially Free.* Old Tappan, N.J.: Fleming J. Revell, 1976.

Guernsey, Dennis. *Thoroughly Married.* Waco, Tex.: Word Books, 1977.

Hancock, Maxine. *Love, Honor and Be Free.* Chicago: Moody Press, 1975.

Hardesty, Nancy, and Scanzoni, Letha. *All We're Meant to Be.* Waco, Tex.: Word Books, 1974.

Lederer, W. J., and Jackson, Don D. *The Mirages of Marriage.* New York: W. W. Norton & Company, 1968.

Lesson, L. Richard. *Love and Marriage and Trading Stamps.* Niles, Ill.: Argus Communications, 1971.

Liftin, A. Duane. "A Biblical View of Marital Roles: Seeking a Balance." *Bibliotheca Sacra* (Oct.-Dec. 1976).

MacDonald, Gordon. *Magnificent Marriage.* Wheaton, Ill.: Tyndale House, 1976.

McRoberts, Darlene. *Second Marriage: The Promise and Challenge.* Minneapolis: Augsburg House Publishers, 1978.

Merrill, Dean. *How to Really Love Your Wife.* Grand Rapids: Zondervan Publishing House, 1978.

Miles, Herbert J., and Miles, Fern H. *Husband-Wife Equality.* Old Tappan, N.J.: Fleming H. Revell, 1979.

Morgan, Marabel. *Total Joy.* Old Tappan, N.J.: Fleming H. Revell, 1977.

_____. *Total Woman.* Old Tappan, N.J.: Fleming H. Revell, 1973.

Petersen, J. Allan; Petersen, Evelyn; and Smith, Joyce. *Two Become One: Bible Studies on Marriage and the Family for Couples and Groups.* Wheaton, Ill.: Tyndale House, 1973.

Peterson, James A., and Payne, Barbara. *Love in the Later Years: The Emotional, Physical, Sexual and Social Potential of the Elderly.* New York: Association Press, 1978.

Popenoe, Paul. *Marriage Is What You Make It.* New York: Macmillan Publishing Company, 1950.

Powell, John. *The Secret of Staying in Love.* Niles, Ill.: Argus Communications, 1974.

Ramsey, Paul. *One Flesh.* Grove Booklet on Ethics, No. 8. Bramcote Notts, U.K.: Grove Books, 1975.

Small, Dwight H. *After You've Said I Do.* Old Tappan, N.J.: Fleming H. Revell, 1968.

_____. *Design for Christian Marriage.* Old Tappan, N.J.: Fleming H. Revell, 1959.

Sproul, R. C. *Discovering the Intimate Marriage.* Minneapolis: Bethany Fellowship, 1975.

Thatcher, Floyd, and Thatcher, Harriet. *Long Term Marriage.* Waco, Tex.: Word Books, 1980.

Timmons, Tim. *Maximum Marriage.* Old Tappan, N.J.: Fleming H. Revell, 1976.

Tournier, Paul. *To Understand Each Other.* Translated by John S. Gilmour. Atlanta: John Knox Press, 1967.

Wahlroos, Sven. *Family Communication.* New York: New American Library, 1976.

Williams, Harold Page. *Do Yourself a Favor: Love Your Wife.* Plainfield, N.J.: Logos International, 1973.

Wright, H. Norman. *The Christian's Use of Emotional Power.* Old Tappan, N.J.: Fleming H. Revell, 1974.

_____. *Communication: Key to Your Marriage.* Glendale, Calif.: Regal Books, 1974.

Marriage: Sexual Relationship

Bird, Lois. *How to Be a Happily Married Mistress.* Garden City, N. Y.: Doubleday & Company, 1970.

_____. *How to Make Your Wife Your Mistress.* Garden City, N. Y.: Doubleday & Company, 1972.

Dillow, Joseph C. *Solomon on Sex.* New York: Thomas Nelson, 1977.

Eichenlaub, John E. *The Marriage Art.* New York: Dell Publishing Company, 1969.

Glickman, S. Craig. *A Song for Lovers.* Downers Grove, Ill.: InterVarsity Press, 1976.

Greeley, Andrew. *Sexual Intimacy.* Chicago: Thomas Moore Association, 1978.

Katchadourian, Herant, and Lunde, Donald T. *Fundamentals of Human Sexuality.* 2nd ed. New York: Holt, Rinehart and Winston, 1975.

Kennedy, Eugene. *Sexual Counseling.* New York: Seabury Press, 1978.

LaHaye, Tim, and LaHaye, Beverly. *The Act of Marriage: The Beauty of Sexual Love.* Grand Rapids: Zondervan Publishing House, 1976.

Lewin, Samuel A., and Gilmore, John. *Sex Without Fear.* New York: Medical Research Press, 1950.

McCarthy, Barry W.; Ryan, Mary; and Johnson, Fred A. *Sexual Awareness: A Practical Approach.* San Francisco: Boyd & Fraser Publishing Company, 1975.

Mace, David. *Sexual Difficulties in Marriage.* Philadelphia: Fortress Press, 1972.

Rosner, Stanley, and Hobe, Laura. *The Marriage Gap.* New York: David McKay Company, 1974.

Small, Dwight H. *Christian, Celebrate Your Sexuality.* Old Tappan, N.J.: Fleming H. Revell, 1974.

Trobish, Ingrid. *The Joy of Being a Woman ... And What a Man Can Do.* New York: Harper & Row, 1975.

Wheat, Ed, and Wheat, Gaye. *Intended for Pleasure.* Old Tappan, N.J.: Fleming H. Revell, 1977.

Selected Bibliography

Marriage: Divorce and Remarriage

Duty, Guy. *Divorce and Remarriage.* Minneapolis: Bethany Fellowship, 1967.
Petrie, Darlene. *The Hurt and Healing of Divorce.* Elgin, Ill.: David C. Cook Publishing Company, 1976.
Small, Dwight H. *The Right to Remarry.* Old Tappan, N.J.: Fleming H. Revell, 1975.
Smoke, Jim. *Growing Through Divorce.* Irvine, Calif.: Harvest House Publishers, 1977.
Young, Amy Ross. *By Death or Divorce: It Hurts to Lose.* Denver: Accent Books, 1977.

Parenting: General

Biller, Henry, and Meredith, Dennis. *Father Power.* Garden City, N.Y.: Doubleday & Company, 1975.
Brandt, Henry, and Landrum, Phil. *I Want to Enjoy My Children.* Grand Rapids: Zondervan Publishing House, 1975.
Daley, Eliot A. *Father Feelings.* New York: William Morrow & Company, 1977.
Deal, William S. *Counseling Christian Parents.* Grand Rapids: Zondervan Publishing House, 1970.
Dinkmeyer, Don, and McKay, Gary D. *Systematic Training for Effective Parenting.* Circle Pines, Minn.: American Guidance Service, 1976.
Dobson, James. *Dare to Discipline.* Wheaton, Ill.: Tyndale House, 1970.
_____. *Hide or Seek?* Old Tappan, N.J. Fleming H. Revell, 1974.
Dodson, Fitzhugh. *How to Father.* Los Angeles: Nash Publishing, 1974.
Drescher, John M. *Seven Things Children Need.* Scottdale, Pa.: Herald Press, 1976.
Duvall, Evelyn. *Evelyn Duvall's Handbook for Parents.* Nashville: Broadman Press, 1974.
_____. *Parent and Teenager: Living and Loving.* Nashville: Broadman Press, 1977.
Felix, Joseph. *Proud Parenthood.* Nashville: Abingdon Press, 1979.
Ginott, Haim G. *Between Parent and Child: New Solutions to Old Problems.* New York: Macmillan Publishing Company, 1965.
_____. *Between Parent and Teenager.* New York: Macmillan Publishing Company, 1969.
Gordon, Thomas. *Parent Effectiveness Training.* New York: Wyden Books, 1970.
Kesler, Jay. *Too Big to Spank.* Glendale, Calif.: Regal Books, 1979.
Narramore, Bruce. *An Ounce of Prevention: A Parent's Guide to Moral and Spiritual Growth of Children.* Grand Rapids: Zondervan Publishing House, 1973.
_____. *Help! I'm a Parent.* Grand Rapids: Zondervan Publishing House, 1972. (Workbook: *A Guide to Child Rearing*)
Shedd, Charlie. *Promises to Peter: Building a Bridge From Parent to Child.* Waco, Tex.: Word Books, 1970.
Skoglund, Elizabeth. *You Can Be Your Own Child's Counselor.* Glendale, Calif.: Regal Books, 1978.
Wright, Norman, and Johnson, Rex. *Communication: Key to Your Teens.* Irvine, Calif.: Harvest House Publishers, 1978. (Teacher's Guide: *Building Positive Parent-Teen Relationships*)

Parenting: Single Parents

Carter, Vera Thorne, and Leavenworth, J. Lynn. *Putting the Pieces Together: Help for Single Parents.* Valley Forge, Pa.: Judson Press, 1978.
Walls, Virginia. *The Single Parent.* Old Tappan, N.J.: Fleming H. Revell, 1978.

Parenting: Sex Education

Baruch, Dorothy. *New Ways in Sex Education: A Guide for Parents and Teachers.* New York: McGraw-Hill Book Company, 1959.

Child Study Association. *What to Tell Your Child About Sex.* Rev. ed. Edited by W. J. Fields. New York: Dutton, 1968.

Duvall, Evelyn M. *Love and the Facts of Life.* New York: Association Press, 1963.

Gordon, Sol. *The Sexual Adolescent: Communicating With Teenagers About Sex.* Belmont, Calif.: Wadsworth Publishing Co., 1977.

Grant, Wilson W. *From Parent to Child About Sex.* Grand Rapids: Zondervan Publishing House, 1973.

Harty, Robert, and Harty, Adnelle. *Made to Grow.* Nashville: Broadman Press, 1973.

Narramore, Clyde M. *How to Tell Your Children About Sex.* Grand Rapids: Zondervan Publishing House, 1958.

Scanzoni, Letha. *Sex Is a Parent Affair.* Glendale, Calif.: Regal Books, 1973.

Schulz, Esther D., and Williams, Sally R. *Family Life and Sex Education.* New York: Harcourt Brace Jovanovich, 1978.

Voland, Arlene S.; Weiss, Caroline; and Talman, Judith. *Sex Education for Today's Child.* New York: Association Press, 1977.

Family Crises

Ahlem, Lloyd H. *How to Cope With Crisis and Change.* Glendale, Calif.: Regal Books, 1978.

Gage, Joy P. *When Parents Cry.* Denver: Accent Books, 1980.

Jackson, Edgar N. *The Many Faces of Grief.* Nashville: Abingdon Press, 1978.

Kooiman, Gladys. *When Death Takes a Father.* Grand Rapids: Baker Book House, 1975.

Neuhaus, Robert, and Neuhaus, Ruby. *Family Crises.* Columbus, Ohio: Charles E. Merrill Publishing Company, 1974.

Pincus, Lily. *Death and the Family.* New York: Random House, 1976.

Smetzer, David. *The Dynamics of Grief.* Nashville: Abingdon Press, 1970.

Family Recreation

Edgren, Harry. *Fun for the Family.* Nashville: Abingdon Press, 1967.

Edwards, Vergne. *The Tired Adult's Guide to Backyard Fun With Kids.* New York: Association Press, 1965.

Eisenberg, Helen, and Eisenberg, Larry. *The Family Fun Book.* New York: Association Press, 1953.

Rice, Wayne; Rydberg, Denny; and Yaconelli, Mike. *Fun 'N Games.* Grand Rapids: Zondervan Publishing House, 1977.

The Family-Life Conference

Brown, S. Autry. *Church Family Life Conference Guidebook.* Nashville: Sunday School Board of the Southern Baptist Church, 1973.

Burke, W. Warner. ed. *Conference Planning.* Washington, D.C.: National Training Laboratory, Institute for Applied Behavioral Sciences, 1970.

Nelson, Virgil, and Nelson, Lynn. *Retreat Handbook.* Valley Forge, Pa.: Judson Press, 1976.

FAMILY-UNIT MINISTRIES

Griggs, Donald, and Griggs, Patricia. *Generations Learning Together.* Livermore, Calif.: Griggs Educational Service, n.d.

297

Selected Bibliography

Hendrix, Lela. *Extended Family: Combining Ages in Church Experience.* Nashville: Broadman Press, 1979.

Koehler, George D. *Learning Together: A Guide for Intergenerational Education in the Church.* Nashville: Discipleship Resources, 1977.

Nutting, R. Ted. *Family Cluster Programs.* Valley Forge, Pa.: Judson Press, 1978.

Rogers, Jack, and Rogers, Sharee. *The Family Together: Inter-Generational Education in the Church School.* Los Angeles: Action House Publishers, 1976.

Sawin, Margaret. *Educating by Family Groups: A New Model for Religious Education.* Rochester, N.Y.: Family Clustering, n.d.

_____. *Resources for Further Research in Family Education.* Rochester, N.Y.: Family Clustering, n.d.